D1448490

Marriage: Studies in Emotional Conflict and Growth

Marriage: Studies in Emotional Conflict and Growth

edited by
LILY PINCUS
with contributions by
KATHLEEN BANNISTER · VALERY GARDEN
JOAN HALL · ALISON LYONS
HERBERT PHILLIPSON · LILY PINCUS
EVA SELIGMAN · JUDITH STEPHENS
and an Introduction by
A. G. THOMPSON, M.D., F.R.C.P.I.

INSTITUTE OF MARITAL STUDIES
The Tavistock Institute of Human Relations

© The Tavistock Institute of Human Relations 1960
ISBN 901882089

First Published by Methuen 1960
Paperback Edition Published by
Institute of Marital Studies, November 1973
Reprinted May 1976

Available from:

Institute of Marital Studies (Publications)
Tavistock Centre
Belsize Lane
London NW3 5BA

Printed in Great Britain by Headley Brothers Ltd 109 Kingsway London WC2B 6PX and Ashford Kent

Contents

Preface to the Paperback Edition

In his introduction to this book, first published in 1960, Dr Geoffrey Thompson comments: 'In the present-day world, our traditional values and patterns of relationships are undergoing far-reaching modifications in response to the radical changes that are taking place in our social environment.' In the intervening years the extent of change has increased and its pace has quickened. Alongside this there has been an increasing amount of criticism of marriage as an institution, and particularly of monogamous marriage. In the current debate views are frequently expressed that it has outlived its usefulness, that it supports untenable distinctions between the sexes, and that it gives rise to unnecessary tensions and conflicts.

Nevertheless marriage remains popular, and many young people still accept, and remain committed to using, the structure it provides for an intimate heterosexual relationship. One change, however, appears to be that many young people go into marriage today not talking just of the adjustment they will have to make to each other, but of the opportunity this committed adjustment to a person of the opposite sex will give them for their own personal development—the need for another to realise parts of themselves. The accent is on personal growth and on marriage being a means of achieving this for some people—not necessarily for all.

This is the particular theme of this book. A variety of disciplines and approaches are relevant to the total study of marriage. But in the Institute of Marital Studies we are particularly concerned with the use people make of marriage as a vehicle for developing maturity. The couples who are described are not basically different from thousands of others who do not seek help, but have failed by themselves to realise their own developmental capacities.

Successful work with marriages enables two people to be richer as individuals in their own right, and therefore to contribute to a richer partnership. Life is not simplified for them. They still have their griefs and sadness, their worries and their difficulties, but their inner resources are markedly increased.

Our thinking on the complex issues raised in this book have

developed since it was first written. A series of monographs, which are listed on the back cover, have been published. They are direct successors of this book, defining some aspects more tightly and opening up other areas of uncertainty. We have decided to reprint this book, however, because it contains the basic theoretical stance from which our later thinking derives. So that the evolution of one approach to a better understanding of the subtle interaction between the inner and outer worlds of the married pair may be traced, we have left the text unchanged.

THE INSTITUTE OF MARITAL STUDIES

viii

Acknowledgments

We wish to thank all those who in many different ways have made the writing of this book possible.

We are grateful to all our clients for their co-operation in the joint task of understanding their problems, and especially to those who have given us permission to use some of the material of their interviews at the Bureau. Although all factual details have been altered to conceal identity, nevertheless we know that to allow the publication of individual and intimate material is never easy, and may be painful. We hope that those clients whose experiences are described here can feel that this is justified on the grounds of its value to others, both to those whose marriages are in difficulties and to those who are trying to help them.

Our thanks must also go to all those individuals and institutions who have made financial contributions to the Bureau, especially to the Home Office and the London County Council, whose constant support and interest have enabled us to do the clinical work on which the case studies and the discussion technique are based.

The work of the Family Discussion Bureau could never have been attempted or developed without its consultants, past and present. We should like to mention in particular Dr J. D. Sutherland, who, despite his heavy duties as Director of the Tavistock Clinic, has for many years given generously of his time and support to the Bureau, and Mrs Enid Balint, who has been associated with the project from its inception. Dr Geoffrey Thompson's introductory chapter will, in part, indicate the extent of his interest in the Bureau; but only the authors know how much he has contributed to their understanding and to this work.

We have also to thank our many casework colleagues, both those who have shared in the work of the Bureau and those who have been associated with us in various training projects, and from whose experience and problems we have learnt much.

Finally, we must express our grateful recognition of the forbearance with which our much-tried secretarial staff endured us and the manuscript during the preparation of the book.

Introduction

By A. G. THOMPSON, M.D., F.R.C.P.I.

Nearly everyone at some time in his life finds himself concerned in a marital difficulty, either his own or someone else's. Those who have had this experience and who have discovered how bewildering marriage problems can be and how difficult it is to give help with them, must end by asking themselves the question, 'What are marriage difficulties really all about?' This fundamental question, and the allied one of how can help be given to those in trouble in their marriages, constitute the theme of this book. In professional marital work one is faced at the outset with very considerable difficulties of a technical nature, not only because the whole field is still relatively unexplored and poorly understood, but also because very great emotional tensions are involved. The people concerned, the married partners themselves and perhaps their relatives, inevitably feel deeply about the situation, and often hold very strong convictions about it or about the sort of action that they think should be taken. In these circumstances the strongest pressures may be brought to bear upon the professional worker, and unless he can resist these pressures he will find himself pushed into premature and misguided attempts at solution. It is vital that he should keep clear of such attempted solutions, which always imply underlying assumptions about the nature of the problem, until he has had time to draw independent conclusions from his own observations.

The aetiology of marital relationships is very complex, and the factors involved operate at different levels. Social, cultural and economic influences all play an important part. The operation of some of these is relatively clear, that of others is much more obscure. There are, however, wide differences between individuals and between individual marriages in their response to social pressures and opportunities. In some marriages a given set of circumstances constitutes a threat which brings about deterioration in the relationship, while in others it calls forth a positive response and a strengthening of the ties between the couple. It is the emotional make-up of the individual and the nature of the interaction between the partners in the marriage which determine the response, and it is with this aspect of the marital relationship that we are here concerned.

The basic theory for the work described in this book is the psychoanalytic theory of personality development and human relationships. The initial assumption, in fact, is that the answer to our fundamental question is to be sought primarily through an understanding of the way in which human relationships develop from their earliest beginnings in infancy, and how these first experiences underlie all later relationships.

Human beings are essentially 'social' animals. They cannot survive in isolation from their kind. By their very nature they need, and strive intensely for, relationships with one another. This inherent biological need for relationships is most clearly evident in the years of infancy and childhood. The first and most basic relationship is that of the helpless and dependent baby with its mother. The baby is born into the closest possible personal relationship with its mother, and it grows and develops, both physically and psychologically, within this relationship, building up little by little its whole inner concept of itself, of other human beings, and of the world it lives in. The mother nurses and feeds the baby, holds it close to her body, handles and tends it, and day by day reacts and responds to all its developing needs and activities according to her own nature and emotional resources. In this primary relationship with its mother, extended later to the rest of its family, the baby lives through its first and most fateful experiences. It commences to feel instinctual excitement, tension, satisfaction and pleasurable feelings of all kinds, as well as inevitable frustration and suffering, and comes to experience its earliest and deepest feelings of love and trust, as well as of hate, jealousy, fear and suspicion. With regard to the individual's ultimate capacity for personal relationships, these primary experiences are formative in the deepest sense. This is not to imply that later experiences, occurring in the years when the child's reality sense is more fully developed, do not also deeply influence his personality development. However, the experiences of early years go far to determine, in conjunction with the nature of the child's hereditary endowment, the kind of adult into which he will grow, the kind of beliefs he will have about himself and other people, the kind of personal relationships he will be able to form with them, and the extent to which he will be able to fulfil his inherent biological and psychological potentialities, upon the fulfilment of which the satisfactoriness and 'worthwhileness' of his life so largely depend.

More and more, then, we are beginning to realize that man's deepest and most lasting concern, that which really dominates him and provides the dynamic of his life, is his relationship with other human beings, both in the directly personal sense, as in the relationships of love, marriage and parenthood, and in the broader social sense, in friendships and work relationships, and in altered and sublimated forms in all the varied activities of his life. Indeed, it is not too much to say that the happiness and fulfilment of a person's life are determined fundamentally by the nature and quality of his relationships with other human beings, rooted in the experiences of the primary and formative relationships of infancy and childhood. As these determine in large measure the degree of happiness and fulfilment achieved in the lives of the countless individuals who make up our society, they are a vital factor in determining the stability and 'goodness' achieved by the social organization as a whole.

In recent years there has been an increasing recognition of the importance of disturbances in human relationships as an essential factor in many of the obscure ills of individuals and of society. Increasing attention is being paid not only by doctors but by sociologists and social workers to the problems of intimate human relationships. This book is concerned with one of the most important of all fields of human relationships, namely marriage. For a great many people the marriage relationship is by far the most important of their adult lives. It is the most direct heir of the intense primary relationships of childhood. For such people marriage, and the family relationships which develop out of marriage, provide their most important opportunity not only for emotional satisfactions but for personality development and maturation.

There is no such thing, outside the realms of imagination, as a marriage that is free from conflict. Such a relationship is not in the nature of human beings. In the depths of our minds we never, throughout all our lives, succeed in freeing ourselves fully from the hates and resentments that first arose in infancy, or from the excessive and unreal demands and expectations of those earliest years. These emotional forces are part of the essential dynamics of our personalities, and they operate intensely in marriage as they do in any deep emotional relationship, and lead inevitably to some measure of conflict, frustration and aggressive reaction against the partner.

Indeed, aggression and hate in some form and to some degree are inevitable in all love relationships, although their operation may often be quite concealed from view. They are certain to play a part, openly or otherwise, in every marriage, and even in the most apparently satisfactory and loving marriages the admixture of aggression and hate in the relationship can often be clearly recognized in certain aspects of the marriage or at certain phases. To an outside observer different marriages appear to vary widely in their degree of satisfactoriness and stability, but the more insight we obtain into the complexities of the relationship the more do we realize that the difference between 'satisfactory' and 'unsatisfactory' marriages is not a fundamental difference of kind. On the contrary, the same basic forces are involved in all marriages, what distinguishes one from another being rather the balance of the different factors involved, their relative intensity, and the characteristic ways in which they play into one another in the endless and shifting complexities of the relationship.

Marriages which appear to be permanently in difficulties and which, for want of a better term, I will call 'unsatisfactory' marriages, show the frustration and hate in an open form. What may be hard to discern in such cases is the love and belief that have disappeared from view. But, on the other hand, in most 'satisfactory' marriages the relationship between the partners, though for many reasons more difficult to study than in disturbed marriages, unquestionably contains strong elements of frustration, tension and aggression as an integral part of the highly complex interpersonal system. These elements may even at times reach an intensity which leads to violent conflict and despair. The truth is that love and hate are inevitably linked, and a happy and satisfactory marriage is certainly not one that is free from conflict and hate. Psychical conflict is an active process in all relationships that are alive and capable of growth and development. Indeed, it may be that it is the experience, extending over many years, of working through the love and hate in conflict, often in quite unrecognized ways, that makes a prolonged relationship such as marriage valuable as a therapeutic or maturational process.

There are doubtless some marriages in which the partners are never aware of being in difficulties at any stage, but in most cases difficulties of some degree become manifest sooner or later. Of course, the majority of married couples work through their problems and conflicts without turning to outside sources for help. Professional experience in the direct study of marriage and its problems has up to now been largely confined to that class of manifestly unhappy or 'unsatisfactory' marriage which either turns to, or is willing to be directed to, professional sources for help. This willingness to seek help, however despairingly, seems to indicate some hope, often quite a hidden one, of still being able to make use of the inherent potentialities of the relationship for growth and development, and a willingness that it should go on and not be finally destroyed. There is a third class of marriage which turns to outside sources only as a final step in bringing a failed relationship to an end.

Unhappy marriages are the cause of much suffering and frustration, both for parents and children, and undoubtedly constitute an important social problem the true extent and seriousness of which is only gradually being recognized, for unhappiness in intimate relationships is often anxiously shielded from the view of the outside world. Serious marital and parental disharmonies can lead eventually to a total break-up of the family, or to a lifetime of unhappiness and frustration for husband and wife, and can produce a crippling effect upon the developing personalities of their children, often leading in this way to a perpetuation of the same unhappy state of affairs in the next generation. A persistent bad relationship between husband and wife can not only produce devastating effects within the intimate family circle, but is a frequent underlying cause of serious difficulties in work and in social relations, and can have subtle and widespread repercussions in many other fields of community life. The family in fact is a vital unit in our society, and when something is wrong in the family, society is not slow to suffer for it. In spite of all the work that has been done with disturbed marriages in recent years, I am sure that we have not yet fully grasped the magnitude and complexity of the issues involved, and their implications for succeeding generations.

When an intimate relationship is in serious trouble it is notoriously difficult for an outsider to give effective help. One of the most important reasons for this is that the true roots of the difficulties that so frequently arise in intimate human relationships are very difficult to reach because they lie in the unconscious bases of the personalities of those involved, and are largely unknown to them. They cannot therefore be easily modified. These are facts that have only gradually been appreciated over the years, largely as the result of psycho-analytic investigations into the unconscious dynamics of human relationships. In many fields of mental health work attempts are now being made by workers who are not themselves psycho-analysts to make use of the understanding that has been gained by psycho-analysts in order to obtain a truer insight into the nature of the difficulties for which their help is sought, and to make this insight the foundation of a more rational and more effective technique of casework. Such a technique would aim at modifying, if only to a modest degree, the underlying basis of the disturbed relationship, and not merely at giving help with what are in effect the results rather than the causes of such disturbances.

Many of the social and clinical problems that doctors and caseworkers in various fields are called upon to deal with can be traced back to the family circle and can be recognized as manifestations of emotional conflict in marriage or in family life. With the increasing recognition of this fact, various organizations have come into being which attempt to give help to marriages and families that are in difficulties. One of the most recent of these organizations is the Family Discussion Bureau, a small body of professional caseworkers which was set up in 1948 by the Family Welfare Association and transferred in 1956 to the Tavistock Institute of Human Relations. The Bureau started its existence as a small pioneering group which set out to study the problems of marital difficulties as they present themselves to social caseworkers, and to try to develop a soundly based and practicable technique of casework.

It was recognized from the start that in marital difficulties one is confronted with the same type of disturbance in human relationships that psycho-analysts study in various settings, and on which psychoanalysis has thrown so much light. It was to psycho-analysts, therefore, that the caseworkers of the Bureau turned for assistance in the twofold task of trying to deepen their understanding of the nature of marital relationships and of developing a casework technique on a rational aetiological basis which could be learned and used by caseworkers who were not themselves psycho-analytically trained. The pioneer efforts of the group along these lines are, I think, full of interest for therapeutic workers in many different fields, but particularly, of course, for those who are themselves engaged in work with marriage and family problems.

A first report of the work of the Family Discussion Bureau was published in 1955.[1] The present book is concerned with the results of further work, and is somewhat differently orientated from the first. Much additional experience has been gained in the past five

[1] *Social Casework in Marital Problems*. Tavistock Publications, 1955.

years, on the basis of which an attempt is now made to describe what appear to be some of the important dynamic factors in the marriage relationship and in the disturbances which so frequently arise within it, and also to try to understand and describe what takes place in the complicated and often very difficult therapeutic relationships which develop during the progress of this particular type of casework.

Something must now be said about the organization of the Bureau, particularly in its relation to its therapeutic work. Though administratively a part of the Tavistock Institute of Human Relations, the Bureau functions as an independent unit whose clients are referred by a wide range of other agencies. In recent years only about 12 per cent of clients applied directly, 60 per cent coming from psychiatric and medical sources and the remainder through non-medical social caseworkers. The actual therapeutic work is carried out by a small group of caseworkers which has varied in number at different times from about six to ten. Clients attend regularly, usually for an hour once a week. Each client has his or her own worker and ordinarily remains with that worker throughout the period of treatment. Husband and wife attend independently of each other unless they wish otherwise. In practice they usually come on different days or at different hours of the day. Sometimes only one of a married pair attends, but experience has shown that it is much more helpful if husband and wife both come, and in fact both usually do, but always have different caseworkers. The period of attendance varies widely from case to case and may extend over a considerable time, sometimes many months.[1] It is only through this regular and continuous work that security can be given for the necessary relationships with caseworkers to be established and to develop in parallel with the changes occurring in the marital relationship itself. This is a central theme in the work of the Bureau, as will be seen from the accounts of casework described in the following chapters.

The same considerations apply to the regular weekly case conferences which are attended by all the caseworkers and by the consultant analyst. They are an essential part of the work and form a regular point of contact between the analyst and the workers, and also between the workers themselves. At these conferences the current casework is discussed and the difficulties met with are as

---

[1] Of the 278 clients, representing 144 marriages, who attended in 1958, 41·7 per cent had under 11 interviews, 50·4 per cent had between 11 and 60 interviews, and 7·9 per cent more than 60.

far as possible worked through. In general, these are difficulties in understanding what is happening in the marriage and in the interviews and also in tolerating the often very considerable tensions that inevitably arise in the work with the clients. The case conferences are not only 'learning sessions' for the workers, but they are also in a very important sense 'therapeutic sessions'. In saying this, however, I do not wish to give the impression that the case conference is a kind of 'therapeutic group'. It is fundamentally a learning group in which the analyst has some knowledge to contribute, as also have the caseworkers. The therapeutic element lies in the group's recognition that anxiety and inner resistances are important factors in making knowledge of unconscious processes difficult to understand, accept and utilize. This applies not only to the worker's capacity to learn from his own on-going cases but also to make use in a more effective and more conscious way of the whole body of his past experience and knowledge, much of which has hitherto remained unrecognized and unutilizable. Increasing knowledge and understanding is also built up through the shared experience of the case conferences. In these conferences many anxieties and difficulties arising in connection with the casework can be experienced, often very acutely, and worked through in a group situation in direct relationship to the case material. Our experience shows that in this way much can gradually be done to lessen the internal resistances and anxieties in workers that interfere with their comprehension and with their capacity for effective participation in therapeutic work. These conferences also provide an opportunity to reconsider from time to time the theoretical basis of the casework and to test out its application in the day-to-day work with marital problems. Indeed, this book is the outcome of a long series of such conferences, although different members of the group have become individually responsible for different sections of the book.

The central part of the book consists of five case studies. These are preceded by a general theoretical statement. In this, the place of the marital relationship in society is shortly considered, and a brief outline is given of the most important psycho-analytical concepts of personality development.

In the arrangement of the book the authors were faced with the dilemma that a certain amount of theoretical background is required to give meaning and significance to the detailed material of the case histories, yet theory is difficult to absorb unless exemplified by such illustration. In a practical training situation, experience and the assimilation of theory can go hand in hand, but it is not possible to reproduce this process in a book. Whether the initial theoretical chapter is read before or after the case studies must, therefore, remain a matter of personal choice.

Following the case descriptions, some of the general theoretical concepts are reconsidered in the light of the detailed material. One of the themes which emerges is that every marriage has a dynamic structure of its own, and a characteristic identity which is not merely the sum total of the personalities of the two partners. Yet, while each couple may deal with their conflicts and tensions in different ways, and each marriage has, so to speak, a distinctive texture of its own, nevertheless the same basic dynamic and developmental processes can be seen to be at work in all these marriages. In the chapter which follows the case histories, therefore, an attempt is made to outline some aspects of the developmental problems and the related processes occurring in marriage.

In the final chapter the implications of these concepts for casework and caseworkers are considered, together with some ideas about the group setting at the Bureau, and the four-person relationship which is central to its casework technique.

This book lays no claim to originality in basic theoretical concepts. Many of the ideas expressed in it have been more fully formulated elsewhere. What I believe is new, and will, I think, be of special interest to caseworkers generally, is the particular type of therapeutic technique that has been evolved. One of the objects of the book is to describe this technique, and the type of casework experience in relation to which it has developed.

The five cases presented here were selected from among those which had most recently been studied in the regular meetings of the working unit, and were felt to be representative both of the type of problems which come to the Bureau and also of the work of the group.[1] No attempt has been made here either to categorize or to

---

[1] The five cases presented were not systematically evaluated in terms of success or failure. However, from a preliminary study of a consecutive series of 100 cases, 'marked' or 'considerable' gains were shown in:

Short-term cases—by 20% of marriages,		20% of individuals
Medium	41%	65%
Long-term	53%	82%

This study also showed clearly associated gains in the individuals' physical health, the adjustment of the children and the effectiveness of the partners in their work life. These findings supported the results of an earlier unpublished study.

exemplify the varying patterns of marital interaction, or to make a comprehensive survey of marriage problems. Indeed, some of what are generally considered to be the most common ostensible causes of marital disharmony, as for instance 'triangle' situations, or interference by in-laws, are scarcely mentioned, though many who come to the Bureau bring these as their problems. Those clients we have described complained in fact of sexual difficulties, serious behaviour disorder in a child, bickering, drinking and violence. But however diverse are the forms of disturbance outwardly manifested in those marriages which seek our help, they all represent the intrusion of unconscious pressures or conflicting elements which the partners feel to be destructive of the relationship. They are symptoms, rather than causes, of inner difficulties and tensions, and it is these with which we are concerned in the case studies.

In studying and delineating the psychological processes which appeared to operate in these marriages, and in the additional relationships that were called into being during the therapeutic work, a further aim has been to increase our understanding of marriage and marital conflict in general, in terms of the unconscious psychological processes which are at work in all human relationships. The thesis implicit in the work is that the more fully we can comprehend these processes, the more effective will be our therapeutic work and the more lasting its results. Needless to say, the whole subject is full of obscurities and difficulties. This is true of all work on emotional factors in human relationships. Many questions are raised that cannot yet be answered, and may indeed never be answered. But even to raise them is a move in the direction of increased understanding and, it is to be hoped, of increased therapeutic effectiveness.

In the present-day world our traditional human values and patterns of relationships are undergoing far-reaching modifications in response to the radical changes that are taking place in our social environment. One result of such changes is that the marital relationship is assuming an ever more important role for many people. The work recorded in this book is a contribution towards meeting the resultant need to make marriage as rich a source as possible of happiness and development for the partners and the family.

PART I

Relationships and the Growth of Personality

Relationships and the Growth of Personality

The love relationship of man and woman that buiids itself into a marital union invites more of our interest and empathy than any other human relationship except perhaps that of parent and child. The seeking for this adult relationship, its preservation and its development towards parenthood are amongst the deepest aspirations of almost everyone. Its rights and its duties are jealously guarded by the individual. The high evaluation of its importance for the individual is endorsed by far-reaching social measures and many institutions.

The unravelling and reknitting of the complex strands which make up this intimate relationship, its conflicts and satisfactions, is the coricern of this book. It is, however, a technical book, and its main purpose is to demonstrate a technique of 'marital therapy', i.e. of helping with emotional conflicts which are felt to be destroying the relationship and the persistence of which indicates that the couple cannot overcome them without outside help. Such a therapeutic technique has a further usefulness; it provides unique opportunities to observe and understand the processes of marital interaction. Indeed, the deeper understanding of such intimate relationships and of individual personalities can only be gained in the context of a professional relationship with those who seek help for their suffering. Only under these conditions can access be gained to the inner psychological forces which make for the conflictful, as well as for the more fruitful, aspects of this close relationship.

Marriage makes possible an interaction of two personalities at greater depth and intimacy than is possible in any other relationships except those in early childhood. For the individual, it recapitulates much from past experience, perpetuating the security and goodness of childhood relationships while providing opportunity for their intimate enjoyment to be transformed from immature and dependent modes of gratification into the give-and-take of an interdependent relationship. For these reasons marriage has great potentialities for psychological and biological growth and for creative attainment. It offers an opportunity for self-realization through relationship with others which can come from no other kind of personal involvement except, perhaps, from vocation in its fullest sense.

Within the family, of which the marital relationship is the core, the past is recapitulated. Thus this broader reproductive cycle ensures that what has proved socially useful in self-expression, and in personal transactions, is transmitted through succeeding generations. That it fulfils this function effectively is essential for the adjustment of the individual and for the stability of society as a whole. As Wilson (1949) has said, the family is the primary school in which human relations are learned. It provides the setting within which the crude impulses of infancy and childhood are regulated and, by constructive experience and example, transformed from self-centred need-gratification to the give-and-take of mature social interaction.

The fundamental role of a permanent marriage relationship for the individual as well as for society is indicated on the one hand by the existence of lasting unions in those societies where promiscuity is permitted, and on the other hand by the historical evidence that instability of marriage and family life coincide with lack of vigour and integration in the community as a whole.

In myths and in the rituals of primitive societies this psycho-biological reproductive function of marriage is clearly recognized and is 'built into' the economic life of the community and into the reproductive cycle of nature. The beliefs and customs evolved to explain and regulate the beneficent forces of nature which give security, warmth and food, and the hostile elements which destroy or deny such goodness, are often applied also to regulate marital relationships. Codes of behaviour are no less rigorously applied in the one than in the other areas of life. The change from this kind of social organization in which man's primary tasks—the psycho-biological and economical—are closely interwoven, to modern social systems in which they are more separate, has added to, rather than diminished, the importance of nurturing offspring who can adapt to rapidly changing conditions.

The quality of marital relationships, and what is required of them by the partners, are influenced by the presence or absence of supportive or complementary opportunities for social satisfaction in work and other areas of the community life. Thus the marital relationship is especially vulnerable to insecurities and pressures from the changing social organization of which it is an integral part. Many writers have shown how the degree of social segregation or isolation of the married couple affects the kind and quality of demands which each makes upon the other within the marriage; how supports and satisfactions which are normally provided by participation in wider social and kinship networks are sought, and often not found, within the resources of marriage; how technological advances have resulted in diminished opportunities for social participation and for social satisfaction in work life, and have brought about a separation of work from social and family life, thus producing frustrations which have repercussions upon the marriage, as well as removing supports which otherwise might have enriched it.

In the past, many interwoven social networks and the closer contact of work, apprenticeship and family life provided a continuity of experience wherein relatively homogeneous value systems ordered the human relationships in all areas of community life. The fragmentation of modern urban society, with the consequent break-up of kinship, religious and social fellowships, puts a greater onus on the marriage to provide the emotional securities and satisfactions which formerly came from these other closely knit relationships.

Thus the family has to provide emotional satisfactions and to contain emotional tensions which formerly could find expression through other social channels, while at the same time it lacks those kinship and social supports which might have sustained it. This means that marriage becomes for many people the chief source of their emotional satisfaction, which in itself is both a danger and a challenge to the further development of the relationship; as Wilson (1949) notes, under modern urban conditions too much emotional current is directed into the marital relationship, which may create stresses and conflicts for the partners and also for their children.

Whereas in communities that were more closely knit in kinship and social and economic transactions and in which satisfactions through direct interpersonal relations were more widely spread, in modern society the need for these satisfactions tends to be directed much more into the marriage relationship. Such increased demands on the marriage to offset lack of personal satisfactions outside it may well increase the likelihood of frustration and conflict. At the same time, modern social and economic life provide opportunities for greater sharing and interchange of roles for husband and wife and thus can make for a fuller and richer life within the union.

This may explain the growing interest in marriage during the present decade, and the considerable effort to develop social services to help marriages in difficulty. The increasingly prominent incidence of marital problems has coincided with a greater readiness on the part of the community and of the individual to seek and accept help for a relationship which hitherto has been regarded as too intimate to bear outside observation or intervention.

This readiness to provide help and to seek it springs partly from the gradual assimilation within the community of knowledge about the nature and importance of intimate family relationships which has come about through the infiltration into so many areas of contemporary life of psycho-analytic concepts about personality development.

In particular, experience in Child Guidance and in the treatment of delinquency has shown how severe tensions within the marital relationship, or family breakdown, relate closely to social maladjustment in children. The increased awareness of the unconscious determinants of such tensions and of the early origins of the feelings of frustration, irrational wishes and anxiety they engender has brought about a greater willingness to explore the deeper aspects of marital interaction. The more open recognition of, and more tolerant attitude to, sexual feelings and functions has also made possible an easier acceptance by both caseworker and client of the sexual components in marital conflict.

Coincident with the increased need for treatment for disturbed marital relationships, and the related changes in social attitudes and knowledge, new concepts have been developed in the social sciences and in preventive mental health work which are particularly apposite in understanding interpersonal relationships and their conflicts. The emphasis has moved from attention to the individual and his capacity for relations with others, to a concern with the kinds of interaction which can exist within various social units, be they two person, three person or larger groups.

The health and success of such social units, e.g. the work group or the family group, depends on the interaction between its individual members rather than on the separate contributions of these individuals. This pattern of interaction can be understood only in the context of an ongoing process which would not exist without the social unit with its own particular purpose.

The parent-child relationship, the family triad and the marital relationship may be thought of as particular instances of such social units. Their primary task is more fundamental than that of any other social unit, by reason of the extent and depth of psychological involvement required to fulfil it. Since the marital relationship has the double function, the self-realization of husband and wife, and the social development of their children, the understanding of its interactions as an ongoing process is of particular importance for the development of preventive mental health work.

In our study of marriage we are concerned with two primary social units: firstly, that of the families of origin in which each marital partner has built up his own individual patterns of conducting relationships; secondly, that of the marriage itself which (like any other relationship, though more directly because of the closeness of its ties) repeats and develops these patterns which were learned during the formative years of childhood. Marriage and the parent-child relationship, more than any other areas of living, focus attention on the overriding importance of a permanent ongoing relationship as a prerequisite for the healthy unfolding of personality, in adulthood as well as in the dependent period of childhood.

In order to understand marital interaction in terms of these related, though different, primary relationships, and to understand also the nature of the conflicts which threaten the inherent securities and potentialities for growth in marriage, the Family Discussion Bureau has drawn considerably on psychoanalytic knowledge and experience. For the aim of this approach is to understand how early experiences may be superimposed on the more mature marriage relationship, leading, on the one hand, to conflict despite the conscious strivings of both partners, and on the other, in more fortunate conditions, or with suitable help, to an enrichment of the marriage in the depth of its fellowship and mutual fulfilment.

It is from such understanding that the method of therapy, described in this book, has developed. Its aim is not so much to produce changes in the personalities of the individual partners as to enable them together to make use of the potentialities for growth and self-realization which are inherent in the marital union.

Psycho-analytic studies have shown how the relationships which are established between parent and child set the pattern for the making of future relationships, and how unresolved conflicts from this early experience reduce the capacity of individuals in later life to build up mutually satisfying relationships. These studies have demonstrated the importance of unconscious factors in making and maintaining relationships, and they have shown how these centres of conflict arise in the early dependent relationships of childhood. From this knowledge of how they arise, it is possible to understand something of the reasons why the conflictful and seemingly irrational behaviour in more adult relationships is so difficult to influence, in spite of the individual's wish to set it aside.

The most important determining factor in the early phases of development is the child's dependence upon his parents, whom he needs not only for physical survival but who also are the most important objects in his world. The quality of his relations with them determine the security and satisfaction with which he involves himself with his external world. From the beginning of life the basic need of the individual, as part of a psycho-social unit, is to maintain good relations with his objects[1]—specifically people with whom he has close emotional ties—for only by doing so can he feel secure within himself and interact successfully with others.

The intense primary relations of childhood are experienced and lived through when the child's capacity for seeing the world as it is, and for testing out its opportunities and frustrations, is very limited. What is experienced in its reality and what is tested out and assimilated as a body of secure knowledge by the child develops rapidly, though precariously, throughout the early years. This is particularly so in his perception and experience of people, for his dependence upon them and the intensity of his feelings in response to them so frequently tend to distort what measure of real experience he has built up. For example, on occasions when a mother has to punish or frustrate him, she may be felt and seen as utterly bad and threatening. In face of such frustration the child may regress to less mature ways of responding to his objects, losing for the time being, in his rage or anxiety, the secure knowledge he has of them.

During these early dependent phases of childhood, a large proportion of all perception and experience is unconscious in the sense that it includes only a measure of tested-out and assimilated experience of reality, which is proportionate to the gradual unfolding of the individual's capacities. In the normal course of development, such experience, often repeated, gradually approximates to what is

---

[1] The word 'object' is used rather than person; it is a general term for a source of satisfaction of needs which may not always be a person. It has the advantage of denoting also the unconscious choice and perception of sources of gratification.

valid and secure knowledge appropriate to each phase of growing up. As such it provides a reliable basis for the extension of experiences by the use of new capacities as they mature, and of knowledge and skills already tried, to extend and enrich his interaction with his world.

This growing body of more conscious, reality-tested experience is organized into what may be called the central ego; it incorporates tried-out and well-assimilated patterns of response and interaction, structured basically in terms of primary relationships between parents and child. Because it is tried out and tested against reality, it has much in common with the central ego experiences of others and thus affords a basis of secure relations with them. The extent to which the central ego is capable of maturation, through the dependent relationships of childhood to the more interdependent personal transactions of adult life, varies with the degree to which it has achieved integration through relationships with objects (e.g. parents) who have consistently confirmed their goodness and secure tolerance of the child's intense and immature ways of self-expression.

If the child's experience of frustration from his primary objects is greater than his capacity to deal with them on a reality level, the intensity of feeling engendered is so great that it may override the already assimilated experience of reality. It may threaten to overwhelm completely the resources of the central ego and negate the knowledge of goodness and security in the object relationships already built up. In such circumstances the object is perceived as completely bad, and responded to with feelings, and impulses to action, which express hate or the wish to attack, destroy or dominate. In extreme instances the child may turn away in apathy and hopelessness.

In order to preserve that portion of the central ego which is thereby threatened, as well as to preserve the external good objects (e.g. the parents concerned), both of which are essential to the biological and psychological integrity of the child, these intense, negative experiences are split off and repressed. With these unconscious sub-systems some remnants of ego (reality-tested experience) may also be repressed. These primitive fixated parts of the ego retain their own drives and attempt to serve their own irrational aims.

It is these latter split-off substructures of personality, which are in varying degree unconscious and therefore not accessible to the central ego for the more healthy process of reality-testing and reassimilation, that produce conflictful relationships.

Even though repressed, these psychological systems are for ever active, and, as it were, seeking resolution of the original dilemma from which they sprang. This dilemma consists essentially of the contradictory and irreconcilable perceptions of the needed object; on the one hand that it is good and to be preserved as the *sine qua non* of a secure unfolding of the central ego, and, on the other hand, that it is bad and frustrating, and to be attacked or forced to conform to the blind untempered demands of the immature child. In order to make more full and secure the central ego's experience of its object world, and to reabsorb those resources of personality which are invested in these unconscious split-off systems, repeated efforts are made to test the conflictful phantasy assumptions they contain. Where the strength and security of the central ego is equal to the task, where some linkages between it and the unconscious system can be established, and where the subsequent experience of the object tends to disprove these phantasy assumptions, a good deal of reintegration may be achieved. This is particularly so within the close dependent relationships of childhood (and as we shall see also in subsequent intimate relationships) where the parents can tolerate this repeated testing-out, and where their tolerant and objective responses to regressive behaviour can disprove the phantasy which is the main cause of anxiety, i.e. that the wished-for destructive, hateful relationship will destroy for ever the needed good relationships. The dilemma which arises from this regressive testing-out manifests itself, therefore, as an effort by the total personality to maintain and extend its experience of, and capacity for, good relationships, while in contradictory fashion a part of the personality still seeks irrationally and compulsively to obtain gratification by destructive efforts which threaten the control systems of the central ego. This process of regressive testing-out is seen, therefore, as an important part of the growth of the individual's capacity for increasingly mature relationships.

As would be expected, the testing out and building up of ways of conducting relationships in infancy and childhood centre around those issues which are predominant for both parent and child at successive phases of development. By the same reasoning, later conflictful behaviour, motivated from the split-off unconscious systems of the personality, is typified by the quality and aim of object relationships which derive from the period in the child's development when the original conflicts were produced. Three important phases in the formative years of infancy and childhood are commonly distinguished in psycho-analytic studies. There is considerable overlap between them, and the transition from one to another succeeding phase will vary in its spacing according to the experience and rate of maturation of the individual child. These phases cover approximately from birth to 1 year, from 1 to 3 years, and from 3 to 6 years. It will be recognized that during the first year the intensity of feeling and degree of undifferentiated response to experience is at its greatest. At the same time the capacity to perceive and assimilate reality is at its lowest. It is only gradually and some-what precariously that a more secure balance is attained, towards the end of the third phase. Henceforward a more sure-footed testing-out of reality experience is possible wherein the patterns of making relationships already learned are consolidated, before the psycho-biological changes of adolescence which mark the transition to adulthood.

In the first of these phases of the infant's development its contact with the mother is overwhelmingly its most important relationship with the external world. In fact, because the infant is incapable of differentiating between what is itself and what is outside, at this stage, this relationship is its world. The main concern in this relation-ship is the satisfaction of the infant's need for food as well as for the closeness and wholeness which contact with the mother provides. The infant is completely dependent, and the satisfaction of his needs is thus a one-way process. On the part of the child it is all taking and no giving; on the part of the mother it is all giving and no taking (though it may be experienced by her, of course, quite differently). The sense of well-being or of total discomfort which the infant experiences according to whether these conditions are satisfactory or not, tends to be an all-or-nothing response in which the infant feels itself and its world to be entirely good, or entirely bad. Its response tends to be an undifferentiated psychological response of the whole organism.

According to psycho-analytical findings which are very much supported by infant observation, the child begins to develop the capacity to be aware of and to tolerate a measure of psychological separation from its object (the mother) at about the time when it is also able to achieve a measure of biological independence, i.e. at around the stage of weaning, towards the end of this first phase of development. The infant becomes dimly aware of what is inside itself, its own very undifferentiated state of being, and what is outside; what is self and what is object. The possibility of making a relationship has unfolded, and with it the nuclear structure of the central ego. Here is the beginning of a two-way process in experiencing and testing out relationships with its objects though it is still very heavily weighted on getting and receiving from, rather than on giving to, the other. Intense greed at moments of frustration (which may depend as much or more on the state of the organism, as on the giving of the mother) now constitutes a problem in human relationships. For with the awareness of the mother as a separate person, such intense greed may devour and destroy the object which is most anxiously needed and which, in its goodness when it satisfies, constitutes the corner-stone of the infant's self, its central ego. To avoid such eventualities, some of this intense phantasy experience may be split off and repressed. It may remain so, or be retested and reintegrated into the experience of the central ego, depending on the intensity and degree of repression and the extent to which subsequent relations with the object tend to confirm or disprove the infant's fears.

At this time, because of the infant's extreme uncertainty as to what is self and what is object, it is normally unable to distinguish clearly whether or not feelings within itself are not also the feelings and attitudes of the external world. At times of frustration, intensity of feeling overrides what little capacity the infant has attained for making this distinction, and it may ascribe its own feelings entirely to its object and, following a splitting-off of such experience, continue to do so in unconscious though ever active perception.

Those systems of the future personality which embody unconscious object relationships from this 'oral' phase of development will show some of these characteristics when they are superimposed on later relationships, in the efforts of the total personality to attain (belatedly) fuller integration.

The second phase of development in childhood is typified by the child's growing awareness of himself, particularly in terms of his increased capacity in bodily functions and in achieving control of them. The attainment of the ability to walk and to talk brings a greater possibility of communication with his objects and with it a greater capacity to control them and make demands upon them.

The intensity of feeling at times of frustration may again make these wishes to control and demand from objects a frightening and conflictful experience, so that repression of these impulses is required. The parents' own value judgments, as well as their personal tolerance of physical demands and aggressions, play an important part in the child's learning of what is good or what is dangerous in the eyes of his objects. This too is the age at which toilet training becomes an important issue in the relationship between child and parent. While the child is now, for the first time, becoming more surely aware of self and object as separate, he is at the same time learning the rudiments of give and take in his relations with his parents. Since his awareness of himself is so much in terms of his whole body, he tends to equate it with his conception of self—both for himself and for his object—so that the products of his body become important to him in this rudimentary give and take. That they are acceptable means that he is good; that they are regarded as dirty and bad means that he is bad. Intense frustration may again override his clear distinction of good and bad in himself, and in his parents, and he may regard the products of his bodily functions as responsible for making himself wholly bad and dangerous to his parents as, on the other hand, they make his parents seem intolerably bad and persecuting to himself. The danger might be that this mechanism of projective identification may become a fixed, as distinct from a temporary, mechanism in conducting relationships.

By the time of the third phase of development, the child's capacity for perceiving his world more realistically has become greater. His intellectual resources have considerably developed. He has extended the range of people with whom he makes contact and he can become more fully involved with them. He is less dependent upon the mother and more aware of the three-person relationship situation (which includes the father) of which he is part. This phase, then, is typified by the child's growing awareness of the difference between mother and father and brother and sister, both as objects who satisfy important needs in his development and also as people of like and different sex to himself. The awareness of physical differences inevitably rouses curiosity and anxiety about his own body and that of the opposite sex. The curiosity about the nature of sexual differences and sexual functions will be the more securely explored, the more the conflicts concerning control of bodily functions in the previous phase of development were resolved.

The child's understanding of sexual differences will depend in large measure not only upon the tolerance of the parents in regard to his explorations, but also on the manner and security with which their own heterosexual roles are taken. From his experience of them he will work out his own heterosexual identifications and build up attitudes about the goodness and badness of his sexual wishes which may considerably influence his making of future relationships.

The conflicts of this phase are the more difficult because of the intrusion and effect of the child's developing sexual impulses, directed mainly towards the parents, and the feeling of rivalry and jealousy arising from his perception that they together have a relationship in which he cannot share. The intensity of feeling when the rivalry dilemma becomes too great may result in phantasies in which he strives to separate the parents, to destroy one or the other so that he may possess one for himself alone, to take the place of one or the other or to achieve a sexual relationship by aggressive and sadistic dominance. A further aspect of this anxiety is the damage that he imagines may be done to him in retaliation for his own destructive phantasies. The anxieties which relate to such phantasies are considerable, for they involve not only the love and preservation of mother and father, but also the preservation of the family unit which provides the secure social base essential for the child's growth towards adulthood.

In so far as he is able to resolve these conflicts and explore the reality of the triangular situation he will make good use of this important phase of learning human relationships. The child may identify securely with the parent of his or her own sex and accept, and feel accepted by, the parent of the opposite sex. But residues of these conflicts and the resultant confusion about masculine and feminine roles may show throughout life.

The child's capacity to deal with these problems of heterosexual identifications, and the resulting feelings about the goodness or badness of sexuality as a mode of self-expression in interpersonal relationships, has important repercussions on the future capacities of the individual to be a confident husband and father, wife and mother, and to express his own loving feelings in the sexual life of his marriage.

It will be apparent that each succeeding phase of development is attempted with the psychological equipment built up in the previous phases. This equipment includes what has been tested out at the level of reality integration appropriate to the child's stage of maturation, and it includes also those areas of the personality not yet so developed or even, in varying degree, split off as previously described, and therefore less capable of integration into the personality as a whole.

Each phase provides an opportunity for re-integration and consolidation as well as a challenge to move forward to fuller and more reality-based relations with his objects. In a sense, each new phase in the maturation process is potentially something of a crisis, as any big adjustment to new opportunities is even in later life. Insecurity and lack of integration from previous experience produces uncertainty in effort and the likelihood of regression to easier, proven methods of dealing with such situations, even though these methods are now inappropriate to the new stage of maturation. These regressions, particularly in childhood, but also in later intimate dependent relationships, may provide opportunity to retest what was still insecure, untested or even split off from the central ego development. Indeed, such regression in childhood is an essential part of the growth process, and is healthy, though upsetting in the intensity of feeling and demand it makes on the object, and in the temporary insecurity and anxiety it produces in the child. It will be healthy and growth-producing to the extent that the parents can tolerate it and help the child to retest his unreal perceptions and irrational wishes against the reality of the situation and of the relationships involved. On the other hand, these regressions in less supporting circumstances, as when the adult cannot tolerate such primitive behaviour and by his own anxiety confirms that of the child, or when the child's unconscious expectancies are otherwise confirmed, may undo such links as remain between the central ego and the split-off, unformed segments of the personality. Such experience may even consolidate the repressed phantasies and make them impossible to retest, except through skilled therapeutic intervention.

The degree of security achieved in each phase of development provides the psychological equipment and the motivation to meet further challenges and extend the individual's capacity to deal with his world. Throughout the individual's life there are possibilities for growth and reintegration, as well as for regression and rigidity, which will consolidate the conflicting organizations of the personality.

In later relations, as in childhood, the essential motivation of the personality is to achieve a greater integration of the previous experience of relations with people; to bring together the more reality-tested experience of these objects, which we have called the central ego, with those unconscious but ever-active residues of experience which are grossly self-centred, destructive and controlling, and thereby irreconcilable with the more mature aims of a give and take relationship. Not only is there considerable emotional invest-ment in these latter split-off, dissociated 'systems' of the personality, and therefore less deep feeling available for constructive relationships, but, in varying measures, some of the resources of the central ego are taken up in controlling them in order to prevent their destructive, irrational aims being brought out in reality.

It will be apparent, therefore, that the balance of forces invested in these potentially conflictful systems of the personality, as against those resources available in the central ego, determines whether repressive and defensive, or more constructive relationships with people are possible.

In a two-person interaction, for example, such possibilities vary according to the circumstances in which the relationship is being attempted, and the conscious and unconscious meanings attached by each individual to the behaviour of the other. Whether the inter-action is conflictful, defensive or creative, depends on what is sought by each, on what is offered, and on what is consciously or unconsciously avoided.

Where the areas of conflict in parent and child coincide or in some important aspect complement each other, it is as if both uncon-sciously conspire together to ensure that the unresolved residues of unconscious experience which they share is never brought to light to be tested out again in their relationship. For example, the child's repression of phantasy experience, in which he sought to attack or control the mother with the contents of his body, may have the defences he has built up to guard against this eventuality strengthened by the mother's obsessional concern over cleanliness (reflecting some similar residual conflict in herself). The rigidity with which the split-off phantasy relations are prevented from finding any measure of direct expression so that they may be brought into the relationship, retested and integrated in central ego experience is thereby con-siderably increased. If the degree of conflict is great in proportion to the total resources of the central ego, there may be little freedom and security to conduct creative and mutually satisfying relation-ships. If, on the other hand, the degree of conflict involves less of the total personality resources, this 'collusive' interaction, in which the defences of the mother lend support to the needed defences of the child, may in fact result in increased freedom of self-expression in other non-conflictful areas of their lives.

There is considerable variation in the ways in which these unconscious 'collusions' have a restrictive, a creative or a conflict-producing function in regulating the interaction between two or more closely tied individuals. For example, a 'fit' in the restrictive ways by which each married partner regulates unconscious greedy impulses may provide a mutual security by the side of which many other satisfactions may be shared. If, however, the intensity of impulse is very great in one or both partners, the restriction may spread over too wide an area of the marriage and conflict will result.

Many other examples will emerge in the context of the adult marriage relationship from the case studies presented in later chapters. There, also, a great deal of attention will be focussed on patterns of interaction where the 'collusive' relationships do not fulfil their defensive purpose, or where they do not allow the partners a sufficient measure of creative outlet. In these cases they intensify conflict within the marriage. This may be because the collusion is so overwhelmingly repressive that it denies one or both partners a necessary measure of self-regard or self-realization in their respective roles of husband and wife (as of parent and child). In some cases the taking of heterosexual roles may be greatly restricted in direct expression as well as more indirectly throughout family life. In other cases the 'collusion' may provide a mutually needed system of regulation in one key area of the relationship, only to leave some other deeply pressing aspect uncontrolled.

So far we have concentrated on the process of conflict and self-realization within the primary relationships of the family, and our attention has been directed more closely to the viewpoint of the child than to the part of the parent. It will be recognized, however, that within the parent-child relationship the opportunities for readaptation and growth in capacity for making object relations is not all on the side of the child. Where the balance of forces within the interaction permits of security and tolerance for the continued process of testing-out, increased freedoms and forms of self-expression will also be achieved by the parents. It is only when the conflict between the hateful and destructive relationships in unconscious systems and the need to preserve loving, good object relations becomes too great to be tested out within the resources of the two or three persons concerned that the twin process of conflict and growth cannot be contained within the primary relationship. In these circumstances mutual regression and intolerance may result which threaten the securities on which the primary relationship is founded. So it is in the marital relationship as it was in the earlier parent-child relationship.

The later phases of childhood provide opportunities by which the pattern of making and maintaining relationships which was built up in the early dependent phases may be modified or in varying ways consolidated, depending upon the experience within the family and with an increasing range of people outside it. The extent to which these opportunities are used for the creative integration of the personality, and for the differentiation of effective defensive ways of making relations whereby the central ego mediates the expression of unconscious systems in socially acceptable modes of behaviour, depends largely upon the amount of security and tolerance within which social learning has been possible in earlier years. It depends also upon the kind and quality of relations with people which is possible outside the immediate family circle. In modern times the lack of integration of family, work and social life which should provide the mores and the motivation for the use of more specific educational opportunities, takes away much from the potentialities within these years for growth and consolidation. The pressure to test out increasing physical and intellectual resources with contemporaries in a social context which embodies, and is seen to embody, secure value systems and standards of behaviour is focussed too narrowly, and too separately, upon the home and the school. In addition, modern life provides a considerably more direct and wider range of intellectual and emotionally charged stimulation without the opportunity to test out 'on the pulses', as it were, its implications for the individual in his relations with his fellows. This stimulation, rich in intellectual and emotional challenge, often carries human relationship implications which conflict with the value systems embodied in the family life, and which indeed tend to support rather than modify the direct expression of impulse so typical of childhood. Thereby also the conflicts inherent in unconscious systems of the personality are fed and intensified, making the retesting of their irrational assumptions inside and outside the family more difficult.

These difficulties, together with a lack of opportunity for integrative experience within the social and cultural networks outside the home, make for a regressive and overdependent reliance upon the immediate family circle, instead of affording a long phase of exploration in which the learned patterns of conducting relations are extended and consolidated before facing the challenges of adolescence.

Thus modern conditions present particular difficulties in the way of establishing a secure belongingness within the family and at the same time a basis for a like sense of more independent belongingness in the world at large, both of which attainments are prerequisites for healthy development through the transitional phase before adulthood.

But these discrepancies within the social milieu of the adolescent— the more direct presentation of opportunities for economic independence and for heterosexual gratification, by the side of a lack of integrative supports within the community—have sharper repercussions during this latter phase of maturation. For at this time the child quickly develops physical, emotional and intellectual resources which for their fulfilment require him to discover ways of self-expression which conform to adult roles in economic and heterosexual relations. In this transition phase, which involves the giving up of much of the earlier dependent relations and the transforming of them into more mature, independent relations, a great many of the conflicts inherent in each earlier stage of dependence are reactivated. For in each earlier stage there was a like dilemma involving the choice between a regressive retention of dependent ties, and the giving up of some measure of such satisfaction in order to meet the challenge of a new step towards independence and self realization.

For the parents, the adolescence of their children may produce, in varying degrees, similar conflicts. Earlier in this chapter we have discussed the importance of collusion between parents and children. The adolescent child may be trying to free itself from restrictive aspects of this collusion and may no longer be prepared to carry some of his parents projections. This, as well as the first indications of the child's maturing sexuality, may reactivate anxieties in the parents about their own sexuality—and thus offer opportunities to review some of the causes of these anxieties. A child's adolescence may well, therefore, become an area for potential conflicts and potential growth in the marriage. On the one hand they may wish to retain too large a part of the child's dependence upon them, either because of their own insecurities, or because the movement of the adolescent out of the family presents them with problems of readjustment within their marriage relationship. On the other hand they may be intolerant of the child's dependence because they tend to measure their own achievement in marriage, as individuals and as parents, in terms of the success of their children in attaining adult independence.

For the adolescent the approach to adulthood is mediated by his experience of the parents in their roles as man and woman, and as husband and wife, not only in their manifest behaviour in these roles but more deeply in the underlying securities or insecurities which determine them. For it is against these deeper attitudes that his own feelings about his sexuality, and its expression as part of a relationship with another person, have been tested out in conscious and unconscious experience.

Sexual maturity holds frightening or reassuring possibilities for the adolescent, depending on the extent to which he has been able to work out constructive, or adequately defensive, methods of regulating his primary dependent needs, because the impulses which he now experiences are of a like order to those which motivated his search for gratification in infancy and childhood. In particular, he is faced with the possibility of realizing, through expression of these impulses, a sexual relationship—a relationship which previously was possible only in imagination on the basis of the knowledge and experience that had come his way, or in phantasy, in so far as such experience had been transformed by unconscious forces into a frightening or destructive possibility. Realization can therefore hold out either the assurance of transforming the sexual experience of the central ego into a satisfying sexual relationship, or the becoming real of phantasy sexual relationships which would be disrupting and destructive in their unconscious aims.

Although the period of adolescence is potentially so conflictful, it contains more possibilities for reintegration and adjustment than any of the previous phases of maturation. Not only has the individual a considerably increased range and depth of emotional response, but he has also greater and more securely established ego resources with which to give his feelings expression in creative effort, thereby realizing his new capacities for empathy and adult identification. The intensity of feeling, which stems largely from the physiological changes of adolescence, stirs the whole range of previous emotional experience, reactivating much that was conflictful as well as much that was deeply satisfying in the dependent phases of infancy and childhood. This provides a new opportunity for a retesting of past dependent relations, including residual unconscious phantasies, in the context of more mature resources and a more adult exchange of experience with parents.

In describing the primary relationship of parents and child we have inevitably anticipated much that throws light on the essential features of the marital relationship. We have also moved towards a clearer understanding of what is contained in a primary relationship in terms of its purpose and the conditions required to fulfil it. The essential motivation in all intimate relationships is for the individual to achieve a more secure and creative self through securely based and mutually satisfying relations with others, even though this drive may take many apparently contradictory forms.

In the continuity of the parent-child relationship, the conflicts which arise from the child's dependence upon the parents, and the parents involvement with the child can become an essential part of the growth process. Although the primary relationship of marriage is an adult relationship, it requires for its fulfilment conditions which match in their dynamic significance the inherent features of this earlier primary relationship. The self-realization of each partner in marriage, as man and woman and as father and mother, is possible only through each other. The attainment of this adult interdependence requires a depth and intimacy of involvement from each partner which matches in intensity the exclusive dependent relations of childhood. Sexual impulses, the expression of which are of central importance to the sense of the completeness which each partner seeks in marriage, epitomize, as it were, the primary nature of the feelings which are brought together and shared within the marriage. A condition of their secure and full expression, as of other intimate aspects of the marital relationship, is the sense of belongingness and the assurance of the continuity of the relationship through which the purposes of the marriage—the self-realization of each partner—may be achieved.

These essential features of the marital relationship are the prerequisites of the adjustment, and of the creative interaction, of the two personalities, as were similar conditions in the dependent years of each partner. Because of the importance of each partner to the other, and the basic nature of the needs which each seeks to satisfy in the other, the interaction is also potentially conflictful and likely to reactivate the dilemmas of earlier dependent relationships. Indeed, as in these earlier phases of growth, some measure of conflictful interaction is necessary, in order that each partner may extend his capacity for good and satisfying relations with the other.

In marriage generally, the more deeply conflictful aspects of the relationship are contained by the central ego resources which each contributes to the relationship in order to preserve the essential purposes of the union and what is experienced as good within it. In many circumstances the secure resources of good relationships within the marriage can make possible the expression of these deeper conflicts in one or both partners, so that the regressive retesting of their false assumptions may be worked through, thereby extending the capacities for adult give and take within the marriage.

When too large a proportion of the resources of the marriage are taken up with keeping out of the relationship the conflicts and potentially destructive residues of earlier experiences, the measure of self-realization possible for the man as husband, and the woman as wife, may be so reduced that the stability of the marriage is threatened. Or where the ways of regulating the unconscious strivings in each partner do not fit in the manner described earlier in this chapter, anxiety about the security of the relationship may not only seriously limit the interaction between husband and wife but also prompt them to seek outside help.

It is because the potentially destructive systems of relations that are activated are unconscious and therefore inaccessible to attempts to work them out 'reasonably' that outside help is necessary for their resolution. To bring them into the normal process of psychological growth which we have described is possible only where these systems are less intense in their dynamic pressure, and where the total ego resources of the individual, or of the marriage as a unity, are proportionately strong in relation to their pressures. In other circumstances the threats to the individual in his relations with his needed object which their full expression might entail are too great for such regressive interaction to be attempted.

The technique of marital therapy developed by the Family Discussion Bureau attempts to decrease these irrational conflicts which threaten the security of the marriage and obstruct the normal process of growth and self-realization which is inherent in the relationship. The focus in the therapy is the marital relationship and the individual's contribution to it, rather than the problems of the individual partner. That this aim is explicit throughout the course of therapy provides a secure background against which work with the individual clients may progress. It can provide an assurance that the unconscious phantasy relationships which threaten the marriage will not in fact destroy it, which is the essential anxiety that prevents the testing out of the phantasies by the partners themselves. On the basis of this implicit assurance it may become possible for the individual clients to test out their phantasies in the quasi-primary relationship which is offered them with a member of the professional staff of the Bureau.

Each partner in a marriage which seeks help works with her or his own caseworker. The two caseworkers keep in touch with each other in order to understand the changing state and progress of the inter-action in the marriage throughout the course of treatment. At the same time, in their actual work with clients they are concerned only with what the client brings to the interviews, and more particularly with the kind and quality of relationship the client seeks to make with them. Because the therapeutic relationship has for its purpose the modification of the client's unconscious conflicts with a needed partner in the marriage, it contains the essential motives of a primary relationship, in which dependence and the need for continuity and exclusiveness play an important part. Within this client-caseworker relationship there is, therefore, opportunity to see and to some extent to test out the irrational phantasy relations, especially their primitive destructive aspects, before attempting their modification within the marital relationship itself.

This latter step is one of the central aims of the therapeutic work. It seeks to make use of the 'therapeutic' or growth potentialities inherent in the marriage to consolidate and extend the opportunities for change which arise from the process of conflict and realization in the client-caseworker relationship.

In this brief review of some of the processes through which the individual's capacity to make relationships with people—and with the world at large—is evolved through a full cycle from the dependence of infancy to the interdependence of adult life, we have frequently changed our focus, from the child to the parent, or from the parents to the field of forces in the wider social environment. By so doing it is possible to illustrate the complexity of the process of social maturation and to show how the stability and continuity which are essential to the unfolding of personality depend upon an interplay of forces between parent and child in the nuclear family, in the context of wider social pressures and supports.

These processes of maturation continue throughout life in the further social and personal relationships in which the individual involves himself. In preventive mental health work we may therefore with advantage focus on those conflicts in the individual which prevent him from using for his own growth and development the potentialities inherent in the primary social groups of which he is a part. The diagnosis and treatment, *within* the family, the marriage, or the work group, of such conflicts, may prove to be more rewarding than more intensive individual treatment of any member of a social unit.

PART II

Five Marriages

Mr and Mrs Clarke

Mr Clarke was referred to the Bureau by his doctor whom he had consulted about a sexual problem. He was twenty-eight, his wife twenty-seven, and they had been married five years. He did not seem able to explain very clearly what his difficulties were, but claimed that his marriage was successful except for his disinclination for sexual relations with his wife.

At this time Mr Clarke was a free-lance architect, making a very small and uncertain income, which he supplemented by evening teaching at a Technical Institute. His wife was working in an advertising agency and earning a much higher salary. She contributed the larger part to the household income and did all the housework of the large and inconvenient flat which they rented furnished.

* * *

Mr Clarke was a slightly built man with fair hair falling over his eyes. In his first interview with Mrs A.,[1] he sat slumped in his chair and seemed able to contribute little to the discussion. He expressed no resentment against his wife, whom he described as attractive, feminine and lovable. He insisted that the problem in the marriage was simply his own sexual failure, which he did not understand, since he had had a number of extra-marital relationships that had been perfectly successful. He said that he sometimes experienced a great disinclination to go home, and he would then stay out all night, without sending any message to his wife, and drink or pick up a woman. He seemed sulky and hopeless, and could not enlarge on this picture or give any meaningful description of himself, his wife or his marriage.

He was much more prepared to talk about his parents, who had opposed his marriage and were still, after five years, making no contact with his wife. He spoke angrily about his mother, who, he said, could not bear to be opposed. She was a successful actress and throughout his childhood she had been much away from home. His

---

[1] In all cases the husband's caseworker will be referred to as Mr or Mrs A., the wife's as Mr or Mrs B.

father was a solicitor and had his office in the house in a small country town where the family lived. It was he, with the assistance of a maid, who had made a permanent home for the client and his two sisters, one older and one younger. He had seemed happy enough about the arrangement, and the mother's visits had been experienced by all the family as exciting and enjoyable. There had been a great insistence by the parents upon the fact that this was a happy family, and Mr Clarke could not remember questioning this in any way until his adolescence. He had done very well at school and at college, and had been his mother's pride. He said that he had always felt that he 'had to be a great success for her sake'.

Mr Clarke said that from about his middle teens he had been conscious of sexual difficulties. With girls of his own type he had been able to make only the most platonic of friendships, but he had had a kind of secret sexual life with others.

He had met his wife when they were both students, and with her he tried to unite what he recognized as his 'split' attitudes to women. The couple were quickly sure that they wanted to marry and planned to do so as soon as they left college. Mr Clarke took home his intended wife and immediately there were family scenes. He said his mother's opposition, though based reasonably enough on the argument that it would be years before he established himself financially, was violent in the extreme. He had been forbidden to continue his association with the girl (although he was twenty-two, having completed his National Service before doing his professional training) and was treated 'like a criminal'. After months of family quarrels, the couple had married on the understanding that his wife should keep them both with her earnings while he tried to establish himself. This she had done for five years, and Mr Clarke was still unable to support himself.

His caseworker, Mrs A., did little in these early interviews except to comment that he had really found it very painful to rebel against his mother in this way. She had clearly been much loved by him in his childhood. He answered this obliquely by saying sulkily that he supposed Mrs A. meant that he had just gone from being dependent on one woman to being dependent on another. Mrs A. said that he seemed to feel that he did not know how to please a woman, or how to stand up to her without losing her love entirely. Again he agreed with this, but in the same sulky and hopeless manner.

*　　　*　　　*

Mrs Clarke presented a very different picture to her caseworker, Mrs B. She was small, attractive and elegantly dressed, but seemed strained and unhappy, a mixture of a successful career woman and a hurt little girl. She seemed very angry at having been asked to come to the Bureau, and made it clear that she was coming only to help with her husband's problems. She said that the marriage was impossible; that her husband was useless and immature and irresponsible, and that she did not think that she could go on with it all much longer. She had stayed with him until then only because she was afraid he would break down without her, and was hoping that the Bureau would make him stronger so that she could leave him.

When Mrs B. mentioned the sexual problem that had ostensibly brought the couple to the Bureau, the matter was dismissed as unimportant.

Only very reluctantly did she describe her own background. She had had an elder brother, never very effective, who was killed in the war, and a younger brother who was a cripple. She herself was the success of the family, healthy and very intelligent, and her father's pride. This father, whom she adored, was brilliant, but she had never felt she could depend on him. He was a business man, and his income and position had varied considerably over the years. Mother was hardly mentioned and, in answer to a question, described as 'conventional, frustrated, harmless'.

Altogether Mrs Clarke gave a confused impression of herself and of her marriage. She was scornful, critical and contemptuous in her attitude towards her husband and towards the Bureau, and yet was quickly touched by any show of warmth and interest from Mrs B. In the marriage, she resented having to carry responsibilities, yet seemed quite unable to make any demands upon her husband, or to complain directly about the many justifiable causes of complaint that she had. She seemed to have to play two parts in her daily life: carrying a responsible job and 'keeping' her husband, and also cooking for him, waiting on him, warming his slippers, and generally mothering him, though despising him for making her take this role. Although Mrs Clarke persisted in her critical attitude towards the Bureau, some of the things about her own part in the marital difficulties, which Mrs B. tried to convey to her, seemed to have reached her.

In the second and third interviews she began to show a great deal of insight and to be able to look at her own problems with considerable courage. She said that she had at first believed her husband to be strong and brilliant, but had known what he was really like before she had married him and had deliberately set out to help him to get away from his mother and to solve his sexual problems. She was able to express her concern at her apparent need to boss and 'make' a man, and showed much anxiety about her brothers and about her position in her own family. Mrs B. tried to understand with her how her experiences with parents and brothers might have affected her relationships with men and substantiated her conception of herself as having always to be in control, and having to suffer for it.

Then she was able to tell her story of the rows with her husband's parents, saying that her mother-in-law had seemed to see her son's marriage 'as if it were the loss of one of her limbs'. She added that her own father had been horrified when she had announced that she wanted to 'marry and have lots of children'.

* * *

Mr Clarke came to his fourth interview looking pale and shaken. He said that after their last visits to the Bureau he and his wife had, for the first time, talked about what had been said there, and his wife had tried to tell him about her problems. He had found himself very uneasy and most unwilling to listen to this, had several times tried to change the subject, and when she persisted had finally become so agitated that he had almost fainted. He had felt sick and ill ever since. He said that nothing like that had ever happened to him before. Mrs A. tried to show him his fear lest his wife should become a 'patient' too. The only pattern of relationship he felt safe with was the one of mixed resentment towards, and dependence on, a powerful woman. He thought a good deal about this, and finally began speculating about his parents, saying that he knew really that his mother's strength was an illusion. She was very brittle, and without his father she would collapse. Mrs A. tried to sort out with him his complex picture of the relationship between the sexes, of the woman who seemed to have taken the power but who could so easily be destroyed, and of the man who had the power but who must never use it. Mr Clarke fell back as usual on a sulky hopelessness, the sort of adolescent and irresponsible attitude in which he habitually took refuge.

Mrs Clarke also spoke to Mrs B. of her attempts to share her problems with her husband. She seemed extremely distressed and cried throughout the interview. She said she knew she had always been full of anxieties that she had to keep under control; she had never been able to give in; she had always had to live up to her parents' expectations and to be successful. In contradiction to her earlier statement, she said she had half imagined when she married that her husband would be dependable and that he would help her, but now she realized that she had chosen someone who could not. She said it was useless to look at her own problem, since the result was so frightening. She could not see how two such insecure people could possibly work things out together. When Mrs B. tried to express the emotional interlocking of these two people in more hopeful and positive terms, Mrs Clarke became bitter and contemptuous again.

She attended on three more occasions, on which she always arrived cold and hostile, pretending to be in control of the situation, became friendly and anxious about herself during the interview, but left with a sneer and an attack on Mrs B. She was scornful of her husband, who had followed up his sickness with rashes and other nervous ailments; and yet now began to show considerable fear that he would, with help, become more mature and would then not need her. Mrs. B tried to show her how much of her contempt was for the weakness and anxiety in herself, and how she had to sneer at her husband and the caseworker when she became worried about herself. Mrs Clarke then complained of her husband's sexual gentleness, which she could not bear, and said he seemed often deliberately to hurt himself and seek pain, and that this alarmed her. She again quickly saw this as one of her own problems too, and worried unhappily about her own conflicting needs to hurt and to be hurt.

In the sixth interview she reported that her husband had decided to find a regular salaried position; and at first claimed to be delighted by this decision which would make her life so much easier. Then quickly she expressed anxiety that he might afterwards feel that she had influenced him or pushed him into it; and finally made it clear just how frightened she was to face the fundamental change in the marriage that his financial independence would mean.

Mrs Clarke started the next meeting by saying that she would not attend any more. Previously her husband had been weak and depressed, and had often wept. Now she was crying, too—in the whole of her life she had not cried as much as during the last weeks. She was quite determined to leave her husband, whom she now felt she hated

and could not stand any longer. All she asked of the Bureau was
that they should help him sufficiently for him to be able to manage
without her. When Mrs B. tried to find out with her why things were
so difficult at this particular moment when her husband seemed to be
getting nearer to the material independence she longed for, she
started to sob—and at first very angrily, but with increasing desperation, talked of her own unhappiness and her anxiety about herself.
When, towards the end of the meeting, she repeated her doubts as
to whether she should come again, Mrs B. did not press her, but
agreed that at the moment all this might be too difficult for her and
that the client should come only when she felt able to do so. In fact,
she did not return for many months.

While his wife was going through this crisis, Mr Clarke had three
interviews with almost no emotional content. He insisted on discussing his problems entirely in terms of his job and his financial dependence on his wife. He ignored Mrs A.'s attempts to show him the
connection between this and his emotional difficulties, yet at this
time he began to apply for salaried positions. He soon obtained a
good appointment and abandoned, apparently without regret, the
uncommitted status to which he had been clinging.

*A good deal had emerged in these first interviews that could help
towards at least a tentative understanding of this marriage.*

*Mr Clarke had grown up in a family where the parents seemed, to
some extent, to have reversed the conventional roles of father and
mother, though there was a complete denial that this might be odd or
might cause any discomfiture or loss to the children. As a boy he had
loved his mother dearly and had been very proud of her. He had
remained unconscious of his rebellious feelings and anger. In some
ways he had modelled himself upon his more passive father, though he
had in fact much of his mother's drive and ability.*

*He would probably have been able to adjust himself to the unusual
pattern, which had provided many satisfactions as well as anxieties,
if he had been permitted to question and criticize a little. In fact, it
seemed as if the parents' own insecurities had created an atmosphere in
which no doubts or criticisms could ever be voiced or even become
conscious in the child. So he had lived with his infantile phantasies,
unable to test them against more realistic perceptions and thoughts as
he grew older, and as a result was extremely confused about himself
and those close to him.*

The very important aspect of a problem which had already appeared, but was to become clearer in later interviews, was his unconscious fear of what he had done by finally rebelling against his mother. He seemed to be saying that it was impossible to cope with women who were powerful and dominating, because if one did so one would lose their love completely and leave them damaged or destroyed. His quite overwhelming panic at his wife's attempt to talk to him about her weakness or 'damagedness' must be understood in these terms.

Mrs Clarke had experienced something similar in the way of role reversal at home, though this was between herself and her brothers. She had been the successful 'son' of her parents at the expense of her brothers. She had apparently been unable to identify with her mother and half adored and half protected her father. She seemed, from an early age, almost to have taken the responsibility for the whole family and to have felt herself to be the only adult one in all family crises. She had struggled towards intellectual achievement, believing that both her parents expected her to put her career first and not really to be interested in marriage and motherhood.

In her husband Mrs Clarke saw initially a man who both needed her protection and yet had high intelligence and considerable strength, but as the marriage went on she could no longer acknowledge this latter aspect of his personality.

Mr Clarke had found in his wife a woman who in some ways resembled his mother, but who had also a very much more warm and feminine side to her. She seemed to offer him a chance to bring his sexuality, which he must previously always have seen as dangerous and destructive, into a loving relationship. Yet he could not use this chance.

It would be difficult to find a marriage in which the problems of the two partners fitted more closely. Each seemed to be marrying a partner who offered a relationship close enough to his family pattern to be familiar, and yet sufficiently different to provide a flexibility and opportunity for growth and development which had not existed in the parental environment.

As it happened, this growth and development had not occurred. Both partners seemed to feel that their parents did not want them to become sexual adults. Although on a conscious level they had rebelled against this, they were unable to free themselves from these inhibitions. Perhaps the fact that each partner had married someone so closely resembling the loved parent of the opposite sex had aroused anxieties that could not be managed and guilt feelings that led to much self-

*punishing behaviour. Neither partner had been able to break out of
the bonds of the past. The husband had become passive and resentful,
hating himself in this role but unable to take any other or to make
effective sexual approaches to his wife because of his uneasiness and
fear of snatching her power and destroying her. She had become
managing and protective at the same time, unable to be dependent or
to make demands, because of her similar fear of the damage she might
do to men. Though both were able and successful academically, they
were unable to allow themselves any success in the domestic and sexual
fields, where they both seemed to see any enjoyment as a direct defiance
of parental wishes. They had organized their lives in practical matters,
to create the maximum amount of trouble and labour, and were still
without a proper home or possessions of their own from which they
might derive any satisfaction.*

*Mr and Mrs Clarke were unusually attractive people with great
potentialities, and at a first glance the couple seemed excellently
matched. In fact, they were both suffering so much pain, and seemed
so unable to stop hurting themselves and each other severely, that the
two caseworkers were uncertain for a long time whether this marriage
could be maintained. Only after many months did it become clear that
despite all their difficulties there were exceedingly strong bonds
between them, and that they needed each other, and indeed could help
each other, in their strivings to overcome their conflicts.*

Mr Clarke changed considerably as soon as his wife ceased to
participate in the work of the Bureau. He seemed extremely relieved
and said that she had found her visits upsetting and was more
composed and normal again now that she had decided to withdraw.
Then he was able for the first time to express anger against her and
to say that the trouble was not all his fault. He said she was always
telling him that he had destroyed her life, but he was now beginning
to doubt that. He talked about all this in a very muddled way,
usually as if he had damaged her and completely let her down, but
occasionally making resentful and spiteful remarks.

At the beginning of this phase, Mr Clarke began to attempt to
come to terms with his parents (who seemed glad enough to end the
unhappy situation) and talked a good deal about his relationships
with them. He felt that he no longer loved his mother and felt
unhappy and ashamed of this. 'I feel as if she is an ageing mistress,
who is trying to hold on to me when I want to get free'. He com-

plained bitterly about his father's weakness and inability to help his son, but then described him as apparently strong and gay and successful in his youth. He seemed to picture his father as changed by his marriage, or perhaps by his own birth. Yet when Mr Clarke related incidents of even minor disagreements with his father or father-in-law, it became clear that he was quite unable to stand up to either, always being very frightened of them and having to take refuge in sulky adolescent behaviour. His sisters figured in his stories in equally confused roles. Usually he described them with anxiety as much less intelligent than himself, always ill, very limp and passive, and insisted that throughout his childhood he had always imagined himself to be the bad one and responsible for anything that went wrong among the children. But occasionally a totally different attitude emerged—of spite and jealousy towards the girls who he had always felt had more of his parents' love without having to do anything to win it. The elder sister had married with full parental approval, indeed had become closer to her mother since Mr Clarke's fall from grace.

He was able to see the relevance of all this to his marital difficulties, and gradually talked more about his relationship with his wife. He said that he consciously wanted to be a good and responsible husband, to settle down and have children, but that he was always 'breaking out' into irresponsible behaviour. He always talked of the moment when he would settle down, buy a house, and so on, as a complete and final surrender. He saw 'proper husbands' as having completely abandoned their powers and independence, and having become exactly like his own father. There was no other way. 'I shall have to promise to be a good boy and to do just as my wife tells me for the rest of my life.' There were several contradictory pictures; sometimes he imagined a worn and sick wife, overburdened with housework and children; sometimes a wife who would give all her interest to their children and leave him completely abandoned and unloved.

During this period he began to make tentative advances towards a new relationship with his wife, but each advance was followed by a hasty withdrawal. From time to time he would be able to have successful intercourse with her, but the following evening he would find himself again unable to face going home to her. Sometimes he would seek another woman. On two such occasions his wife left him and the couple remained apart for several days.

In the interviews he was often sulky and childish (he described himself as feeling 'like a delinquent adolescent') and gradually talked to Mrs A. more and more about his 'delinquent behaviour and destructive feelings'. He would quickly retreat into his sulky manner if he felt any kind of disapproval, and showed very real concern to have Mrs A.'s support and interest and to try to work through this with her. On one occasion, when he had become very upset, he said, 'Oh, I wish I didn't care what you or anyone else thought of me.'

He told his wife very little about his interviews, and she made no direct attempt to find out about them, but as their relationship generally improved and as Mr Clarke became established in his new job and became apparently more mature and capable, he said that his wife was complaining that he withheld so much of himself from her. He was able to understand this and to link it up with his sexual fears and with his need to protect himself from the supposed destructiveness of his wife and mother, no less than to protect them from his own.

After six months Mr Clarke said that his wife had asked if she could come again to see Mrs B.

By this time Mr. Clarke had revealed a good deal about himself. He seemed to be more than usually hampered in his functioning as an adult and as a husband by phantasies and problems carried over from his childhood. In his discussions with the caseworker he seemed to be continually concerned with these problems and particularly with his anxieties about the differences between men and women. This concern was conscious, but was built upon earlier unconscious phantasies the intensity of which dominated his relationships, so that in all aspects of his marriage, and to some extent outside it, his responses and behaviour were never free from the influence of these primitive feelings. The pattern that manifested itself in his sexual difficulty could be seen in every other aspect of his marriage.

The couple, in their domestic arrangements, had created a situation in which there was the maximum of drudgery and the minimum of satisfaction, and they behaved in this self-imposed frustration each in his typical way, Mr Clarke with depression and incompetence, and his wife with endless futile effort. They seemed never to be able to relate to each other with spontaneity and enjoyment. Bearing in mind our knowledge of the normal problems and phantasies of childhood, we could at least guess at what lay behind these frustrations and prohibitions.

Mr Clarke's situation may have been a particularly inhibiting one. His mother had appeared to him to be so powerful and yet so weak, so threatening to him and yet so vulnerable, that he had always been extremely frightened both of her and of his own aggressive feelings towards her, which he saw as incompatible with his predominant need to retain her love. In his unconscious phantasies he seemed to feel that he had stolen her masculinity (and perhaps his sisters' too) and that women were castrated by men and would naturally try to take their revenge upon them. He must then submit to this revenge, or must carry an intolerable burden of guilt towards these damaged women, and of course lose their love. Mr Clarke's marriage had apparently represented to him a supreme act of aggression towards his mother, in that he was taking the potency he had stolen from her to another woman. (It will be remembered that it had been described on one occasion 'as if it were the loss of one of her limbs'.) Before his marriage, his successes had been an offering to her and had added to her pride and strength.

In addition, he seemed to fear that any potency on his part would be a threat to his father, who seemed to him both to have submitted to his wife and to have propped her up at the same time. However, his father seemed able to control and check his mother's destructiveness and to some extent to protect her, and he had retained her love. Mr Clarke saw himself as a failure even in this respect, and so felt towards his father confused feelings of jealousy, anger and contempt. The only possible escape from all this was to remain a rebellious adolescent, permanently in a position of irresponsibility and impotence, though this, of course, did not satisfy his conscious needs, for he was, at another level, an intelligent, capable and even forceful man.

Mr Clarke was essentially a lonely person whose relationships had been dominated by these bewildering phantasies and who had never felt that anyone cared for him for his own sake. He felt himself to have no rights, and most of his pleasures had to be clandestine. He seemed not to know what kind of a person he was, but was sure that whatever was inside him was bad. He seemed also to know little about other people, their feelings or their motives, and spoke of them with astonishing naïveté. He thought of his sexuality always as damaging, never as an expression of adult fulfilment or of love. He seemed surprised at Mrs A.'s interest in him, and apparently in his relationship with her was able to feel angry and sulky and weak and vulnerable in turn without experiencing this as a threatening situation. It was totally new

*to him that his childish and 'delinquent' bits could be accepted, and
not be used as weapons against him to keep him ineffective. Mrs A.
must have shown both that she could share his phantasies and also
that she could free herself from them. She must have said things that
he experienced as an attack on him, but also spontaneously have shown
that she did not believe they would injure him. She enabled him to test
out with her some of his anger and rebellion against his mother without
the distressing scenes that had always been the result of such testing-out
with his real family, since his mother, though she looked so strong,
could not bear any criticism or hostility.*

*Even as he made progress, any successful love-making with his wife
stirred up so many anxieties that he needed to escape from her and seek
an outlet and reassurance elsewhere. He had to withhold himself from
her in many ways, and indeed could risk giving to his relationship with
her only his dependent, depressed, impotent self and his impersonal
intellect. As his fears began to diminish a little he was less compelled
to force upon her the role of a powerful and indestructible 'mother' and
was able to tolerate her as someone also in need of help. It was then
possible for his wife to return to the Bureau.*

Mrs Clarke returned to Mrs B. in a very changed mood. She had
apparently derived considerable benefit from the growth in her
husband, and had been able to use the insight that she had gained
from her first few interviews. She made no attempt now to deny her
own part in the difficulties or to take refuge behind practical problems.

Nevertheless, during the first few minutes she said that she had
come back to ask whether it would now be safe for her to leave her
husband, since she was fed up with him. Mrs B. commented that she
seemed always to start interviews by asking permission to be unloving, and Mrs Clarke quickly changed her mood and admitted
that she knew she needed her husband. Again in the next sentence
she contradicted this, saying that she saw him now as very much
changed, 'a much better man, but not necessarily a man I can live
with'. If he had been like this two years before, all would have
been well, but now she no longer wanted him. Then she expressed very great fear that he would leave her. Mrs B. tried
to show her the uncertainty about a dependent relationship which
was so clearly expressed in her many conflicting statements. She
wondered if this was what had brought her client back at this

point when such a possibility was for the first time really offered
to her.

Mr Clarke, in the interview immediately after his wife had revisited
Mrs B., returned to the subject of her complaints about his withholding himself, then suddenly presented a quite new image of his
father. He said that his father was like this, he withheld himself
completely, never made any suggestions, never showed any feelings;
in his own passive way he remained completely invulnerable—one
could never know him properly. In talking of his father, Mr Clarke
began to understand a little of his own behaviour towards his wife,
and of how rejecting and frustrating such an attitude could really
be. There seemed also to be some awareness on his own part that
he needed something from his father but could not get it. It was only
at this point that he was able to say that he had imagined, in his teens,
that his mother's love for him was an unnatural and sexual one—
that, because his father had been so passive and weak, she had
wanted her son to replace him and to be her lover. Mrs A. tried to
sort out with him this surprisingly conscious phantasy, the fear that
by becoming sexually adult he would in fact push aside his father
and have his mother for himself.

In the next interviews, Mr and Mrs Clarke both continued to show
anxiety about the other's vulnerability. Each expressed the feeling
that if only the other were perfect—he completely masculine,
powerful, stable; she completely feminine, loving, contented and
happy—all difficulties would disappear. While the two caseworkers
tried to deal with this, the couple had many rows and again talked
seriously of parting. Then Mr Clarke began to express anger with his
wife's caseworker, whom he pictured as a powerful and critical
woman, brilliant, omniscient and impossible to deal with. He took
it for granted that she was telling his wife he was worthless and that
she should leave him. This completely unrealistic picture showed
clearly how little Mr Clarke could yet disentangle his experience
and his perceptions from his phantasies, and suggested again how
coloured by his unconscious needs and anxieties his ideas about all
the people close to him might be.

At this stage, Mrs A. and Mrs B. felt that a joint meeting might
be helpful, and suggested this to the Clarkes. Mrs Clarke, while
clearly wanting the meeting, said: 'I am afraid it will be too humiliating for him. He will cry and that will be awful.' Mr Clarke made it
clear that he saw it as an attack on him by his wife's caseworker, and

when this was talked about, inquired: 'How can you come to terms with mothers?'

However, they both agreed to come together to the Bureau.

During this period Mr Clarke made a very close relationship with Mrs A. Only gradually did it emerge that he was also building up a strong sense of Mrs B.'s being hostile to him. He seemed to have separated at the Bureau his two images of women. His own caseworker became the woman to whom he could bring his weakness and his delinquency, his impotence as well as his positive achievements, without losing her support and her concern, while his wife's caseworker became in his mind the 'impossible' threatening condemning one. This was particularly hampering to further progress in that he himself despaired of the situation. He assumed that his wife's caseworker, in her imagined hostility to him, in fact judged him rightly, while his own caseworker, since she seemed able to continue to be interested in him and to behave as though she saw him as fit to be a man and a husband, must still be unaware of his true character however much he had tried to show her his degradation. He seemed to feel that any love or respect for him must be associated with self-deception and denial, and that when he was 'found out' he could be only despised and rejected. In a way, this situation seemed to protect him since, if he had nothing, nothing could be taken from him.

Mrs Clarke did not appear to be using the two caseworkers in this way, but she too seemed to be faced with endless contradictions in her perceptions of the people around her and of herself and her future aims.

There was the additional problem with these clients that, although Mr Clarke had begun to communicate easily with his caseworker, he was still not able to talk very much with his wife. There had never been between these two people the sort of 'honeymoon' which so often occurs at the beginning of casework, when the marriage shows a great if temporary improvement and the couple have long talks about their difficulties after months, or perhaps years, during which communication had almost ceased. Between the Clarkes there had always been a great deal of communication on an intellectual level—even in their worst crises they were able to enjoy theoretical discussions with each other on impersonal matters—but they seemed unable to risk communication on a feeling level.

It is not the regular custom at the Bureau for the two caseworkers and the two clients to meet together, unless there seems to be some special reason for this. In this case, Mr Clarke's splitting of his feelings and phantasies between Mrs A. and Mrs B. so that he avoided bringing any direct hostility to his own caseworker was creating a bar to his further progress and resulting in a general sense of frustration. It was therefore decided to hold a meeting of all four. In individual analysis such projecting and splitting can be slowly worked through with the patient. At the Bureau this is not always possible, and the arrangement of a 'foursome' provides an opportunity for all four people involved to do some reality testing.

The joint meeting was preceded by a week of tensions and crises. Mr Clarke had stayed away from home twice during that time and, on one of these occasions, had telephoned the Bureau, slightly drunk, demanding to see Mrs A., who was not there that evening. He had not gone home at all the night before the meeting, and when Mrs Clarke arrived she did not know whether or not he would come. He did arrive, in fact, in good time. Both Mr and Mrs Clarke looked extremely tired and strained.

The meeting started with Mr Clarke saying, very aggressively, that he supposed that this was the end of the marriage and that he and his wife had come here to part. When both caseworkers expressed surprise, and asked why he felt like this, he turned angrily to his wife's caseworker, and said: 'That is what you have said, isn't it? You tell my wife that I am hopeless and not fit to be a husband, don't you?' Mrs B. said she wondered why he felt that she was so much against him, and there followed a confused discussion between husband and wife about Mr Clarke's 'bad' behaviour as to whether it was neurotic and compulsive, or was quite within his control and was a deliberate expression of his lack of love and consideration for his wife. Mrs Clarke said that she could put up with his behaviour if she knew it was an 'illness' because then she would not feel so hated and rejected. Mr Clarke refused to accept the excuse of 'compulsiveness' or 'illness' and utterly disclaimed the 'patient' role which he seemed to feel the three women were trying to put on to him. Then Mrs Clarke entirely abandoned her superior, guardian-of-a-neurotic-child manner, and dissolved into tears, saying unhappily: 'I only want my husband's love. I can't bear him to be so unloving and so rejecting. If it is not illness in him, what is the matter with me?' At this point Mr Clarke took charge of the meeting, became manly and dignified and very warm and protective towards his wife, saying: 'There is nothing wrong with you, you are perfectly all right.'

After this both clients were able to talk about the whole problem with much insight and sensitivity, although Mr Clarke continued to be hostile towards Mrs B. and tried to provoke her into saying that he was not fit to have a wife. In the end he said: 'I only want to be able to make love to my wife, like any other husband.'

There seemed to be a great bid on both sides for a recognition of adulthood and of lovableness both from one another and from the two caseworkers, and when the caseworkers both finally commented on this, Mr Clarke turned in surprise to Mrs B. and said: 'You don't mean to say *you* think that?'

It is clear that something very important happened at this meeting. Both clients seemed to react strongly to the arrangement immediately it was suggested, and before it actually took place both showed signs of great apprehension. At the beginning, when Mr Clarke said 'I suppose we have come here to part', he seemed to express his sense of condemnation by the three women and was probably meaning 'I have come here to be thrown out, to be shown by all of you that I am not adult or lovable and not fit to have a wife'. Later he put this on to his wife's caseworker only, and seemed to do his best to re-create in her the mother who would forbid him to grow up and to marry. (It seemed likely, indeed, that to a large extent the young couple had provoked the parental opposition at the time of their marriage. That was the way they had to have it.) In the foursome, however, this provocation did not produce the expected attack and rejection, and Mr Clarke's projections on to Mrs B. could not be kept up. He was able, as a result, both to display his aggressiveness in a more adult and manly way and also to be loving and protective towards his wife.

Mrs Clarke had appeared to hope for something from this meeting, if only that she could show her needs to her husband in circumstances in which he must listen and could not rush away from her. She seemed to need, too, to be assured by both caseworkers that he was not mentally ill and that she could safely relinquish her dominant protective role. Yet this knowledge was also very disturbing to her as she had then to face the fact that many of her reasons for taking up this role were in herself. She did, however, seem to get some feeling that the feminine and dependent side of herself was perceived and valued by both case-

workers, and was able to show her weakness and her pain without finding it an intolerably humiliating experience.

Perhaps, too, these clients sensed something in the relationship between the two caseworkers which helped to undo some of their phantasies: for instance, that Mr Clarke's hostility to his wife's caseworker did not seem to worry Mrs A. and that she did not need to defend or protect her colleague from him as his father had always seemed to have to protect his apparently strong mother whenever his son dared to oppose her; that both caseworkers could accept the needs of this couple for one another, without reacting jealously or possessively each towards her own client.

This joint meeting would not have been such a valuable experience unless each client had had basically some confidence in the support of his own caseworker, and some feeling of being acceptable and lovable. In Mr Clarke this confidence had been shaken by the very suggestion of the foursome and his telephone call had arisen from his desperate need for reassurance. (He said later that when he had tried to contact Mrs A. he had felt 'completely alone and unloved, an outcast'.)

Certainly this foursome seemed to be a supreme testing ground for their phantasies, and made possible the further expression of important feelings which had so far been withheld or denied. Mrs Clarke's ability to ask for her husband's love and support and his to respond in so affectionate and protective a manner was in such striking contrast to the incidents that had occurred at the beginning of the work in this case as to be extremely moving to all four people concerned.

Mr and Mrs Clarke left this meeting in a loving mood, and Mr Clarke told his wife for the first time what he did on the occasions when he did not go home. From this time they developed an ability to communicate with one another in a quite different way. Then followed some months of new adjustment during which Mr Clarke continued to attend regularly while Mrs Clarke kept a looser contact. He was much more cheerful and relaxed and also much more aggressive and active, being very argumentative and taking pleasure in correcting his caseworker and in demonstrating her stupidity. All the people he talked about, particularly his parents and his sisters, seemed to have become more real to him and were less obviously projections of his childhood phantasies. During this period Mrs Clarke gave up her job and the couple discussed finding a house and having children, but this new pattern of life was not achieved without renewed anxieties. On the day that his wife handed in her resignation, Mr Clarke stayed away from home, although he was, consciously, delighted by her decision and looking forward to an ordinary domestic life.

Although Mrs Clarke, too, had consciously very much wanted to give up her career, the change from an overactive professional life to that of a housewife brought her problems to a head. Three months after resigning her job she asked for an interview, making it clear that she now wanted help for herself. She was very depressed and said that being 'only a woman' offered her little satisfaction. She did not complain about her husband, blamed only herself— although she did say that he had not helped her to feel valued as a woman, and had, in fact, been very angry with her when she had turned down a part-time temporary job that she had been pressed to take. He had always blamed her work for the difficulties in the marriage, but now that she had given this up, he did not like it either. On the other hand, she was quite aware that she did not appreciate his growing masculine efforts. She showed no enthusiasm, and offered no co-operation in his attempts to buy a house, although she realized how very important this was to him. Nor did she show pleasure in his sexual approaches, rather the opposite. He had become much more loving, but although she desperately wanted to be loved by him, she often rejected him sexually and was never encouraging.

During the next few weeks she talked a great deal about her fears of how the change in her life might affect her parental family. She linked her depression with the fact that she had given up the role of the successful career woman which she felt her parents had designed for her. It seemed to her that all kinds of difficulties had developed in her family the moment she had done this, and that she would still not be allowed to be a wife, since she would need to give up her own life in order to cope with them.

In exploring with Mrs B. how her parents' apparent prohibitions and expectation had affected her life, and had formed the picture she had of herself, she spoke again of her childhood.

As the only daughter, she had been loved and cherished but, with her delicate brothers and parents who had always seemed to her so vague, she had felt that no one but herself could cope with illness in the family and with the many upheavals of the war years. She had had to carry some of the responsibilities of a grown-up woman when she was in fact only a girl. Everyone else had seemed delicate and vulnerable, so she had always to be strong. She had always felt that she had to be in control to prevent disaster. Later on in her marriage she had felt just the same, and said she realized now that this was partly her own fault, but she seemed unable to sort out what was really needed of her. Mrs B. tried to show Mrs Clarke how she had both competed with her father and had pushed her mother aside, taking over the latter's position, but feeling very guilty about this. She had tried to cope with this guilt by doing a great deal for those around her. She seemed to have to go on repeating this pattern with her husband and to invite from him the sort of behaviour which would seem to make her controlling attitude inevitable and therefore excusable. Mrs Clarke answered this only by starting hurriedly to talk about love and hate. She said that she really loved her husband, but that if he frustrated her, she loathed him; it was always one or the other, and in fact both were equally frightening. If one showed love one was weak and vulnerable, but if one showed hate it led to disaster.

After this Mrs Clarke was able to work with her caseworker over some of these conflicting feelings about men and women, love and hate, power and dependence. She was as co-operative and as willing to accept her own part in the marital difficulties, and to try to understand it, as she had been previously elusive and determined always to blame everything on to her husband. In her relationship to Mrs B. she seemed to swing over, at this time, from the professional woman who consulted another professional woman, to a loving daughter who wanted to have her femininity valued by a warm feminine mother. Mrs Clarke, who always had an astonishing capacity to use any new understanding and insight in a most effective way, was able to recognize these swings in herself and to link them with her difficulty in reconciling her apparently conflicting needs. She expressed this most clearly at length by saying that perhaps if one became more feminine one need not necessarily become stupid and throw away all intellectual ambitions or share in the masculine world.

At this time Mr Clarke began to show increasing impatience with himself for continuing to need therapeutic help, and interviews were spaced further and further apart. The couple seemed ready to move forward into full adulthood and parenthood.

It is interesting to look at the 'boxing and coxing' which this case involved. Mr Clarke was seen on many more occasions than his wife and for long periods was attending alone. He seemed, in many ways, to be a much more deprived person than she, and apparently expressed at the beginning of the contact the more sick and socially unacceptable parts of both their personalities. He seemed to need a period where he could have his worker to himself, and had to feel sufficiently secure with Mrs A. before he could begin to criticize his wife and face some of her problems and difficulties and the way they affected the marriage. Mrs Clarke was able to make a great deal of use of her own early interviews, and somehow, too, of the work with her husband, although she fully committed herself to therapy only at the very end when her husband was more able to tolerate his recognition of her difficulties.

It is important to allow flexibility of this kind and to make it possible for clients to use the Bureau in their different ways; even though the caseworkers are aware that their clients' needs and wishes are often contradictory and ambivalent. Mrs Clarke, for example, was almost certainly begging for help for herself from her caseworker as well as from her husband on the occasion, after the third interview, when the disturbing scene occurred between them. Perhaps her caseworker should have responded to this instead of accepting the client's pattern of dealing with her anxieties by withdrawing into the role of the competent woman. Yet, although Mrs Clarke was partly ready to express her own dependency and need, it was probably true that the marriage itself could not have supported two 'crying babies' at once. Her husband's later growth and strengthening, though it appeared on the surface to increase her anxieties, in fact created a safer situation in which Mrs Clarke could face the crying, demanding baby in herself without endangering the marriage; only then could she begin to give up the denial of her own needs and begin to free herself from her rigid pattern of behaviour—a mixture of self-sacrifice and domination—and the resulting resentment and guilt.

There came a point at which the situation seemed to be completely reversed—when Mrs Clarke said: 'Everything is upside down. I am now totally incompetent; I can't take any responsibilities', and Mr Clarke asked plaintively: 'Why did I marry this weak, neurotic girl?' They seemed to need to exaggerate these opposite aspects of themselves as they had earlier needed to deny them in themselves and exaggerate them in their partner. At the same time they were ceasing to react to one part only of each other's personality and were rapidly moving towards a freer and more loving relationship.

We have seen in this case that these two people had chosen each other partly because each fitted so well the other's needs to project on to the partner those parts of his personality which he had hitherto disowned in himself. Each, then, in using the partner to carry his or her own repressed parts, contributed to the exaggerated expression of these by the partner—which then invited condemnation, and evoked guilt and anxiety. They had chosen partners who were only too able and willing to accept and react to these unconscious projections, thus giving to one another an initial feeling of acceptance but at the same time perpetuating the denial and restricting the growth and adaptability of both personalities. It seemed impossible for either to come to life in a full and imaginative marital relationship.

The work at the Bureau enabled them slowly to recognize those aspects of themselves—which they had in the past condemned or denied in response to their parents' real or phantasied expectations of them. Stumblingly, step by step they were able to gain confidence in the acceptability and manageability of their personalities including these hitherto repressed parts. It is not easy for anyone thus to accept himself as different from the picture that he has previously had of himself and which he has needed as a defence against his guilt and insecurity, but it is perhaps easier for a husband and wife to do this where both are being helped at the same time towards inner adjustment through which a more satisfying equilibrium in the marriage can be achieved.

Mr and Mrs Webb

This couple was of a type well known to social workers. Their marriage had been unhappy almost from the start, and they had sought help, over the years, from almost every agency and clinic in their district. At the time of their referral to the Bureau they had been married for nine and a half years and had two children, the first conceived before marriage. The husband complained of his wife's behaviour with other men and of his own headaches and insomnia. The wife complained of her husband's jealousy and suspicion and of his violence towards her. She had been refusing intercourse for some months before this time and was daily threatening to leave the family.

Mr Webb was a qualified electrician working for a local Board. He had studied for his National Certificate during the marriage, having been previously only a labourer. He was thirty-five, his wife twenty-eight, and they had a son aged nine and a daughter aged four.

* * *

Mr Webb was seen first. He was a tall thin man, shabby and untidy, with a strong cockney accent. He seemed nervous and confused and spoke in an extremely subservient manner. He gave no impression of having the necessary intelligence to qualify for the job he in fact held.

He began by expressing gratitude to the caseworker for seeing him, and called her 'Madam'. Then he poured out his complaints against his wife. He told stories of her flirtations with other men, and particularly of her interest in 'inferior' men, for instance, dustmen and coalmen. He said she delighted in humiliating him before such people, and added that she had had a bad mother who had had children by several men. He went on and on pouring out these confused stories, endlessly detailed but often mutually contradictory, but when his caseworker, Mrs A., made any comment, however trivial, he immediately returned to his subservient and placatory manner, turning the comment into words of wisdom: 'Oh, thank you, Madam. You would advise me to do that, would you, Madam?' After some time Mrs A. commented on this, and said that her client seemed to be trying to pretend to himself that he was already getting a lot of help and advice from her. She said she wondered if he was expecting nothing, and was trying to ward off his disappointment and the anger and despair he would feel about it. Mrs A. had thought hitherto that he was too nearly deluded to make any actual contact with her, and was surprised when he reacted to this. He did not answer directly, but left the stories about his wife and began to talk more rationally. He told Mrs A. that he had been discharged from the Army with psycho-neurosis and that between that time and his marriage he had lived with his parents, quarrelling with them most of the time. 'I was awful to my mother. I don't know how she stood me,' he said. Then he quickly asked if his interviews could be arranged at such times that his employers need not know about them. He was frightened that they would think him neurotic or mad. Mrs A. said that he seemed very uneasy about what people would find out about him and was perhaps trying to warn her that she might not be able to stand him either. Again he looked at her as if he had heard what she said and seemed relieved by it. He could not leave without shaking her hand at the door and thanking her warmly.

*   *   *

He opened the next interview by saying that he had read books on psychology and had tried to explain to his wife why she behaved as she did, but it was of no use, she just wouldn't understand, and that made him furious. Mrs A. said that he was perhaps wondering whether it would make her furious if he 'just wouldn't understand', or whether he was afraid he would get furious and frustrated when she failed to understand him, as she often would. Again he seemed relieved and then asked if he might take notes or be given definite problems to think about between meetings. Mrs A. said that she felt it was hard for him to bear the slowness and vagueness of this work and that he seemed to be trying to find a way of keeping at bay his frustration and anger about it. This time he replied directly, admitting his impatience and saying desperately that there wasn't much time to spare. He didn't think he could bear the situation much longer.

Then he began to talk, unasked, about his own history. He had been the youngest of six children in a very poor family; his father had had long spells of unemployment. He felt he had always been 'picked on', blamed for everything, and made into the family drudge. He said finally that his mother had had a breakdown when he was

born, and had been in hospital for six months. He did not know
how he had been looked after, 'I don't think I was properly fed as
I was always going into convalescent homes later on'.

Then he suddenly returned to his stories about his wife's behaviour
and went on pouring these out until the end of the interview. They
were of an even more confused nature than those he had told before,
stories about the sexual depravity of other people not connected
with his wife, stories about his colleagues, and about people whom
he met in the course of his work.

Again he shook hands warmly before leaving.

*Many readers may wonder why Mrs A. said the things she did, and
will think of other possible comments. Clearly many different things
could have been said which would have been equally relevant and
helpful. The important thing seemed to be to cut through the outpourings
of this distressed and almost deluded man, and to make contact with
him at some level at which he could feel the caseworker's recognition
that he was trying, despite all his difficulties, to make a relationship
with her. His material was too confused to be used helpfully, but he
seemed to respond to the awareness of his needs and fears and, although
he rarely replied directly, he gave the impression of 'hearing'. Even in
the first interview he was then able to stop abusing his wife and to
comment on his own 'awfulness' and, in the second interview, to mention
his own anger with a 'bad' mother who had deprived him of food and
severely damaged him.*

Mrs Webb came to her first interview looking drab and untidy
though she was a tall and quite nice-looking woman. She seemed to
be at the end of her tether and said that she had no love left for her
husband and could not stay with him much longer. His irrational
jealousy and tempers were quite impossible. Every day he made
scenes about nothing, and had recently begun to smash crockery and
damage her possessions in his outbursts. He treated her as an inferior
and continually accused her of being a 'bad woman'. She said that
there was really no point in talking about the marriage. The only
problem for her was how to get away, since there were two young
children whom she did not want to leave.

Mrs Webb then expressed considerable uneasiness about the
purpose and methods of the Bureau, and said that her husband had
told people that she was mad and that he was bringing her here for

treatment. The caseworker, Mrs B., discussed this with her and then, listlessly, and apparently only because she thought this was wanted, Mrs Webb outlined her own story. She said she had been the younger of two daughters and had been extremely fond of her mother. When she was seven she had gone into hospital with diphtheria and had returned home to be told that her mother had died while she was away. Her father had remarried two years later, but she had hated her step-mother and had left home at seventeen. Soon after this, she had had a love affair, but the man had left her after a few months, and she became promiscuous for a time. Then she had met her husband and become pregnant by him and married him as a result. She said that the only time she had had any satisfaction from sexual intercourse was before marriage. Mrs B. said that Mrs Webb seemed to have experienced a number of desertions in her life and the client replied that she had felt 'utterly abandoned' when her mother had died. She said that her husband accused her of not being fond enough of the children, but she felt it was wrong to give 'too much love'. She added that he was himself very good with them, and very concerned about the effect the situation in the marriage would have upon them.

*   *   *

At her second interview Mrs Webb still looked dreary and showed little animation. She reported further scenes at home during the week. Her husband complained that she was interested in everyone except him, and she couldn't give anything to him. She admitted that she could hardly bear him to touch her and felt quite dead sexually. She repeated her statement that she was remaining with him only for the sake of the children, as she did love them, although she could not show it.

Mrs B. commented on this difficulty in showing love, and then Mrs Webb said that the only person she had ever wholly loved was her mother. She added, with a rush, that she had learned later (when she was about fourteen) that her mother had not died at the time she had been told this, but had gone off with another man—but this had not made any difference at all to her feelings for her mother. Mrs B. said gently that Mrs Webb must have been very upset about this, and that some bit of her must have been very angry with her mother and might perhaps feel very guilty and very muddled about this and about sexuality in general. Mrs Webb entirely denied the anger, but said with some relief that she always felt herself to be bad

sexually. Then, looking a little brighter, she asked if she might bring
her little girl to the Bureau next time as she was 'such a lovely, happy
child.'

*A good deal of what was going on in this marriage seemed very clear,
though it was less easy to see what could be done to help. Mrs Webb
seemed to have had a severe shock in her childhood which had left her
both despairing about the value of giving or asking for love, and very
unsure about her sexuality. In her late teens she had indulged in rather
promiscuous affairs, probably in some muddled way both punishing her
mother and yet seeking to justify her behaviour by copying it. By
conceiving a child before marriage, she had ensured that she should not
have a husband entirely for herself for very long. The man she married
she knew to have been discharged from the Army with a nervous breakdown and she consciously saw him as someone for whom she could be
sorry. She seemed thus to have tried to solve her confusion about her
own goodness or badness as a woman by hoping to mother him and help
him, but also by having a 'bad' sexual relationship with him. She must
have been partly aware that his instability would result in considerable
suffering for herself and to have unconsciously sought this kind of
punishment for her feelings about her mother, and perhaps, too, about
her love for her father. But she had also played the part of the unloving
abandoning mother to her husband, whom she knew to be very dependent
upon her. In her relationship with her children, too, this anger about her
own abandonment proved an inhibiting factor. Though she very much
wanted to be a good mother, she found it hard to show them any love,
and in her interviews usually talked of 'the children', not distinguishing
them by name or sex.*

*She was clearly not able to show love to her husband at all; she soon
began to dislike sexual intercourse and hated being pregnant. It seemed
fairly certain that she did to some degree provoke and increase her
husband's jealous phantasies by her own need to identify with the under-
dog and the outcast, and to associate with, or seem to flirt with, men of
that kind.*

*Mr Webb seems to have found in his wife an ideal object on which to
put his divided feelings about his mother, the good woman whom he
needed to love him and wanted always to placate, and the depriving,
rejecting woman who starved him and deprived him of strength and
manhood. This latter picture of the bad woman seemed also to include
the sexual woman though, in fact, this client was obsessed less by*

*suspicions about his wife's actual sexual behaviour (he did not really
believe that she had intercourse with other men) than with much more
infantile images. He seemed to see her as the mother who gave her milk
to others and not to him.*

*His despair at being deprived and rejected by her drove him into
childish furies in which he abused her and occasionally attacked her
physically—this behaviour driving her still further away from him.
Her lack of response to the sexual relationship and her hatred of
pregnancy increased his doubts and guilts about his own sexuality and
his potency. Her misery and failure to defend herself against him were a
continual reproach to him, and both increased his fear of his own
destructiveness and made it harder for him to control it.*

*Despite the chronic difficulties in this marriage and the degree of
disturbance in the husband, there seemed a ray of hope in the attachment of both partners to the children. There seemed, too, to be some
real search for help.*

After these initial interviews there was a period of anxiety and
frustration for both clients and caseworkers. Mr Webb came each
week and poured out his complaints about his wife which became
wilder and wilder. He was more violent at home and had outbursts
in which he hit his wife and smashed china or broke windows.
Mrs Webb seemed more and more depressed and began making plans
to leave her husband. Both clients pressed for a joint meeting in
which some of the practical issues could be thrashed out, and the
caseworkers finally agreed to arrange this.

* * *

At the joint meeting both clients were extremely nervous and at
first found it difficult to say anything. Then Mr Webb turned to his
wife's caseworker and poured out his troubles to her, making a great
appeal for her support. He claimed that his wife did not love him
and was always threatening to leave him, and this was unbearable.
He said he must have a decision one way or the other. Mrs Webb
then became very angry and there was some cross-talk between
husband and wife in which each demanded from the other promises
of absolute love and no further bad behaviour of any kind. The two
caseworkers tried to intervene and to show the clients how difficult
they both seemed to find it to bear the ups and downs of marriage,
of alternate love and rejection, kindness and anger, but they were

not able to listen to remarks of this kind. Mrs Webb became very upset and said that there were no ups and downs as far as she was concerned, she hated her husband all the time. Then, half weeping, she said she was 'absolutely sick of it all' and rushed out of the room and out of the building, although the couple had brought their four-year-old daughter with them and she was playing in another room.

Mr Webb made no attempt to follow his wife, but simply said contemptuously: 'Now you see what she is like. What can you do with a woman like that?' Mrs B. then withdrew (still hoping to have a further word with Mrs Webb), and almost immediately Mr Webb's mood changed. He began to sob, and continued to do so for some time. Mrs A. tried to comfort him, and tried also to show him his confused behaviour towards his wife, his great longing for her love and yet his apparent need to see her as hateful and bad. He gradually pulled himself together and, when able to leave, collected his little daughter, who was inevitably very uneasy about her mother's disappearance. With her, he showed himself as quite a different person, considerate, sensitive and capable.

The joint meeting opened a new phase. Mrs Webb cancelled her next appointment. Mr Webb came to his in a very subdued mood. His wild stories and accusations ceased and he became much more consciously worried about himself. He continued to have outbursts of violence at home, but came to his caseworker childishly and pathetically to confess about these and to beg for her help. She tried hard to make more direct contact with her client's destructiveness and despair, and to help him to recognize his fury with her and with all the women who frustrated him and deprived him, but he remained placatory and anxious, and seemed dull and stupid in the extreme. The only subject in which he was much interested was that of getting his wife back to the Bureau. While he rationalized this by arguing that there was no point in his working at his marital difficulties if she was not doing so too, it was clear that his uneasiness went much deeper than this.

Mrs A. tried to show him that his wife, in walking out on her caseworker and thus expressing her anger with the Bureau and her feeling of being let down, was perhaps expressing these feelings for him too, and that this was what made him so alarmed by her absence. He denied this completely, but, as usual, seemed relieved that it had been said, and then in a half-frightened, half-provocative manner began to report various critical or sneering remarks that his wife had made about the Bureau. Always Mrs A. put these back to him as being partly his own feelings that he was unable to express directly for fear of destroying the relationship that he had made with her. She tried to link this up with the situation within the marriage and to show him his need to drive his wife to do and say things for him.

After a month, Mrs Webb returned to Mrs B. and for a short time there was a great improvement in the marriage. Mr Webb became much calmer and, for the first time, began to try with his caseworker to understand his problems. He began to talk about his work as well as his marriage and made it clear that he had great difficulties with colleagues and superiors. He was able to talk about his uncertainties of himself as a man and about his own father, whom he saw as lovable but weak and pathetic. He talked about his own children, in particular his son, and expressed considerable anxiety about what he was doing to him. In talking of him he told many stories of the boy's sexual curiosity and anxiety about himself and his body. He talked also of his greed, of his tantrums and jealousy, and yet could see the boy's attempts to make amends for this and to show love for his parents. In this way Mr Webb was gradually able to come to discuss these things in himself.

Mrs Webb, after her return, seemed relieved that she was able to come back and find Mrs B. still there for her. She, too, began to co-operate in interviews and to talk about her husband as a real person with whom she had a relationship and not just as a persecutor. She expressed anxiety about her own sexual frigidity, and seemed distressed about her general inability to show warm feelings. She continued to talk of her mother only in idealized terms, always to deny any suggestion of angry feelings about her. In the same way to refute any suggestion of anger or frustration in her relationship with Mrs B. Towards Mrs A. she often expressed hostility. During this short period of improvement Mrs Webb had her birthday and received from her husband two loving birthday cards, one from 'Your Husband, Alf', and the other from 'The Same Bloke Again', which seemed to express some kind of drive on his part to bring to her the contradictory aspects of himself and to have them accepted. Mrs Webb was indeed touched by this, and for the first time for many months responded affectionately to him.

As it happens, joint meetings were arranged in the two cases so far discussed although, in fact, this is not the usual practice at the Bureau.

It may be interesting to contrast these two joint meetings. With the Clarkes the casework was already well advanced and each client had developed a secure relationship with his caseworker. With the Webbs, the work had barely begun, and the arrangement was made because it seemed impossible to proceed any further without it. It seems probable that Mr Webb's anxieties were such that he could tolerate further work only if all four people concerned were brought together in actuality —that is if all his splittings and contradictions could be resolved at least momentarily. He had to show his 'bad' wife to Mrs A. and to try to make contact with Mrs B.

For Mrs Webb this meeting proved a very disturbing experience. She said afterwards that she had felt let down and 'abandoned' by her own caseworker. She had followed this up by abandoning her husband and child. She did not return to the Bureau for a month—abandoning her worker too.

Unlike Mr Clarke, who could not, at first, bear his wife to be a patient, Mr Webb seemed to feel terribly unsafe during this period when his wife was not attending. The contradictions in his behaviour, and in his conceptions of himself and his wife, occasioned him such anxiety that he could bear to talk about them only if all were brought together somehow at the Bureau. He could not bring his hate and violence to Mrs A., but he seemed to need his wife to bring them for him. He could not see any good in his wife or give her any affection, but he needed Mrs B. to be in contact with the good side of her and to support and protect her from him.

The 'honeymoon' in the Webb family lasted about four weeks, then Mrs B. was due to go away for her summer holiday, and Mrs A.'s holiday was to follow immediately on Mrs B.'s return. Both caseworkers feared that the withdrawal of help at this point might undo all the good that had been done so far in this marriage and, after some discussion, they arranged that each should make herself available to see the other's client during the holiday period if Mr and Mrs Webb themselves wanted this.

At his first interview after Mrs B.'s holiday had begun, Mr Webb reported a severe domestic upheaval. He said he did not know how the row had started, but it had ended in a fight in which he had broken a window and blacked his wife's eye. She had gone to the police and to her doctor, and was now talking of applying for a separation. Mrs A. tried to understand with him what had happened

—perhaps as a result of his anger at the Bureau workers' apparent lack of concern for them and his uneasiness now that his wife was no longer supported and that he felt that he was not sufficiently controlled. He could make little contribution to this attempt to understand the situation and again seemed very dull and remote. He could present himself only as a frightened and pathetic little boy, wanting forgiveness and love, and wanting to be told that all would be well.

After this scene, things calmed down again though there was no further movement towards a better relationship. Mr Webb continued to come to his interviews, but seemed quite unable to make any further attempt to understand himself or his marriage. He came like a little boy, begging for instructions. He seemed to understand almost nothing that was said to him and said again and again: 'I don't think I quite follow that.' Mrs A. accepted his need for support, but tried a little to show him the fear of his anger and destructiveness which lay behind this. He would admit no reaction to his caseworker's approaching holiday, always making admirably reasonable remarks about it.

When Mrs A. went on holiday and Mrs B. returned, Mrs Webb came back to her caseworker very depressed and unhappy again. She said that her husband was as bad as ever and that she was terrified of what would happen during Mrs A.'s absence. Mrs B. spent the whole interview working over with her client this recurrent theme of abandonment and all the anger and fears which surrounded it for both Mr and Mrs Webb.

Mr Webb's first interview after Mrs A.'s return was extremely difficult. He kept his overcoat on (it was early September), turned his chair to face away from Mrs A., and replied to her conventional polite greeting: 'How am I? Frightened. I'm always frightened.' His caseworker made an attempt to get him to say more and to try to explain himself, but he sat silently, still turned away from her.

Finally she said that he seemed to be frightened at this minute since he had remained wrapped up and was apparently unable to talk to her. She said that she thought he was very angry with her for going away, and, as always, very frightened of his anger which he imagined would harm her, or, at best, destroy her interest in him. She wondered, too, if a little bit of him was wanting to walk out on her, in revenge, and perhaps that was why he had kept his coat on. Mr Webb laughed and relaxed. He denied every word of this, but

took off his coat and settled down to tell his caseworker what had
happened while she had been away.

*This whole period of holidays and 'abandonment' in the casework
seemed to be of immense importance to Mr and Mrs Webb. The
experience, for both clients, of feeling utterly let down and furious about
it, and of being helped to express this and to understand it a little,
seemed to be a very meaningful one. They had managed to make a
good relationship, had lived through a crisis occasioned by separation
and yet had managed not to destroy it.*

*The arrangement that was made, that each could see the other's
caseworker, is a rare one at the Bureau, since it might be expected to
create jealousies and anxieties which could undermine the therapeutic
relationship. In fact, both Mr and Mrs Webb made use of the invitation
on one occasion each. These interviews were curiously alike in that they
were in a very low key, both clients bringing stories of their suffering and
misery, but making no real accusations against the partner and little
attempt to bid for support for themselves! Each seemed relieved to
establish that the other had a good and supportive relationship at the
Bureau, and needed only to be certain that they could both be acceptable
to both caseworkers.*

*Even Mr Webb, whose tendency to persecutory ideas must have
made him very suspicious as to what his wife was doing with Mrs B.,
seemed to have an overriding need to have her protected and seen as
good by someone. Only thus could he feel accepted himself. Mrs Webb,
who at the time of the joint interview had felt so attacked by everybody
and so abandoned by her own caseworker, seemed now only to need to
assure herself that she could make contact with her husband's caseworker, and was able to face the partial rejection inherent in the
situation. Perhaps, too, some of the division she had made in her
childhood between the mother who must be seen as good at all costs,
and the step-mother who could not be loved at all, made this meeting
with 'step-mother' of great importance to her.*

From this point the character of the work in this case seemed to
change. At the next two interviews both Mr and Mrs Webb reported
continued scenes and smashings, with the astonishing difference
that now Mrs Webb was hitting back and smashing things herself,
and that the rows ended with tears and reconciliation. The caseworkers both commented upon the ability of their clients to be

loving and reparative after rows, when the hatred had all been shown and there was little left to fear. Mrs B. tried to explore with her client the relation between her masochism and her sexual difficulties. She said that her client seemed frightened to think of sex in terms of love, and while unable to allow herself any intercourse with her husband, seemed almost to invite him to beat her. Mrs Webb said that sex had always seemed to her like an attack. Then she began to cry and said that she could remember the violent quarrelling that had gone on between her own parents. She hastily followed this with further insistence upon her love for her mother and said that fortunately her husband had never said bad things about her mother. 'If he does, that will be the end, I shall go berserk.' Mrs B. again tried to show her client her misery about her mother's behaviour and her denial of this feeling. For the first time Mrs Webb was then able to express some of her shame and anger about it.

After this the violence subsided. The couple resumed sexual intercourse after almost a year during which Mrs Webb had completely refused it, and the removal of this frustration, and of the utter rejection and condemnation of his sexuality which it seemed to mean to Mr Webb, helped him very much. They were both able to tolerate the fact that it was not immediately very satisfactory. Mrs Webb began to come to life in the marriage, and the couple started sharing activities and taking the children out together. When they quarrelled it was on a realistic level, as the result of genuine grievances which they had against each other. Mrs Webb seemed to be able to stand up for herself more while, at the same time, doing less to provoke her husband's phantasies. Mr Webb seemed able to see his wife again as a real person and to relate to her as such. He was able to look at some of the projections he had made and understand some of his own behaviour in the marriage—his very great demands, his fury when he was rejected, his terror about this, and also his need to see his wife as bad and dirty just because she was his sexual partner. At this stage he dropped both his servile manner and his pathetic childish stupidity and began to show in his interviews the intelligence and ability that had been so completely hidden before. His appearance changed remarkably and he began to look like a pleasant and capable man.

These clients continued to attend weekly for several months, then asked if they could come fortnightly and, later, monthly. By this time it seemed that they had found ways of giving some support and satisfaction to each other and were taking pleasure in their children's development and activities. Their internal tensions seemed to have been partly relieved and it seemed that the much freer and more realistic relationship that they had now established might be able to absorb and contain these anxieties in the future. The pressure might at some time mount up again, but it seemed almost certain in this case that the clients would be able to avail themselves of further help if the situation in the family showed signs of deterioration.

*   *   *

The work with the Webbs went on for almost the same length of time as that with the Clarkes, but the objective was a far more limited one. Mr Webb's near-delusions and the probable phantasies behind them were not dealt with directly. The work was concentrated entirely on the difficulties which these clients experienced in making and maintaining relationships with one another and with the case-workers.

As will have been seen, Mr Webb's behaviour towards Mrs A. was never at all violent, demanding or bizarre; he showed real distress only at the joint interview and anger only at the first meeting after the holiday break. This anger was of the most passive and terrified kind. Although he did not try to hide his bad behaviour from Mrs A., and always 'confessed' that he had been making scenes, he did not bring details of these, and certainly did not bring into the room the furious crazy creature who broke windows and smashed up his wife's possessions. It seemed as though, while he had to report violence and destructiveness at home, he could present himself to Mrs A. only as a pathetic little boy asking for forgiveness, in that way half denying any adult responsibility for what he had done. Only when he was no longer in danger of destroying his marriage, was feeling less ashamed of his behaviour as a husband, and was able to be adult and loving towards his wife, could he bring himself to Mrs A. as an intelligent, potent and loving man. It might perhaps seem that this relationship was of a rather 'phoney' kind and could not possibly help the client, but the counter-balance was clearly provided by the four-person situation, by the fact that Mr Webb knew that Mrs A. knew the worst about him. When his wife was not attending the Bureau, he was always extremely anxious and unable to deal with his relationship with his caseworker. He seemed to feel that his wife was acting out his own hostility and his own desire to walk out on the Bureau. Although his caseworker verbalized this feeling for him, he continued to find the situation too disturbing.

In the Webb family there were two children who were loved by both parents and who appeared, on the surface, to be remarkably undisturbed. They mediated between their parents and constantly tried to persuade them to 'Kiss and make it up'. Both Mr and Mrs Webb seemed to see them as wholly good, and to give them all the love that they could not give to one another. The last part of the casework was concerned largely with the clients' relationships with their children, and with some of the confusion of rejection, guilt and reparation in their feelings towards them. As the tensions between the parents eased, the children could give up their 'false maturity' and showed more signs of the strain that they had undergone.

It is possible that work with marriages provides a way of helping clients of this degree of instability. While their childishness and violence at home are the focus of the work at the Bureau, in the relationship with their caseworkers they often remain polite, reasonable and co-operative. It seems that neither clients nor caseworkers can risk the degree of regression which might result if these 'bad' aspects of themselves were brought directly into it.

For such clients, it seems extremely reassuring that they can come to the Bureau in their roles as husbands and fathers, or wives and mothers, and that this part of them is recognized and accepted side by side with their 'madness' and their oddness. They seem able to preserve their self-respect in relation to their caseworkers, on the basis that the knowledge of their destructiveness or dirtiness is brought into the Bureau by their partners, who at the same time find protection and support there. These people have an immense need for and dependence upon their family relationships, but are in constant danger of destroying these by their demands and destructiveness. Their worst fears are of losing their capacity to be husbands and fathers, or wives and mothers, or having these basic relationships taken away from them. Often their contact with other social agencies has had to be in connection with threatened or actual separation—and caseworkers may be associated for them with the anxieties and guilt which accompany such family crises. At the Family Discussion Bureau an important part of the work with these clients consists in the caseworkers' acceptance of them as marriage partners and parents, and this cuts across their dominant anxieties and provides an opportunity for them to test out with some measure of safety the less frightening aspects of their personalities, and to reconcile to some degree within themselves their splits and contradictions.

Cases of this kind present very great difficulties, especially where there are outbreaks of violence in which the clients themselves are terrified as to what will happen next. It is impossible for caseworkers not to share this terror, and not to wonder whether it would not be better if these people could separate from one another before serious damage is done. On the other hand, the experience at the Bureau may often make a greater impact upon these clients than upon more sophisticated and more stable ones, and if this experience is interpreted and understood to some extent, there may be considerable permanent gain. Many of the individual difficulties may remain untouched, but if some of the projections within the marriage are withdrawn, both husband and wife can gain the strengthening experience of discovering that their loving feelings are not destroyed by their hate.

Mr and Mrs Price

Mrs Price approached the Family Discussion Bureau as one of innumerable agencies which she had consulted over the last year or two to complain about her 'drunken' husband, whose 'violent temper and dirty habits' she could not stand any longer.

Her first visit was preceded by a long letter written 'in desperation'. She wrote that her health had been undermined by her husband's drunkenness and aggressive, dirty behaviour, and that he threatened to throw her out of the home for which she had saved every penny she had earned. Her doctor had suggested the Family Discussion Bureau and she prayed that they could do something about her husband as she 'had reached breaking-point'.

When she came to see Mrs B., her manner was in curious contrast to her desperate letter. She was polite, quietly spoken, anxious to please—a tall well-built woman of forty-nine, simply but carefully dressed, very neat and tidy. She brought a packet of papers with her, letters, testimonials from employers, even paper-cuttings from women's magazines to which she had written for advice. She explained that she had brought all this so that Mrs B. could see what a clean-living hard-working woman she was, and what she had to put up with in her husband. When Mrs B. took no notice of the papers, which were pushed towards her across the table, and invited the client to tell her story, her first words were: 'We had to get married because Betty was on the way.' She added hastily: 'Betty didn't suffer from it. I saw to it that she had the best of everything, and a good education—she's a fine girl!' Betty was now twenty, and there was a boy, Gerald, aged eleven. 'He is a good boy, and very helpful to his Mum—not at all keen on playing with other boys.' Mrs Price went on to talk about the children with a mixture of pride and anxiety, telling Mrs B. how she had striven to give them 'ever such a nice home' which she kept spotless: 'In my house you can eat off the floor!' Her husband had ruined all her efforts, made everybody unhappy, and would drive the children out of the home; for they dreaded the week-ends when he was drunk, unreasonable and objectionable. She described disgustedly how he wouldn't wash or bath or change his underwear. He would sleep in his dirty vest, and sometimes, when drunk, he would wet himself, losing control before he got to the lavatory. He had no table manners; he snored—she really could have nothing to do with him. And for many months now she had slept in a separate room.

On weekdays, when he wasn't drunk, he was not so bad—and, as Mrs Price went on talking, it became clear that the children were, in fact, very fond of their father, and that she did not find it easy to accept this. She admitted that he was good at his job—he was a fitter in an aircraft factory. 'He works much too hard, till late at night, and often Saturday or Sunday; he's never at home—either at his job or in the pub. When he's at home, he only watches television and doesn't talk. He earns good money, but spends it on his love—his beer.' At this point she picked up the papers from the table and handed them to Mrs B. to read. The caseworker had by now begun to sense the client's need to make the husband carry the projection of her own 'badness' and her anxiety when she had found herself talking about his good qualities. So instead of reading her 'testimonials', Mrs B. asked Mrs Price why she was so uncertain of herself that she had to insist on all these proofs of her goodness. The client was startled; then began to talk of her husband's unreasonable attitude towards Betty. He got so worked up when the girl stayed out late, which, admittedly, she often did. It was true that she had a lot of boy friends, not always of the best sort, but that was 'no reason to suspect the worst'. Mrs B. suggested that Mrs Price, too, might be worried about Betty—perhaps she and her husband had felt so guilty about having this baby before they were married that they almost expected the girl to turn out badly. Mrs Price denied this. Betty was all right, only her father was wrong. Her own family had never liked him, never wanted her to marry him. She told Mrs B. that she was the eleventh of thirteen children, with one sister very much older, and eleven brothers 'who teased the life out of me'. One brother, a year younger, whom she 'idolized', died when she was four. And when she was eight, another brother was born, but that one she always hated.

In fact, a great many things had happened when the client was eight, but Mrs B. only learned about them much later. A brother one year older, whom the client called her 'twin and favourite', was run over by a car, and her elder sister got married. The brother sustained severe leg injuries and was permanently crippled. This kept him away from girls, and he only married in his forties. The sister lost

her husband with pneumonia within six months. She had to share
her sorrow and the hours by his deathbed with another woman, a
previous girl-friend for whom he had asked when he was dying.
The young widow, who could never get on with her mother, confided
to her little sister her grief and humiliation, her disappointment and
her disgust with men.

In this first interview Mrs B. knew nothing about all this, nor did
she know how rejected her client had felt by her mother, who had
cared for many neighbouring families in trouble besides her own
thirteen children, giving to these other children the time, the concern,
the food, even the actual clothes, which her own should have had.
But although Mrs B. did not yet know any of this, her client's despair
about her unworthiness, her anxiety about her badness which
seemed to harm those near her, and her desperate need to be loved
and accepted in spite of it, came through the façade of righteousness
and intolerance.

By her attitude, Mrs B. conveyed this acceptance. Disregarding the
papers and testimonials, she showed that she did not need these
written proofs of her client's goodness, and that whatsoever badness
might emerge, it would make no difference to her interest in and
concern for Mrs Price.

At the end of the first meeting, Mrs Price said that she felt much
better—perhaps her husband would see reason after all. Mrs B. felt
that this remark expressed her client's first fumbling attempt to see
her husband as a person who reacted to her and not just as a hateful
unchangeable object with which she had no real connection. Mrs B.
wondered whether Mrs Price might now be able to let her husband
come to the Bureau in his own right, and asked whether she would
like him to be invited. At that the client got agitated: 'He wouldn't
dream of coming—and he wouldn't be any use either, as he can't
express himself.' Anyhow, they were just going on a holiday and she
would contact Mrs B. after her return.

*   *   *

She was in no hurry to do so. Her next visit, five weeks later, was
again preceded by a frantic letter (six pages this time) with an
enclosure of all the papers which she had tried to make Mrs B. read
during the first meeting. The letter contained the news that Betty had
left home—apparently after a quarrel with her mother. It was a
confused account of how this had happened, mixed with more
complaints about the husband's 'disgusting habits', and expressions

of anxiety that she herself was to blame for the girl's leaving. When she came to the interview, she quickly expressed her real fear—that she was a bad mother and had produced bad children. She described Betty this time as irresponsible, untidy, disobedient, a trial to her mother, and oscillated between relief that she had not to put up with her any longer; fear that she had failed her daughter; hopes that the girl would be happier away from home; dread that this might really happen and thus prove that mother was at fault, and, above all, fury with her husband who blamed her for it all. Later in the interview, she told Mrs B. that, for many months now, she had refused to sleep with her husband as he was disgusting—just like an animal, and, anyhow, she had always detested sexual intercourse. Mrs B. remarked on the client's sense of her own sexual badness, saying how difficult it was to tolerate what one felt to be so bad inside oneself, and how one often saw, fought and hated these bad things in another person—the husband and the daughter. This time, Mrs Price accepted the worker's comment and then began to speak more positively about her daughter and her husband. Only now did she bring a message from the latter that he would like to come to the Bureau, too. Mrs B. agreed to invite him, and he was soon given a date with Mr A.

* * *

When Mr Price came he turned out to be a large, solidly built man, with a quick abrupt manner of speech which made him difficult to understand. He was neatly and carefully dressed. He sat on the edge of his chair, not looking directly at Mr A. and clearly expected to be told off. The general impression he gave was of a rather withdrawn personality. As the interview progressed, however, he was able to relax and even to smile, though the jerkiness of speech persisted. He spoke first of his wife's tempers, which had killed his love for her and made things so difficult for the children that now Betty had left home. Betty herself he described as a sort of extension of his wife, also with a vile temper, and when the two of them got together. . .! He added that although his wife quarrelled so much with Betty, and nagged her all the time, he knew that she really loved the girl. So perhaps his wife's nagging of him might not necessarily mean that she no longer cared for him. A little later he said that his wife needed a lot of appreciation; it was quite silly how she wanted to be praised and admired for everything she did—he 'couldn't be that sloppy to do that'. Then he complained that his wife would not understand that he had a thirsty job in which he worked hard; he was entitled to his drink, and whatever happened he wasn't going to give that up. Mr A. made it clear that he was not expecting his client to do this, but suggested that they might understand together why he and his wife had to be so unyielding to each other. After that, Mr Price expressed anxiety about Gerald, whom his wife alternately petted and smacked, and whom she was turning into a cissy. Mr A. took this up with him in terms of his own anxieties about being a father, and wondered what his relationship to his own father had been.

With some help, the client overcame his reluctance to talk about his parents and described his father as a 'brute of a man' with a wife who was good and patient and who had to put up with a great deal. They were a large family and the client came somewhere in the middle. When he was about ten, Mr Price said, he got into some sort of trouble and appeared before a Court and was sent to an Approved School. He did not have to go, but it was put to his parents as a possibility and his mother thought it would be better for him since this would protect him from the beatings he had been receiving from his father, as 'the black sheep of the family'. So he went to an Approved School, where, he said, he was very happy. Later he went to a farm and thence into the Army. In this first interview he spoke as if he had had little contact with his family from an early age though in later interviews it transpired that this was not so, and that in fact he had more than one important period at home.

A particularly significant time for him was the period just before he married, when all his brothers and sisters had left the home and he was alone with Mum and Dad. Now he was stronger than Dad, who anyhow had calmed down a bit, and there was no need to fight him in order to protect Mum. For this was what the client felt had happened when he got himself into trouble in childhood. The importance of this time to Mr Price emerged in a much later phase of the casework contact when it became clear that he might never have made up his mind to marry had his wife not become pregnant; in fact, it seemed that he had to make her pregnant in order to be able to leave his mother. During that phase it also became clearer that Betty's leaving home had reactivated his anxieties about this earlier situation. Betty, to him, was perhaps the seductive and seducing girl which his wife had been when she came between him and his mother, and thus seemed to be some threat to the security of his marriage. Perhaps still more important, Betty's departure brought about a direct repetition of the earlier threesome, but this time between himself, his wife and his son, and produced a confused sense of identification with Gerald.

There was no mention of all this in the early contacts with Mr A., although the client had indicated in the first interview how much he identified with Gerald. What came across most strongly in the first meetings was Mr Price's sense of helplessness in coping with his powerful wife and powerful daughter; there were also first indications of how he could only deal with this by withdrawing and 'letting the wife get on with it'. His attitude of withholding himself was carried into the relationship with Mr A., to which he found it difficult to commit himself. He always found some reason to avoid weekly meetings; there were parents' meetings at the boy's school, or he was 'not feeling too grand'. However, he soon made it clear that he was not entirely passive and did not want to be so passive at home either; in fact, he did not feel helpless as a father if left to it by his wife.

Against his wife's expectations and in spite of his own ambivalence he seemed to get a good deal of satisfaction in coming to the Bureau. Yet he insisted that the only important thing was her response to it. So far this was favourable and, as long as this lasted, he was content to fall into line with her about it. Mr A. tried to show him how his falling into line and 'letting her get on with it' was, in fact, his way of expressing anger with his wife. In doing so, however, he sometimes seemed to hurt himself and to put himself at a disadvantage. It was difficult for Mr Price to accept the idea that his withdrawing into the pub and withholding himself and his money was his way of getting back at his wife, and the implied suggestion that in this way he was punishing himself as well as his wife was ignored. It was easier for him to see some of this when Mr A. talked with him about the time when he went to the Approved School, and commented that he must have hurt his mother as well as himself by getting into a position in which he had to be sent away. This he could only hear at the second mention, and then said: 'You know, I have only just thought of that.' It obviously meant much to him that he might have some power with his womenfolk, even though he had to hurt himself in order to hurt them.

In the early stages of this case, Mr A. let the client set the pace, and interviews were arranged at three- or even four-weekly intervals. Yet, almost from the beginning of the contact the marital situation

steadily improved, there was less nagging, more ease at home. Mr
Price reported that while in the past he would stay away from home
as long as possible, he now wanted to get there quickly 'just because
I like to be there'. It was 'a miraculous change', but he insisted that
it was his wife who was 'different'—he was just the same as always.

*   *   *

Meanwhile, Mrs Price, with only a few setbacks which in each
case were followed by long frantic letters to Mrs B., had built up a
strong positive relationship with her caseworker. She told her that
she always got on better with women. Her mother had warned her
of men, who were 'all brutes', and the client had never trusted them.
She did not mention her father, and when asked about him said he
was kind, very fond of her, but quiet, and never seemed to get
anywhere. 'In our home, you first noticed Mum—Dad was in the
background.' When she talked of her brothers, it became clear that
she felt misused and denigrated by them and that she had taken her
revenge on the only weaker one, the much younger brother. She
had no boy-friends until she was twenty-three, when she became
friendly with her best girl-friend's brother and let herself be seduced
by him. Immediately after this he jilted her, leaving her ashamed and
terrified at what he must have discovered in her that could have
turned him against her. Was she different from other girls?

At this time of unhappiness and confusion, she had met Mr Price
at a party. He had been engaged to his best friend's sister, a girl he
had never seen, but got engaged to by letter. He had just broken the
engagement, also by letter, when his pals had made him feel that she
was no good, something of a prostitute. He had never been interested
in girls before. These two people, who both felt utterly bewildered
in relation to the other sex, confided in each other, each trying to
gain reassurance through the other one. They soon started a sexual
relationship and she became pregnant. In telling this story Mrs Price
kept on saying she only wished she had never married him, even
though she was pregnant. Mrs B. explored with her her doubts about
herself and about her own bad sexuality, and linked them with her
anxieties about Betty, who was so attractive, but also so messy and
rebellious. She tried to show her client that she had always been so
frightened of these feelings that she had to disown them, and put
them on to her husband—and men in general. At the next meeting,
Mrs Price reported proudly that she was now always remembering

Mrs B. and repressing her bad temper at home. Immediately after she mentioned 'splitting headaches', and Mrs B. said it sounded as if wanting to please her had given her the headache, and then spoke of how repressed, condemned, split-off feelings may affect oneself, as well as one's husband and one's children.

From then on, whenever Mrs Price complained about her marriage or her husband, Mrs B. related this to the client's guilty feelings, showing her at the same time how these complaints were often about things which had good and loving aspects. For example, the client spoke angrily about the husband's generosity in the pub, where he liked to treat everybody to drinks, and Mrs B. recalled her feelings when her mother was so generous to all the neighbours' children. She showed her that she hated her mother—and her husband—for being generous to others at her expense, and yet was proud of them. A few weeks later, when Mrs Price spoke of her husband's attempts to please her by redecorating a room—and how he then spoilt it all by the mess he left behind, Mrs B. said that the 'mess' seemed always to be spoiling the attempts they both made to keep things nice and clean, and why was the messiness really so terrifying? It was on this occasion that Mrs Price asked anxiously whether it was perhaps her own constant cleaning that made the children and husband so uncomfortable at home. She then talked more about the way she had to clean up after everybody, particularly Betty, who would leave her dirty, disgusting underwear all over the place, especially on her 'days'.

Throughout all this, Mrs B. would try to help her client to tolerate both the good and the bad in herself. While accepting the reality of the client's fears about her own badness, Mrs B. showed in her attitude that she could tolerate this without losing her awareness of the client's good qualities. Almost from the beginning of the casework contact, Mrs Price showed her acceptance of the links which her caseworker made between the 'bad' which she saw in others and the 'bad' which she rejected in herself by illustrating this with further material. But, inevitably, a few minutes later she would make a remark such as: 'What my husband is like in drink needs to be seen to be understood.' Mrs B. would then let her know that she recognized the husband's part in the mess and muddle, as well as her client's feelings that she herself was to blame—and would say something to show how much she understood and valued her client's tremendous efforts to be 'good' and 'clean'.

By this time Mrs Price was obviously much less aggressive towards her husband, could more easily tolerate his need for a few pints and was very surprised by the fact that his visits to the pub became much shorter, that he was staying at home more frequently, was taking more interest in the boy, and was more helpful in every respect. Betty was still living in digs, with a nice family, where she seemed to behave well. She came home frequently with a boy-friend of whom both parents could approve, and the relationship between mother and daughter seemed much easier. Gerald was now allowed, and able, to spend more time with his pals, bringing them home, or going out with them and, for the first time in his life, he did not insist on going with his mother when she went to her sister's for a week-end.

The Prices came to the Bureau just at the point when Betty was about to leave the home, and this seemed to have brought to a crisis the discontent and strain of twenty years of marriage. Both parents had projected on to this daughter much of their guilt about their own bad sexuality, and the girl's uncontrolled and provocative behaviour in turn increased the parents' anxieties. For both of them the daughter's growing into a woman, her boy-friends and escapades, revived their anxieties about their own sexuality, which they had always felt was dirty and bad, and their feelings of guilt associated with their own parents.

Mrs Price had tried to deal with this by building up a picture of herself as such a very good woman, by her continual scrubbing and cleaning and by projecting the badness on to dirty men, in particular, her husband. These defences were now threatened by the fact that, in Betty, feminine sexuality seemed to be getting out of control again.

In her childhood, the only men she could love were her ineffectual father, the injured elder brother, and the idolized younger one who died in infancy. All other men were avoided as 'brutes'. It must have seemed to her that only damaged men could be safely loved—but then, had love damaged them? In making her son into a cissy, she was, perhaps, trying to stop him from growing into a man so that she could keep him lovable and safe and protect him from becoming a target for her bad projections and destructive impulses. The alternate cuddling and smacking of the boy were an expression of her ambivalent feelings.

In her previous search for help, Mrs Price had always managed to get support for the denial for her 'badness'. Mrs B.'s refusal to look at the written proofs of her 'goodness', and her offer to look at the client herself, implied an acceptance of her as she was, and seemed to offer a possibility of safely relaxing some of her defences which she so anxiously maintained.

Mr Price had hitherto been prepared to accept and use his wife's projection of her own badness and dirtiness, because this suited his own unconscious needs in relation to his mother. In his marriage he could express his resentment by withholding himself and his money from his wife, who represented, for him, the bad aspects of his mother. In his uncontrolled drinking and his dirty habits he behaved much as a small child who wanted to punish a frustrating mother. But his wife also carried, to some extent, the projection of the loving mother whom he needed to keep clean and good. By taking the badness on himself he both punished and preserved her, but at the expense of his own degradation. At the same time he was perhaps identifying himself with his 'brute' of a father.

The absence of benevolent control in his childhood family made it particularly difficult for him to come to terms with the goodness and the badness inside himself, and with his feelings of love and hate. When he loved his mother, he had to protect her not only from the dirty brutality of his father but also from his own forbidden sexual feelings. In getting himself sent away as a boy he had produced a situation in which he could feel safer and, at the same time, punish his mother for her inability to control the dangerous relationships at home. At the Approved School he experienced benevolent control of his destructive impulses, but was robbed of the opportunity to test them out in relation to the members of his family who had evoked them. At the Bureau, within the safety provided by the special setting of the four-person relationship he could re-experience some of this benevolent control and, at the same time, was offered an opportunity to explore his aggressive feelings in the context of his family life.

When the improvement in the Price family had lasted about five months, Mr A. and Mrs B. began to consider terminating the case although they knew that a great many of their clients' problems had not even been touched. This was, however, a middle-aged couple whose marriage had never been very satisfactory; that, by now, the tensions in the family had lessened considerably was, perhaps, all that could be expected.

In the next meeting with Mrs Price, five weeks before Easter, Mrs B. hinted that the Easter break might be a good point at which to stop meeting, and the client seemed to accept this. A few days later came one of her frantic letters—the first for several months—describing a scene which arose because the husband had been late for Sunday dinner. Mrs Price wrote that this quarrel had made her feel that she could not go on with the marriage although she wanted 'to be loyal to everybody'.

Obviously the letter was connected with the threat of losing Mrs B., and the question of whether termination might be appropriate was brought to a Case Conference.

Case Conference

The discussion started with the question whether Mrs Price's last letter really indicated a deterioration in the marriage or was a response to the suggestion of closing the contact. A crisis often occurs at the point when the workers begin to withdraw, as if the clients are trying to hold them in this way. Was Mrs Price's continuing need òf her worker therapeutically useful? The Consultant Psychiatrist pointed out that this client needed to take from her caseworker into herself a good deal more of what a good mother could give her before real improvement could be possible.

That both these clients were happier with members of their own, rather than the opposite, sex was important in considering the potentialities of this marriage and of the casework.

The anxieties in heterosexual relationships were stressed, and it became clear that, although both workers had been aware of this, they had avoided taking up the question of their clients' feelings for their own sex for fear of raising anxieties with which they might not be able to deal.

In further discussion, members of the group recalled similar cases in which a compulsively clean and tidy wife came to complain about a drunken husband. One of these women had told a story of her beautiful little daughter who, in a white dress, was distributing flowers in a hospital ward 'while her dirty swine of a father was lying drunk in the gutter'. All these women had soon revealed feelings of guilt about their own sexuality—all had had pre-marital sexual relationships or illegitimate children, and their doubts about their own worthiness could, in all these cases just as with Mrs Price, be linked with feelings of rejection and unwantedness in childhood. They all seemed to project on to their husbands their feelings of their own dirtiness and badness in a desperate attempt to keep these feelings away from themselves, their children and their home.

In the cases which were recalled, none of the husbands had been as bad as their wives had made them out to be. While they all liked more drink than they could easily take, and withdrew into the pub from their domineering wives, none were alcoholics. They all worked hard in good steady jobs, and were liked by their mates. In the group discussion an attempt was made to understand more clearly the husbands' part in the difficulties. The way in which they accepted and used their wives' projections indicated how this fitted in with their own needs. Mr Price's witholding attitude was commented on. Mr A. spoke of the feelings of frustration and rejection which this client's attitude provoked in him, and how this helped him to understand the wife's reaction towards her husband.

In the other cases which had been mentioned, all the husbands had stopped coming to the Bureau when, after a few interviews, things at home had got better. In each case the wife continued to attend, making everybody feel, once again, that all depended on her. There was first a feeling that Mr Price, too, wanted to withdraw and that he should be allowed to do so, until male members of the group pointed out that, in these other apparently similar cases, the husband had worked with a woman caseworker who seemed to have only too readily accepted his withdrawal. Might Mr Price not be able to make use of his contact with a male worker to explore his confusion?

The conclusion which emerged from the group discussion was that such homosexual impulses as the Prices seem to have were not so deep-seated as to be a real hindrance to the marriage, and that to bring them into the open would help the clients' development towards a more mature adjustment in the marriage.

*   *   *

When Mrs Price next came for an interview she was looking surprisingly well and wearing a new outfit which she wanted Mrs B. to admire. She said that her husband had bought her this for his niece's wedding, and settled down to describe the wedding in great detail. Betty had looked lovely—by far the prettiest girl there, and 'so proud of her Daddy' and he of her. Gerald had 'carried the whole congregation away' with his singing, and everybody had remarked on how he had grown and what a nice boy he was. Her husband had been most helpful with everybody; 'he is the best of the lot, has a heart of gold'. Mrs B. listened to all this and then said how glad she was that the difficulties which Mrs Price had mentioned in her letter had been overcome. 'Oh, yes, that letter . . .' and then, half-heartedly, she described the incident, when her husband was twenty-five minutes late for Sunday dinner, and she went 'almost mad with rage', and could not get over it for nearly a week. When Mrs B., with the client, tried to find out what had been so upsetting in this trivial incident, Mrs Price did not know. She said she had since wondered herself what had made her react in this way. Mrs B. asked whether she might have wanted to show her caseworker how much she still needed her, and the client replied: 'You are very important to me because you don't use things against me.' Then she told a long and involved story of a woman at work to whom she had once remarked that Betty looked very attractive on top but was messy and dirty underneath—and this woman 'always rubbed it in'. Mrs B. suggested that she herself must have made the client feel that she did not want to look at the 'dirt underneath' and only wanted to see what was good on top; and yet it was, perhaps, just the 'dirty bits' in herself which she needed to feel accepted and valued. Mrs Price started to cry, which she had never done before, and said pleadingly: 'I need you very much'.

In the interviews through the next month or so, the client talked almost entirely about the bad side of herself. She told Mrs B. what a naughty rebellious child she had been; punishment had made her only worse—'I gave my mother hell.' She spoke of her hatred of the youngest brother, who was born when she was eight; she had tipped him out of the pram and trodden on his hands when he was crawling. A bit later she talked of the way her elder brothers had teased her—how they had given her first silk stockings to the dog to play with, and sprinkled her first face powder into the sink. It was as if they didn't want her to be pretty and feminine. Until she married she shared her parents' bedroom—never had a room of her own, and this was humiliating and hateful, although 'I never noticed anything.' It was in this bedroom that she had to lie when she first discovered that she was pregnant. She didn't tell anybody, did not let Tom (her future husband) know—but got ill 'probably from worry', and 'when he came to see me there he had to drag the truth out of me, I was that proud'.

During these weeks the client's reports on the situation at home were very positive. Even sexual intercourse, which she had always hated, became enjoyable; her periods, which had stopped for two years, returned, and she looked much younger.

* * *

The effect of the case conference had been equally important for the work with Mr Price. Mr A. had not fully realized before to what extent he himself had accepted his client's withholding attitude without discussing the implications of this with him in relation to the interviews. At the next meeting he was able to do this and to show Mr Price the connection between what he was doing at the Bureau and what he was doing at home, and how he was rejecting his caseworker as well as his wife by withdrawing from them. This helped the client to understand how the impact of his own attitudes affected other people, and this seemed to be a startling discovery for him.

Although Mr A. had not previously discussed the sexual relationship with Mr Price, the client started the following meeting by saying: 'You're quite right—you know—the sexual turn-out. . . .' Mr A. wondered what made him say this and he replied: 'I've been keeping my wife short of love, I can see that now.' Thus, he himself made the link between his general frustrating and withholding attitude and the sexual difficulties in his marriage. He made this still clearer when, later on in the same interview, he spoke about his mother. Formerly he had described her as a near-perfect figure who protected him from his father by sending him away. Now he was able to face his anger with her for not being able to avoid the dangerous involvements without sending him away. The new understanding of how hitherto he had coped by withdrawing from situations which raised his anxiety and guilt, helped him to see how, in relationship with his wife, too, his sexual guilt, his anger and withdrawal were all connected.

In this phase, Mrs Price brought to her caseworker her badness and her feeling of guilt with the same pressure as she had formerly insisted on her goodness and blamelessness. As she reviewed the picture she had made for herself, she began to feel that neither she nor the people around her were all good or all bad; that she could also love what she had hated, and accept the good things that she had denied herself and felt that others had denied her, as well as those bad things she had repudiated in herself. She was only able to make this move after the importance of the relationship with her caseworker had been discussed and acknowledged.

Mr Price, too, was only able to make a conscious link between his pattern of behaviour and the way this affected his relationships after he had become aware of the interaction between himself and Mr A. This client had tried to defend against some of his own anxieties by picturing himself always at the mercy of other people. In the security of his relationship with his caseworker, he discovered his own power in relation to others. This discovery came to him as a flash of light,

*and was of tremendous importance to him both in relieving him of his
sense of impotence, and in facing him with new burdens and dangers.
It seems to have made it possible for him to look at himself and the
important people in his life in a different way. Subsequent material,
in particular the spontaneous link which he made with his sexuality,
and the developing change in his relationship to his wife, showed that
much had been understood that had never been discussed. Unsophisti-
cated clients like Mr Price, who may have difficulties in verbalizing
their feelings, can nevertheless often use the unconscious communications between themselves and their caseworkers in a very profitable
way.*

*The same applies to Mrs Price. Throughout the contact, Mrs B. did
not respond to this client by attempting to make her more conscious
of the phantasy element in her material, but rather talked about it at a
level which the client could accept. In order to make a meaningful
communication on that level, she had nevertheless to be aware herself
of the inner content of these phantasies. For example, when Mrs Price
talked about her feelings of 'humiliation' when sharing her parents'
bedroom, Mrs B. did not explore the client's sexual phantasies about
this situation, and her feelings of exclusion and jealousy. She simply
accepted her client's sense of deprivation in having no room of her
own, and linked this with the present situation in which she was so
sensitive to her husband's 'snoring' that she could no longer share a
bedroom with him. Yet, whenever Mrs Price came back to the question
of whether she had a 'right' to a bedroom of her own, usually in connection with Betty's possible return home, she stressed how much the
sexual relationship with her husband had improved since Betty had
been away. It was as if her daughter's return home would really
reconstellate the situation in her own childhood when she wanted, and
was afraid to, come between her parents.*

After a couple of weekly interviews in which he worked hard with
Mr A. and things at home steadily improved, Mr Price used the
bus strike, which made coming to the Bureau difficult, though not
impossible, as an opportunity to fall back on the three-weekly
interviews. But now both he and Mr A. could see his reluctance to
come more often as an indication that he wished to work things
out slowly and that this was somehow in accordance not only with
his own needs but also with the needs of the marriage, in which his
wife had to be a step ahead. Now the client could tolerate this

without getting too angry and having to retaliate by withdrawal, just as he could stay away from Mr A. without feeling guilty and making excuses.

Mrs Price, too, had cancelled her dates during the seven-weeks' bus strike. When buses were running again, she telephoned Mrs B. to say that all was well, and later wrote a note to tell how beautifully her husband had redecorated the house. It was another five weeks before she came to see Mrs B., and this was on the whole just a chatty meeting. Things continued to be better at home. Betty was 'more sensible', thinking of marriage, and consulting her parents about her plans.

The prospective son-in-law had become an important figure in the family; he seemed to represent the acceptable aspects of masculine sexuality and could not only have good relations with each member of the family, but seemed to bring them all more closely together. He teased and pleased Mrs Price, had drinks with Mr Price, and an occasional game with Gerald who 'all of a sudden' had turned into a big boy, went for cycle rides and 'ganged up' with his father.

Husband and wife could show each other more clearly now how each needed the other one. Although Mr Price seemed to express this mainly in terms of being jealous of the insurance man and other callers, it greatly pleased his wife. And she had been able, though again only after she had dreamt that her husband was dead, to tell him how lonely and miserable she would be without him.

Although more might have been done with this couple, both caseworkers fell in with their clients' evident desire, neither to embark on further and more intensive work, nor to terminate the case altogether. Both clients clearly wanted to feel that they could now manage on their own, but at the same time that their caseworkers were still available if they needed them. In fact, only Mrs Price made direct use of this availability, first by asking for interviews at longer and longer intervals; later by an occasional letter or telephone call. Each contact was occasioned by some sort of crisis which was overcome as soon as Mrs B. showed her continued concern. A year later the improvement in the family had been fully maintained.

The Price family present a pattern which is well known and sometimes very puzzling to social workers, who often wonder why these clean, hard-working women marry and stay with drunken husbands whom they despise. They also ask themselves why casework efforts to help such families are so often unsuccessful. We certainly have our share of failure, although our special setting, including the use of the case conference, helps us to remain aware that a vital factor in the treatment of all cases is the ability of the caseworker to tolerate the projection on to her of the 'bad' as well as the 'good'.

This is especially difficult in cases such as these where the wives have so frantically to deny their own badness, and therefore have the urgent need to appear so good and to make such good positive relationships with any parental figure. For them to bring together the good and the bad in themselves represents a terrifying demand, and the worker is faced with the gruelling test of being drawn into this or giving in to her own need to avoid the distress, pain and aggression of a negative transference.

* * *

It might be helpful to include a brief note on another marriage where similar processes of projection were evident in such extreme form that they can be seen even more clearly. In this case the wife had responded to severe deprivation in her childhood by delinquent behaviour in adolescence, until a wise and understanding employer showed her that she was 'not only a devil but could be an angel too'. Since then, she felt she had been alternating dramatically between the two. When her marriage failed to help her to bring these extreme facets of her personality together, she dealt with them by projecting the 'dirty devil' on to the husband.

He had been a premature baby and a sickly child, and his mother had 'kept him in cotton wool'. He had felt very restricted but, as she was doing all this 'for his good', he could never express his anger as a child. His anxiety about what his anger might do to women had been much reinforced when he married this wild hysterical girl. Later, when his mother died in an accident, and again when a sister had a mental breakdown, he felt himself somehow involved and to blame. He began to drink more heavily, and would come home, and soil himself or urinate against the wall. He withdrew from home and children and had little interest or success in his job.

The wife kept herself, her home and her five children, of whom at least one was not her husband's, beautiful and exaggeratedly clean. All her love and warmth went to the children, who co-operated with her needs by being exceptionally attractive just as the husband co-operated in accepting the aggressively dirty part allotted to him.

In this case the wife spontaneously made a strong and dependent relationship with her caseworker. She saw in her, as she had done in the good employer who had first made her aware of her angel and devil bits, the good mother she was longing for. With her help, she was quickly able to see how she had dealt with these contrasting parts of herself in her marriage; and how this affected her attitude to her husband.

The husband explored, with his caseworker, his terror of what he was doing to women and women to him—and how he had responded to feeling at their mercy by behaving like a dirty uncontrolled baby. He eventually felt free enough to bring his guilt and his anger to his caseworker without fear of damaging her, or to stay away without having to feel too aggressive. It seemed that it was of great importance to him that his badness and messiness was accepted at the Bureau, and he was helped to feel that these disturbing aspects of himself might be contained within his marriage As soon as his wife withdrew some of her projections from him, the husband seemed to throw off a burden which had stopped him from developing the stronger side of himself. He gave up drinking within a few weeks, took a more active and responsible role both at home and in his job, and soon he gave his caseworker to understand that he could cope on his own. The wife continued to attend for several months, and all seemed to be going well, including the sexual relationship.

About a year after the wife's last visit, she had to have an internal operation. This she felt as 'having gone bad inside' and blamed the husband: 'He has put poison into me'.[1] In her interviews, which she resumed through her husband's initiative, she presented a completely reversed picture of the marriage. Now she saw the husband as rigid, bossy and persecuting: 'He always nags, nothing I do is good enough'. As she was not able to fall back upon her old pattern of projection because her husband was no longer prepared to accept it, she now exaggerated his growing strength, feeling it as persecuting, just as in the past she had so used his weakness. During a few weekly sessions it became clear that her feeling of 'having gone bad inside' was connected with her old fears about her own badness which, she felt, had made her mother desert her. She had experienced the end of the casework contact as a desertion by her caseworker. By the time she had recovered from the after effects of the operation she had also worked through some of her frightening feelings, in particular her fear that her caseworker could not possibly care for such a 'bad'

---

[1] Clients often use this expression: see Mrs Robinson, p. 111.

person. This time the husband had got less involved and was able to give her support, and the couple achieved a more stable adjustment. Two years later, when they approached the Bureau for a 'reference', this had not only been maintained but further strengthened.

In this case the same processes are at work as in the case of the Prices, but everything is more highly coloured. Both partners, especially the wife, had much more severely disturbed backgrounds; the inter-action between the couple had led to extremes of behaviour in both husband and wife; the reaction to the casework was alarmingly drama-tic—both became 'changed' people in a relatively short time. This wife's breakdown after her operation provided a new therapeutic drive; it offered an opportunity to work through some of her feelings about the idealized 'good' and the deserting 'bad' mother in relation to her caseworker, and this helped towards a further phase of adjustment.

In the case of the Prices, both partners had, in spite of bewildering and ambivalent feelings in their childhood, evidently experienced sufficient love to be able to attempt a more gratifying relationship in their marriage and with their children without such violent reactions and reversals of behaviour as those which we have just described.

Mr and Mrs Robinson

Mr and Mrs Robinson were referred to the Bureau by the Child Guidance Clinic at which Martin, aged nine, Mrs Robinson's son by her first marriage, was receiving treatment. The boy was reported to be a disturbing influence at school, stealing, lying, and indulging in sex play, and it was thought that difficulties between Mr and Mrs Robinson might be a factor contributing to his delinquent behaviour.

The following facts about the family were contained in the referral letter from the clinic. Mr Robinson was thirty-one, his wife thirty-four, and they had been married for seven years. Mrs Robinson's first husband had deserted her for another woman, leaving her pregnant with Martin almost immediately after marriage. She had returned to work after Martin's birth and, when the boy was about a year old, she had met Mr Robinson, a Chartered Accountant, who was working in the same office as herself, and had married him after a short courtship.

Mrs Robinson's mother had died within a year of the marriage and her father had remarried soon afterwards.

Mr Robinson's father had died very recently and he now saw a good deal of his mother, who lived nearby.

The couple shared a large house with Mrs Robinson's sister and brother-in-law and their children.

There was a longer delay than usual before Mr and Mrs Robinson could be offered appointments at the Bureau. As they had only just begun to face the fact that Martin's difficulties might be connected with those in their marriage, this delay may have involved considerable strain for them. Both these facts may also have had some bearing on the urgency with which they each expressed their feeling of 'oddness' in their early interviews.

*   *   *

When Mr Robinson came to his first interview he gave Mrs A. the impression of a shamefaced little boy who was expecting to be ticked off. He sat nervously screwing and unscrewing his gloves, or unsuccessfully attempting to light his pipe while he talked. He seemed very uncertain of himself and most anxious about what kind of impression he was making.

During the interview, his attitude was that he was useless and stupid, and that anything he did was bound to be wrong. He frequently asked Mrs A. whether he was talking about the right things, or remarked: 'I expect that sounds silly to you.' If Mrs A. did not seem to know all the answers, or to understand him, he immediately assumed that it was due to his own stupidity in not being able to make himself understood. His attitude, however, also implied that Mrs A. was not telling him all she knew because she did not think it would be good for him, and this had the effect of making her seem to be either deliberately withholding help from him or else to be completely useless.

He spoke of his marriage with utter hopelessness, saying that the situation had become quite impossible. 'We will bicker tomorrow morning and the morning after and the morning after that.' His relationship with his wife he described as 'like driving a car and coming to a T junction, my wife watching to see which way I am going to turn the wheel and then saying it's the wrong way.' If on the way home he were to buy strawberries because he thought his wife might like them, he would be sure to have made a mistake for it would be raspberries she would want. Although, while telling Mrs A. this, Mr Robinson's tone of voice showed his anger with his wife, he acknowledged none, and insisted that he must be at fault in some way. He told Mrs A. that he and his wife had bought their present big house in the hope of 'filling it with our children', and only when this had not seemed possible had they asked Mrs Robinson's elder sister and her family to share the house with them. He felt very much to blame for their not having managed 'even to have one child of our own'.

He had, he said, taken Martin to the doctor that morning because the boy had a lump in his groin which both he and his wife thought might be due to a rupture. The doctor had told him that it was nothing to worry about, but Mr Robinson was sure that his wife would say that he had not managed to make the doctor understand. Mrs A. suggested that he was perhaps expressing some of his doubts about being able to make her understand too. This led to their discussing his apparent feeling of uncertainty in connection with Mrs A. as well as his wife. He said that he had been happy and much more self-confident in the Forces—he was in the Air-sea Rescue

Service—and accepted very easily the suggestion that he seemed to feel particularly uncertain with women.

When Mrs A. tried to indicate the anger with his wife and herself which lay behind his attitude of hopelessness, he immediately turned the blame back on himself, saying: 'Of course, my "poor, poor me" attitude must be pretty awful.' His wife told him he was mother-tied and he thought she was probably quite right, he had never been able to 'stand up to' his mother. He stopped quite suddenly at this point and said that he felt frightened because Mrs A. seemed to know so much about his feelings. He was, he said, very afraid of what she might be seeing—'I suppose I must feel guilty or something.'

At first, Mrs A. had found herself trying to avoid being made into the useless person who did not understand her client, and had felt herself almost forced into proving her willingness and ability to help him by showing him all she could about his difficulties. She had been concentrating on showing him the similarity in his attitude to his wife and to herself, pointing out how he expressed the same uncertainty and feeling of uselessness in both relationships and also trying to show him how he was forcing both his wife and herself into the domineering role that angered and frustrated him so much. He responded by such remarks as: 'How stupid of me not to have seen that myself, but still I must be pleased to learn from you.' Mrs A. began to see that in order to avoid feeling useless herself she too was letting herself be forced into this role of the domineering woman who knew everything. So she tried to be less dominant herself in the interview situation and to help her client to feel safer in taking a more dominant role with her. Throughout the contact Mrs A. concentrated on this, in consequence leaving untouched or unseen many points that she might otherwise have taken up.

During the rest of this interview, Mrs A. tried, by her attitude, to help Mr Robinson to be aware of the fact that neither he nor she was infallible, and that only by working together could they attempt to sort things out. Towards the end of the meeting he gave a different picture of the relationship with his wife; he said that he felt awful when his wife cried because he knew he ought to comfort her, but, 'I am very bad and ignore it by reading the paper or something.' When Mrs A. asked him why he felt he did this, he spoke of his feeling of inadequacy and said that he felt he could never be the sort of man his wife really wanted 'someone who would sweep her off her feet'.

*　　*　　*

When Mrs Robinson—a tall, slim, dark woman—came to her first interview, her dress and gesture accentuated her angularity rather than her litheness, the severity and tautness rather than the dignity of her appearance. She sat down abruptly and proceeded to stare at Mrs B. for a few tensely drawn out moments; then, suddenly and violently, the flood gates seemed to fly open and to release a rush of talk, accompanied by mime and rolling Rs, which all but seemed to burst through the walls of a small interviewing room. This impression was further heightened in that her theme seemed singularly out of key with such a dramatic presentation. It was a detailed description of the oddities and the peculiar modes of life and background of her workmates in the office where she worked, the only woman in an all-male 'madhouse'. This post was formerly held by her father-in-law and, whenever he was too ill to go to work, Mrs Robinson would help out. So it was only natural, she felt, that after his death she should take over his job. She went on to talk about her own father, towards whom she felt very bitter. He never gave her mother anything; he would deck himself out in the most beautiful clothes, which he made her mother finger—and she did so admiringly and with envy; in contrast, she was left with the responsibility for dressing three children as well as herself, and was not able to buy new clothes. The client mentioned in this connection that, besides her and her sister, there was a brother, three years younger than herself. Her mother had been considerably older than her father, and had died five years before, leaving Mrs Robinson desolate in the realization of her irrevocable loss. She could never forgive her mother-in-law, who had promptly announced, 'I shall have to be your mother now.' Her father found himself another wife, a woman many years younger than himself and just as sweet and good and gentle as her mother. Mrs Robinson had expressed her anger by telling her father that he 'really did not deserve it!'

Still not mentioning her husband, or the problem that had brought them to the Bureau, Mrs Robinson went on to speculate on what her father would do when his second wife reached the 'change of life', as the client had been told that he would have nothing to do with her own mother thereafter. She went on to describe her father's disgust at 'women's physical dirtiness', he would insist that women should change their underwear every day, but here again her poor mother, like other busy housewives, could only manage a change of clothes once a week.

Eventually, Mrs B. was able to deal with her client's anxiety sufficiently for this flood of words to subside and it then became possible to talk about the marriage problem.

This problem was the constant arguing between her husband and herself. She wished she could say, 'Yes, dear', like other women. Her husband was undoubtedly intellectually her superior and, in an argument, would so confuse her that she never knew what she was saying. On the other hand, he had none of the deep feelings and emotions which she felt were the basis of marriage. He would forget their wedding anniversary, and for her last birthday he had given her a jumper which his mother had knitted; 'Surely this should have been my mother-in-law's present to me, not his!' On the one occasion when he gave her flowers, they turned out to be a bunch of flowers another man at his office had intended for another woman there. About sexual intercourse, Mrs Robinson said that this could not be right, as she had read somewhere that a woman should have successive sensations, and while she thought that she must have some of these, she could really start intercourse all over again the moment it was over.

When Mrs B. commented on her client's evident anxiety about her femininity, Mrs Robinson, as though something had been triggered off by this remark, exclaimed that she had often thought that she might well be one of those women who could suddenly change their sex, one only had to look at her, she was so tall and flat-bosomed. Moreover, as a little girl, by way of gaining her father's approbation, she had always excelled at sports and games while her younger brother—the apple of father's eye—had been a delicate unmuscular boy. In fact, this brother had had an accident at the age of ten when playing football and, as a result, was laid up in hospital for a year or more. Worse than that, it soon became apparent that his operation had been delayed too long and he had to have an artificial kneecap which left him permanently lame.

Terminating her interview seemed to present as dangerous a hurdle to Mrs Robinson as beginning it, and on this first occasion she snatched her coat from its hanger with some violence, saying breathlessly, 'I'll put my coat on outside.'

The most striking impression both clients left after their first inter-
view was of their need to make themselves sound interesting and of
their anxiety about whether they could be loving and lovable people and

have anything good to offer to their partners. Both Mr and Mrs Robinson seemed uncertain of their own worth, and this must have made the period of waiting particularly disturbing for them. Interestingly, there was no mention of Martin's difficulties by either of them, and they launched into their own problems and those of the marriage with great urgency.

It is clear that both were feeling desperate about their ceaseless bickering with one another which seemed to make a loving relationship impossible for them. Mr Robinson felt that he could not please or satisfy his wife, while his wife resented the fact that he dominated her intellectually, but deprived her emotionally. Mr Robinson's description of the impasse between them when driving the car illustrates their conflict about dominance and submission. Each partner was reluctant to take control and yet was resentful at being controlled by the other; frantically trying to avoid either situation, they were disagreeing over everything.

Since sexuality expresses itself through all aspects of the functioning of personality, it may colour even the apparently most trivial things that are said and done in a marriage. What we know so far about the Robinsons and their difficulties suggests that their bickering reflects the nature of their sexual conflicts, and this is confirmed by the little that Mrs Robinson told her caseworker about her uncertainty about her role as a woman in their sexual relationship.

With Mrs A., Mr Robinson attempts to assume an attitude of self-depreciation and submissiveness, and to put her into the role of the knowing woman whom he must try to please, under whose domination he can perhaps feel more justifiably angry and possibly safer. If she does not accept this role, his attitude is that she is rejecting him or useless to him. It appears that his wife, because of her own problems, slips readily into the dominating role. When he feels that control of the situation is demanded of him (by his wife when she cries, or by Mrs A. towards the end of the interview), Mr Robinson feels hopeless about having anything to offer and resentful that something is expected of him, so he just 'reads the paper'. His behaviour expresses his anxieties about his potency in relation to women. Loving a woman seems to him to involve the risk of losing one's personality. Perhaps it is best to deny that one has any.

Mrs Robinson, who finds it impossible to comply and say 'Yes, dear', like other women—yet is equally afraid of being the dominant partner— tries at the beginning of her interview with Mrs B. to hold on desperately to the active talkative role, perhaps in order to ward off any criticism or attack from her caseworker. But her anxiety about these aggressive, masculine aspects of herself is shown towards the end of the interview in her expression of fear lest she should turn into a man—i.e. become like her bullying father—and in her story about her injured brother. She sees active rivalry with the male as dangerous, but how else does one set about winning father's love?

Already, in these first interviews, we can see how both Mr and Mrs Robinson are attempting to relate to their caseworkers in the same way that they are relating to one another—not because this pattern brings them any conscious satisfaction, but perhaps because it has so far been their only way of dealing with their conflicts and anxieties.

When Mr Robinson came for his second interview, he reported that he and his wife had had 'a seven-day good patch', but that he had not been sleeping because he had been worrying about what Mrs A. might find out about him. He wondered if it was 'odd' of him to worry about this, and then expressed his doubts about whether his reaction to his father's death had been 'odd' too. He told Mrs A. that his father had been ill for some time and had asked the client to help him out of bed; but when, on doctor's orders, he had refused to do so, his father had tried to get up by himself and had fallen back dead. Mr Robinson had not felt guilty about this, but other people seemed to think that he should have done and that he should have been more upset than he was.

When Mrs A. tried to find out more about his fear of her thinking him odd, he said that he was afraid she might send him to 'a Mr Someone-or-other, your psychiatrist'. When she wondered what it was that he was really so afraid of her finding out, he told her in a rather exhibitionist way that he masturbated, laying considerable stress on his feeling of wickedness and how horrified he expected her to be. He said that when, as a child, his parents found out about his masturbating they were neither angry nor did anything to help him, 'They just suggested that I should try not to do it so often.' Mrs A. remarked that perhaps he expected her reaction to be similar to his parents'; he replied, with considerable feeling, that he did not care what she said or did about it provided she did not ignore it and treat it as a matter of no consequence.

The following week, he said that he had been worrying about what Mrs A.'s reaction would be 'to what I told you last time'.

Mrs A. suggested that he was wanting her, as he had his parents, to accept his masculine sexuality as something of real importance. He said that as a boy this had mattered to him a great deal. It was 'as if I had desperately wanted my father to accept me into "The Club" and my mother to realize how much this meant to me'. But no one took much notice of him. He felt that his much older sister had his mother's confidence because she was a girl, and his younger brother her love because he was the baby of the family.

He remembered how as a child he had been whizzing a stone along a wall to make it spark and his brother had taken it away from him; also how he used to want to play a drum, but felt afraid that if he did so he might lose the drum stick. He really preferred reading to playing with other children and said that he thought this was because books and learning were something one cannot lose. Mrs A. suggested that masturbating was, perhaps, a little like reading, a satisfaction which he felt could not be taken away from him. He replied that the difficulty in putting your faith in a heterosexual relationship was that your wife might stop loving you and go away, or become ill or even die. When Mrs A. commented on his fear of trusting his own or his wife's loving feelings, he asked whether Freud's theory of repression was still accepted. Mrs A. showed him that even in telling her about his repressed loving feelings, he had to do this in the form of a question implying in this way that she had more knowledge of the subject than he had, before daring to show her the knowledge which he knew himself to have. Perhaps he only felt safe enough to show a woman his ability and power if he had first made her into a powerful person who knew best. He replied that this was just what he always did with his wife. Even over such details as putting the coal on the fire, he would say, 'Shall I put some more coal on, dear?' instead of telling her that he was going to do so 'or even just doing it'.

During this interview, Mr Robinson managed to get his pipe alight for the first time and said he would be 'tickled pink' if Mrs A. were to tell him that she felt he was 'getting somewhere' in their talks.

Very early in the contact, Mr Robinson began to use his relationship with Mrs A. in a constructive way by 'testing out' his feelings, first with her and then with his wife. He soon became aware that he was doing this and consciously attempted to work through his difficulties in this way.

For a few weeks the only quarrels between the couple occurred just before Mr Robinson's interviews with Mrs A. Mr Robinson reported these quarrels to Mrs A., saying that he felt he had now failed her as well as his wife. He explained that he and his wife had been attending dancing classes and that having become quite confident during the lessons, he had for some time felt ready to take his wife to a dance and put himself to the test. The other evening he had done so, but had been unable to remember any of the steps he had learned once they arrived at the dance. Although he expressed feelings of guilt and unhappiness at having let his wife down again, Mrs A. sensed a mixture of relief as well as despair in his manner. It seemed as if in spite of his wish to succeed, he felt relieved at having failed in the leading role and having, once again, only remained successfully in the role of the protected pupil. He said, 'I suppose I feel that if I cannot be the best dancer on the floor I might as well be the worst.' Mrs A. suggested that this might be how he was feeling about coming to the Bureau. Just as he seemed to have felt that he had not been good enough to gain his mother's love in competition with his older sister or baby brother, and that the only way to gain her attention was to be her worst child, perhaps now he felt that he had to be Mrs A.'s worst client, or at least to have quarrels with his wife to report to her, in order to hold her attention.

Gradually, in the context of his relationship with Mrs A., Mr Robinson began to see how having to show himself as a failure expressed his frustration with women for not appreciating his qualities as a man; whenever Mrs A. took this up directly in terms of his anger with herself he denied it, at the same time showing his anger with her by resorting to intellectual argument which resulted in confusing the interview.

He described his father as a quiet man who did not 'stand up' to his mother, who, through her charm, always got her own way. He said that, as a boy, he would have liked to stand up to his mother himself, but 'I never did because it wouldn't have been fair to Father'. Instead he used to think about all the awful things that he would like to do to her if only he could. Mrs A. linked this with his present behaviour towards his wife; he had adopted a 'Yes, dear' attitude to her, but he expressed his frustration in his masturbating and by punishing her by withholding from her what was good and positive in his masculinity.

He replied that he was afraid he might 'go too far' if he tried to take a more definite line with his wife. Arguing with her was 'a different matter'. Here he could 'beat her' without any danger. He clearly enjoyed arguing with Mrs A. too, and would readily have spent all his interviews in this way. In his own words: 'When we are discussing things in a reasoning way, it is like talking to Father, but when we begin talking about feelings I get angry and upset because then it is like talking to my mother.' Through becoming aware of the similarity between his behaviour with his wife and Mrs A., Mr Robinson was able to see how he resorted to argument when he felt insecure and angry in his relationship with women.

Gradually, in this way, he began to acknowledge first 'his anger with womankind' and then with his wife, especially in connection with their sexual relationship, where he felt rejected and cheated out of the satisfaction of satisfying her. His anger with her was mixed with feelings of inadequacy in contrast to her first husband whom he imagined as the dominant 'he man' that he dare not be himself.

He then talked about his frustrated attempts to compete with his brother who was athletic but less intelligent. His brother belonged to a sports club, but when Mr Robinson wanted to join it, he did not reach the required standard. Later, he could have gone to University but was not allowed to because his parents thought it would be unfair to his brother, who might not manage to do so. Talking of one of his acquaintances led to the theme of homosexuality and his anxiety lest he himself might have effeminate tendencies. Mrs A. wondered whether to be effeminate and like the sister whom mother preferred might have seemed to him as a boy to be the only alternative to competing with his father and brother for his mother's love. At this point Mr Robinson asked her most earnestly if she felt that it would be safe for him to go on and really see what sort of person he was, and asked for Mrs A.'s reassurance that he would not turn out to be 'too odd' if he did so. Mrs A. said that he seemed to be seeking the reassurance from her, that he felt he had not had from his mother that it really would be all right for him to grow up into a man.

In his eighth interview Mr Robinson said that Mrs A. had taken the scales from his eyes so that he was able to see his wife's faults. Now he saw that it was she who was in the wrong and not himself. He supposed that he had better accept this and learn to put up with it and that there was no point in his continuing to come to see Mrs A.

For a while he spoke angrily of his wife. She had slipped and cut her leg and blamed him for having parked the car in the wrong place. He had apologized, as usual, but had not felt at all worried and regarded her reaction as being due to her 'nasty nature'.

Although, for the first time, Mr Robinson was able to blame his wife and to give up trying to gain his caseworker's attention through being the one in the wrong, this change in him seemed to have made him so anxious that he sought reassurance about continuing. Discussing this, he said that he often wondered what Mrs A. and Mrs B. had thought about him and his wife when they first came to the Bureau: 'Did you see us as all good or all bad, or something so middling that we couldn't be seen in a fog?' Thus he seemed to express his feeling of despair at not being good enough to earn love; now he felt he was losing his claim to attention as the bad one.

From then on he tested out his aggressive feelings with both his wife and Mrs A. in various ways. One evening he told Mrs A. that at last he had safely had a row with his wife. The quarrel had occurred the same morning. Later in the day, he had telephoned his wife and told her that he loved her. Much to his surprise, she had replied that she loved him too. Mrs A. wanted to mention a holiday break during this interview; immediately she did this her client became angry, showing this by misunderstanding everything she said and making the discussion very muddled and confused. Mrs A., too, found herself feeling angry and frustrated, and became involved in a wrangling argument, conducted in a reasoning way but with considerable feeling on both sides, until she realized, towards the end of the interview, that in mentioning her holiday just at the moment when Mr Robinson had shown her how he had been able to take a firm line with his wife, she ignored and rejected his potency much as he felt his mother had done. She put this to her client, linking it with his feelings towards his wife when she, too, rejected his potency by not enjoying intercourse with him. Mr Robinson ended this interview by paying Mrs A. a compliment and left saying that he must rush off to show his love to his wife.

At this stage, he told Mrs A. he felt the main remaining difficulty was in connection with Martin. Perhaps he expected too much of the boy, 'But I feel I am the boy's father and I would like Martin to feel this too.' When Mrs A. suggested that he was, perhaps, trying to avoid remembering the existence of Martin's own father, he replied that he had done this to such an extent that he only referred to him as 'that man' and never by name. He began talking about his feelings of inadequacy as a man, saying that he had not 'even been able to father a child' and that, under the circumstances, he felt that if his wife criticized his handling of the boy he could not say anything. Martin's aggression worried him a good deal and he and Mrs A. discussed his own problems about masculinity in connection with the boy's difficulties. Whenever Martin was in one of his uncontrollable moods it made Mr Robinson feel like a powerless little boy. At other times he felt afraid that he himself had turned into the overpowering father. The situation between himself and Martin was, he said, always much more difficult when his wife was present; having to share the 'mother' seemed to take Mr Robinson back to the time when he himself was Martin's age.

One day about this time, when Mr and Mrs Robinson were going out together, Mr Robinson asked his wife what she would like him to wear. She jokingly replied, 'Oh, the silk dress, I should think.' Mr Robinson felt sexually stimulated by this and told her so. She was horrified and said he must be abnormal and he anxiously asked Mrs A. if this were really so, adding that it was certainly a masculine reaction that he had felt and not a feminine one. Mrs A. suggested that his cloak of femininity was perhaps a way of protecting his penis. He replied, 'You mean that by doing this I was saying "I haven't got one so you can't cut it off".' When Mrs A. asked what reaction he would have liked from his wife, he said he thought that he really wanted her, figuratively to rip the dress off him and say, 'You can't wear that—look, you are a man.'

His doubts about himself were also reflected in his feelings about his job. He felt dissatisfied in his work, but had no idea what else he could do. 'If only I knew that I really wanted to be a plumber or a hurdle-marker, for instance, it would be simple.' He did not think he had any doubts about his ability in either of these roles, but supposing he made hurdles in his back garden, people might remark, 'What odd things are going on in the Robinson's back garden!' Similarly, in the sexual relationship, he would have liked to be more assertive, but was uncertain about 'what is the accepted way'. He discussed with Mrs A. at this stage not only his fear of what he might do to women but also what they might do to him in retaliation, and how his need to pretend that he was impotent in many spheres was his way of protecting his potency so that they would not take it away from him.

It was after this that he told Mrs A. he felt he had got as far as he could—and then immediately added that he had been so angry during the week, when two of their cats had torn up a rug that had meant a good deal to him in his childhood, that he had thrown the rug away altogether. Mrs A. related this to the work with her and spent the interview helping him to express his anger with her. In the end he acknowledged that at last he had really been able to let himself feel angry rather than rush into an argument when faced with his emotions towards Mrs A. This experience, he said, was a new one to him; if he was angry with his mother as a child she used to say, coldly, that she did not love him any more.

Once Mr Robinson felt safer in showing aggression to women, he began to reveal his fear of 'being led on by their wiles' if he allowed himself to have loving feelings towards them. He also began to show his jealousy of Mrs A.'s other clients and his wife's friends. This was linked with his feelings of jealousy towards his brother and sister who were such close rivals for his mother's love. Together, Mrs A. and her client explored his feelings of anger and despair as a small child when he had to give up to his younger brother his right to his mother's attention as the baby of the family.

At this time he mentioned that his feelings about his father's death had changed; he now felt truly upset about it. He reported that he was feeling more confident about taking a decisive role with his wife, and that, much to his surprise, she did not seem to mind. When, one day in the car, he turned the wheel firmly in the direction he thought they should go, although his wife said it was the wrong way, she later told him that he had been right after all, and the incident passed off easily. Altogether, whenever quarrels did occur, neither of them felt as intensely as they had done in the past; it seemed that they were both able to take a more realistic view of what had happened.

*   *   *

The tangle of material presented by Mrs Robinson in her succeeding interviews might best be unfolded in terms of her relationships. Although, in the context of the Bureau's work, focussed as it is on the marital problem, the client's most significant relationships are those with her husband and with her caseworker, these can perhaps in Mrs Robinson's case be most clearly understood in the light of her childhood relationships with parents and siblings.

The extent to which Mrs Robinson's childhood phantasies affected her adult relationships and family life was very striking. The 'people' of her childhood still seemed very real to her and were kept more alive by the fact that, after marriage, she chose to live in her parents' house and that, later, she had invited her older sister and her family into her own home.

Her father, whose more than life-size figure dominated the first series of interviews, she saw as tyrannical, selfish and brutal, particularly towards her mother, whom he often reduced to tears. She felt he had made her mother into a drudge, forever catering to his demands which, even when he was asleep (after night shifts), imposed themselves on his family in terms of 'Hush, hush, Father's asleep' and no one must dare to move.

There were stories about her father's 'over-sexed male lasciviousness' that related to the period immediately after her mother's death, when he told his daughters bawdy stories about the brothel he went to in the First World War.

Mrs Robinson described her father as a rebellious person who had no time for rules and regulations, or for religious beliefs, but, in spite of her apparent disgust and condemnation of him, it was clear that he had seemed to her a dashing and exciting figure. When Mrs B. tried to show her client her underlying feelings of excitement and of adoration for a father who was a law unto himself, and who seemed (by virtue of his being so God-like himself) to have no need of moral and religious commandments, she rejoined with more commiserations with her poor mother. She had been reduced to an entirely submissive 'yes-dear-no-dear' wife to her controlling husband. Mrs Robinson saw herself as the only one in the family able to stand up to her father and argue with him. Yet at other times she described him as controlling her too absolutely, body and soul, her pleasures, her money, her clothes. She spoke of her heartbroken disappointment when her father prohibited her attendance at a charity fête because it was 'against his principles'. At a later period, when working in her first job, she had, she said, to give up all wages to her father, who gave only half a crown to her mother for her keep; and when, with her first Christmas bonus, she had wanted to buy herself a pretty feminine coat, he insisted that she should buy a useful but dull tweed one instead.

Mrs B. suggested that it might make her client feel safer to see herself as irrevocably controlled and dominated by her father. Perhaps she had to see him as such a bad, bullying person in order to make it 'safe' to fight him back and to argue with him; for then she need have no doubts that he would win, being the stronger—that indeed father was unassailable and indestructible.

Each time Mrs Robinson expressed her outraged resentment of her father for controlling her 'body and soul', Mrs B. substituted 'mother' for 'father' and slowly it became clear that Mrs Robinson had to describe her mother as angelic, gentle, long suffering and sweet because of the feelings of guilt and resentment that were mixed up with her love for her. Reluctantly the client admitted that it was with her mother that she fought a terrific battle over control of her bodily functions. She told Mrs B. that she would defaecate into her bath, and her mother would have to let the bath water run out, and begin all over again. She was incontinent up to the age of twelve; and her mother had to 'wash my pants and lay them out, eight in a row, on the lawn'.

What came across most vividly to Mrs B. almost from the first meeting was the exaggerated nature of the picture the client presented of her parents—the one having to be so tyrannical and the other so angelic—and the pressure of her anxiety about them. These anxieties had been carried into and interfered with her relationships with her husband and her child, and Mrs B.'s main concern was to help her client to recognize and accept her own contradictory feelings in relation to her parents so that she might become able to tolerate the opposing feelings within herself, and make more realistic relationships in her present situation. Therefore, whenever Mrs Robinson's material made this possible, her expressions of hatred, horror and condemnation of her father were discussed in terms of her unacknowledged love for, admiration of and even infatuation with him; and her expressions of love and pity for her mother were discussed in terms of her unacknowledged resentment and envy of her.

Another of her childhood conflicts discussed with Mrs B. was her jealousy of her younger brother. In an interview during which Mrs Robinson had been talking about her parents' relationship in terms of her father's cruelty causing her mother's tears and of his selfishness being degrading and destructive to her mother, she related the story of the birth of her brother, Martin, who was born when she was not quite three.

Her mother went to hospital for what seemed no longer than a single day and, on her departure, promised her younger daughter that she would come back bringing 'a surprise'. The client looked forward to her mother bringing her a nice slab of chocolate and consequently when she returned, holding something white in her arms instead, the little girl was so disgusted that she 'never took the slightest notice' of her baby brother.

In the casework situation Mrs Robinson was able to express some of her anger with her mother in connection with this brother, and Mrs B. discussed with her client her feelings about her mother having given the next-born child a penis, while depriving her of one. This had been even more difficult for the client because Martin, who became the apple of her father's eye, had arrived at an age in her own development when it was a matter of passionate urgency to the little girl to make a place for herself in her father's heart. As it was, the only achievements that seemed to her to earn her father's approval were boyish activities and ability at games. The only acknowledgment of her physical attributes that she felt to be favourable was of her square shoulders and long thin legs.

Her brother, in contrast, was delicate and, moreover, it will be remembered, had been lame since he was ten. It is interesting to note that the time at which the client believes she gave up wetting her knickers coincides with his accident, and it seemed that in her own mind, at any rate, these two events were linked.

The client's other attempts at having a share in her brother's masculinity, in something of the same way as mother had in father's, were also doomed to prove to her, all over again, that she could never hope to have anything for herself. Mrs Robinson told Mrs B. how she asked her brother to come into the lavatory with her and 'to put it into me', but Martin only laughed, 'not knowing where to put it'.

Her feelings about her husband's relationship with Mrs A., whom she seemed to see as very much like her own mother, reflected her anxieties as to whether she could win and keep mother's love in competition with men. To her it seemed that her husband was always given more time and concern at the Bureau than she, and she was envious of his relationship with Mrs A. Throughout the work, Mrs B. tried to help her client to see how these feelings which stemmed from her relationship with her brother were affecting her attitudes, both in her marriage and in the casework situation.

It will be remembered that Mrs Robinson's sister occupied the top part of the Robinson's large house with her husband and children. Her brother-in-law was away from home a good deal and at these times Mrs Robinson's sister participated in the client's household and marriage to a quite extensive degree. If ever Mr and Mrs Robinson wished to go out together without the sister, they would have to use every subterfuge and creep out of the house like 'thieves in the dark'—and, indeed, the client made it clear how guilty they felt about these clandestine outings. Mrs B. suggested that her client might have needed to put her sister in the place of her mother who was now dead and could no longer exercise her vigil over her 'outings with men', and, more generally, her sexual activities.

There were also, on the other hand, stories to show that the client took a protective role towards her sister, whom she saw as helplessly and hopelessly feminine. She described her disgust at her sister's physical dependence on her husband to whom she devoted herself exclusively while he was at home, although there were also noisy quarrels.

Mrs B. showed the client how her description of her sister's marriage seemed to be a faithful replica of what she felt about her parents' relationship with one another which she saw in anger and in love as a unique and desirable one based on, and having its object in, the client's exclusion from this mysterious union.

Other stories, which described the sister as helplessly looking to Mrs Robinson for guidance and support, the client seemed to have interpreted to herself as a demand on her to be a brotherly, masculine protector to the sister, thereby finding another way to be like her brother Martin. Linking these stories with those told on previous occasions, in which the client had expressed her sense of failure whenever she tried to compete with Martin, Mrs B. suggested that perhaps she saw her sister's requests as an opportunity of proving herself a better brother than Martin had been.

This led to Mrs Robinson describing how both mother and sister had contributed to her disgust about sexuality; mother by bathing all three children together and referring to her brother's penis as 'the tail', and sister, with whom she had shared a bed during childhood, by asking her to smell her genitals under the bedclothes. Later, her sister had 'initiated' her into the 'secrets of sexual intercourse' by showing her books on the subject, but Mrs Robinson felt disgusted at the thought of 'the tail' touching her, 'because it wee-wee'd'.

That Mrs Robinson's interest in and disgust at sexuality, which in the interviews she continually linked with her childhood experiences, were an urgent problem in her present situation was apparent from everything she told about her sexual relationship with her husband.

She often spoke of her dread of being 'overmanned', or 'mastered'—and came to recognize, on the other hand, her great need to be thus controlled. In the first phase of her treatment, pondering on this theme, she said that people maintained that if a woman had a proper climax, a man would never leave her. But, as for herself, she felt it would be dreadful if she let herself lose control; her husband would then be in control of her. At the same time, she complained of his giving her nothing of value, feeling herself to be as deprived as her mother was. Much later, she saw her fears in terms of a threat of being overmastered from within herself by her own sexual depravity, which would make her husband leave her. The other horn of this dilemma was that if she fought against being mastered, her husband would surely leave her for a sexually more exciting woman. Yet to enjoy sexual intercourse and to have feelings as a woman were tantamount to 'going mad', to losing her intelligence and judgment—in short, losing everything she valued and called 'I'.

Her disinclination to talk about her son Martin who was after all, the main reason for the couple's referral to the Bureau, was an equally important sign of her present difficulties. She rarely mentioned him, but when she did, it was never as if she was talking about a real little boy. It felt rather as if she was talking about a part of herself in which she needed to control her own bad masculine and feminine propensities. She spoke of the 'poison' which her first husband had put into her and saw Martin as the result of her bad sexuality with a brutal man whom she could not love. At one point she said she feared that Martin's stealing might land him in prison and added, she had caught herself thinking, when reading in the papers about a recent bank robbery, that she could have done it so much better and, consequently, would not have been caught. Throughout, Mrs B. tried to show her how the feelings about her own 'goodness' and 'badness' were connected with her feelings about her sexuality, and how they influenced all her relationships.

Naturally, the casework relationship, too, reflected the client's difficulties in coming to terms with these conflicting feelings. In the earlier phases of the contact she needed to keep Mrs B. and the image of her own mother good. Later, when her angry feelings with Mrs B. could no longer be contained, she appeared to transfer her 'good' feelings to her husband's caseworker, whom she now saw as having all the good things, while her own caseworker seemed to assume the 'bad' features of her mother-in-law.

During this phase, the client talked a great deal about her 'hateful and despicable' mother-in-law, using much the same tone of voice and similar phrases to those she had used when talking earlier about her own father. It seemed as though her father personified the essence of masculinity, which was not for her, whereas mother-in-law stood for the essence of femininity to which she must not aspire either.

Mrs Robinson saw her mother-in-law as a woman 'who makes all her children, and everyone else she can get round with her wiles, dance attendance on her', while the client, like her own mother, was fearful of making demands, and tried to be independent rather than helplessly in need of support.

By this time the bickering in the marriage had ceased to a large extent, and the sexual relationship had become more satisfactory. About this time, too, Martin's therapist at the Child Guidance Clinic reported that the boy's behaviour had improved and that he no longer needed to attend for treatment.

Mrs A. and Mrs B. considered the possibility of terminating the case within a few weeks and arranged to discuss this with their respective clients. As it happened, the first date was with Mrs Robinson, and therefore it was she who told her husband of the caseworkers' suggestion. At his next meeting Mr Robinson was withdrawn and difficult, behaving like a sulky child, and saying he felt 'bristly'. Although to begin with he denied feeling angry with Mrs A., he later showed his aggression in a very lively way, remarking at the end, 'I will come and spar with you again next week.'

The following week he spoke of his anger and boredom when his wife and her sister talked together at home. Whenever he felt particularly annoyed with them he would go into the kitchen and make coffee for them. Mrs A. linked this with his sulky withdrawal the previous week when he felt that his wife and the two caseworkers had left him out of the termination plans, and with his childhood feelings of being excluded from the 'women's world' when his sister, who was so much older than he, and his mother had adult conversations together.

After this, he began to express positive feelings both towards his wife and towards Mrs A. and, at the same time, began talking about his fears of designing women who would lead him on, as well as his concern about having illicit relationships with women. He was concerned because he found himself talking to one of the men at work in order to avoid meeting a particular woman with whom he

would really have liked to talk. This was discussed in terms of his
fear that if he showed his positive feelings towards women they
would either reject him or lead him on until he was entirely in their
power. At this time, too, he began telling both Mrs A. and his wife
how much the other meant to him, and he spoke quite frequently
about other women to whom he felt attracted. Mrs A. suggested that
this was partly in order to prevent herself and his wife from becoming
too powerful now that he had become aware of his positive feelings
towards them, partly to gain her permission to be interested in
women and also to show her that he did not care, too much, about
being rejected by her.

When his conflict about daring to show love to his mother was
linked with his difficulty in showing love to his wife, Mr Robinson
said that he had always been afraid of being ensnared by women,
and recalled a girl with whom he had become friendly before meeting
his wife. As soon as she had assumed that he wanted to marry her
he had withdrawn from the relationship, feeling 'trapped'. He had,
he said, been very concerned at the time at the thought of having hurt
the girl. Talking about this during the interview, he became quite
anxious about what he might do to women he loved. Would he
commit adultery, give them babies, or even rape them? Mrs A.
pointed out his fear of being in the power of women and his ambivalent desires both to love and to hurt them; perhaps, too, he had
these mixed feelings towards his caseworker, especially now that she
was withdrawing from him.

As the holiday of Mr and Mrs Robinson was followed by that of
Mrs A., the termination date was fixed just before this time and a
follow-up meeting was arranged for three months later.

Mr Robinson suggested that, instead of meeting Mrs A. at the
office for the follow-up interview, he should take her out to dinner.
While not accepting the invitation, Mrs A. tried to show him that she
appreciated his wish to have a more mature relationship with her—
at the same time helping him to see that such a 'different' relationship
would be both unrealistic and inappropriate. She talked of this, too,
in terms of his feelings towards his mother; he replied that he had
always felt very strongly that his mother depreciated his sexuality,
and in adolescence he even felt guilty about thinking of girls in case
she disapproved. Now, he said, he would like to feel that his wife
'cares enough to want to control me, and to be jealous of my interest
in other women'.

After this, he frequently paid compliments to Mrs A., and showed his love more openly to his wife, making it very clear that he wanted Mrs A. to recognize his part in relationships with women as an adult and potentially seductive one. When Mrs A. said that she thought that he perhaps wanted her to recognize that he was a man and not a little boy, he replied that he did not think that he was worried about being a boy rather than a man, but of being a woman. As a child, he had felt envious of his sister, who could have boy-friends, be attractive and grow up with his mother's approval. 'Perhaps I was not only afraid because I thought my mother would not allow me to have an adult penis, but also jealous of my sister who had breasts.' The following week he wanted Mrs A. to admire a blouse which he had bought as a present for his wife. It was as if, in this way, he was showing what he felt to be the more feminine side of himself and testing out her reaction to it.

In his last interview before the three months' break, he expressed real regret at having to give up the idea of establishing a different relationship with Mrs A. He saw for himself that this would be inappropriate, just as his desires towards his mother had been inappropriate. 'But it does not mean that one does not wish it were possible.' On the other hand, he saw that relinquishing this idea was necessary to finding his own way of becoming an adult man with his wife and he said that, naturally, it was this which mattered to him most.

On his return three months later, he took control of the interview all the way through. He reported that his relationship with his wife was continuing reasonably well; both had, to some degree, managed to come to terms with the mixture of masculine and feminine within themselves and that he felt that this was gradually becoming less of a problem in the marriage. He and his wife were, he said, finding their own way of coping with things 'which may not be yours but which I feel is right for us' through having joined a religious group.

*   *   *

Mrs Robinson reacted to the suggested break in interviews through Mrs B.'s holiday and the arrangements for the approaching termination as many clients do, by arriving late and by saying that everything was all right and she had nothing to report. Mrs B. suggested that this was the client's way of showing her anger towards her for going away; by making no demands and stressing her independence, she was, perhaps, safeguarding herself against the risk of Mrs B.'s not coming back.

Five weeks later, when Mrs B. returned, her client described 'a complete change in my relationship with Father'. She told Mrs B. that in the interval she had discussed her parents' marriage very frankly with her father and now she knew that her parents' relationship had been a loving one and that their sexual life had been satisfying and pleasure-giving to her mother. Mrs B. suggested that her client now seemed to feel safe enough to explore a little of the reality of the relationship between her father and mother. Mrs Robinson replied obliquely that she still had no sexual feelings and would gladly do without intercourse altogether. This worried her all the more since she had read somewhere that a woman should 'want sex at certain periods when the seed detached itself'. Mrs B. picked up her client's use of the word 'seed' as indicating some of Mrs Robinson's confusion as to whether she had seeds or eggs inside her body, to which Mrs Robinson at once added her fear of changing into a man; she said her masculine build was proof of this possibility. Yet she was a fervent feminist. It did not seem to her that women in Western countries could rest contented with their achievements towards emancipation while their sisters in the East were still subjected to all manner of social and sexual humiliations and endured subservience, not to say slavery; she had read accounts of their degradation, the idea of which caused her intense horror and indignation.

Mrs B. discussed her client's avowed feelings of horror and indignation at this state of affairs in terms of Mrs Robinson's excitement and sexual wishes; her conviction that, under these 'humiliating' conditions, she too would experience sexual feelings. Mrs Robinson acknowledged this by saying that she could only allow her husband to penetrate when she herself was absolutely 'motionless and paralysed'. Mrs B.'s suggestion that it might be permissible for her to express herself by being more active in intercourse, without endangering her husband's penis, seemed to come as a great relief to her.

After this interview Mrs Robinson seemed to be calmer and less anxious. Her appearance had changed considerably during the casework contact. Now she was taking pleasure in her clothes and had a pretty new hairstyle which she said her husband had set for her after a home-perm. She described what seemed to be a solid improvement in her marriage. She also spoke more positively about her father, telling Mrs B. how very fond he was of Martin, and how good he was to the boy in whom he took a grandfatherly interest.

She went on to talk about her son more fully than ever before, and he began to emerge as a real little boy, no longer merely as a vehicle for her anxious theorizing. It seemed that since she had been able to see her parents more realistically, she was also more able to see herself as a better parent.

It was in the following interview, three weeks after Mrs B.'s return, that, with tremendous feeling, the client told the story of her mother's death. Mrs Robinson spoke of her 'sister upstairs' who had been away at the same time as Mrs B., and described her relief during her sister's absence, as well as the subsequent irritation at her recent unwelcome return, for her husband and she could no longer feel free; both resented her renewed 'interference'. Mrs B. linked this with the client's feelings about herself and the discussion went from Mrs Robinson's resentment of her elder sister's and Mrs B.'s interference and control over her relationship with her husband, to her anger with her mother for exercising similar control in the past, and then on to Mrs Robinson's resultant feelings of guilt and protectiveness towards sister, mother and Mrs B.

It was towards the end of this interview that Mrs Robinson told Mrs B. how her mother had died. The client had arranged with her mother to go and visit her brother Martin, who was in hospital at the time. As her father had arrived at the hospital before them, she and her mother went to see her maternal grandmother, who was sick in another part of the building instead. On the way there, her mother suddenly collapsed and died within a few moments, and the client was charged with the frightful task of breaking the news to the male members of the family.

Mrs B. said that in the way she told her story Mrs Robinson seemed to accuse herself of being responsible for her mother's death. The client responded by saying that ever since that moment she had lost faith in an after-life as she had felt that she would never be worthy of it. Mrs B. then discussed with her her feelings of unworthiness, culminating in her conscious anxiety that she had killed her mother and the resultant perpetual remorse which made her feel that she had no right to be a happy mother and a happy wife herself.

Mrs Robinson closed this interview by saying that she could

hardly bear to come for the last time the following week, and Mrs B. accepted her grief at this loss, as well as the connection between this and her misery and guilt about the loss of her mother.

At the final interview, Mrs Robinson reported a row with her husband, the first for many weeks. She had given him the money she had saved towards their holiday—much more than he had expected—but, after a first reaction of pleasure and gratitude, he had gradually become sulky and had ended up by nagging and being critical, and by hitting Martin.

Mrs B. discussed this characteristic interplay over giving and taking with her client, and Mrs Robinson soon made it clear that she had understood it herself. The couple had quickly made up this row and had been able to explain to one another how each had felt about it.

Mrs Robinson did not come to a suggested follow-up interview three months later, but telephoned her caseworker instead. She, too, reported that things were going well and that both she and her husband were feeling very much helped by their membership of the religious group.

*   *   *

The marriage relationship between Mr and Mrs Robinson was, as we have seen, affected largely by the problems arising out of their childhood situations and their phantasies about themselves in relation to their parents and siblings which the passage of time and the reality of their parents' attitudes had not been able to dispel in this particular couple.

It is striking how similar these phantasies were for both of them. They each saw the parent of the opposite sex as frighteningly powerful and yet intensely fascinating and attractive persons and the parent of the same sex as ineffectual. In their childhood, it must have seemed to them that loving and being loved by the parent of the opposite sex was both frightening and dangerous. They might really be able to steal the love from the parent of the same sex to whom, they felt, it rightfully belonged. Nevertheless, it was vital for Mr Robinson to be loved by his mother and for Mrs Robinson to be loved by her father and to find some way of expressing love for them. Each attempted to deal with this dilemma by tending to deny the goodness and allowing themselves to see rather the powerful badness in the desirable parent—turning their love for them into envy of the qualities of the opposite sex which they themselves did not possess. In order to win the love and approval of the desirable parent, they felt they must give up their identity as a boy or a girl. That the reason for the referral to the Bureau was initially anxiety about Martin's sex-play and stealing; that both parents of the same sex had died more or less in the client's arms in circumstances which perpetuated their guilty feelings, and the way in which these clients still feel involved with their brothers and sisters indicates the dynamic interactions between the three generations.

In their marriage the couple seem to have been trying to deal with their problems by choosing a partner who was as unlike the seductive and exciting parent as possible. Mrs Robinson chose a man who appeared to be just the opposite of her domineering father, and Mr Robinson a woman whom he felt was unlikely to lead him on with her feminine wiles. Thus, in their choice of a partner they repeated the denial of love for the exciting opposite sex and were able to maintain the bi-sexual identifications which they had developed as a way of coping with their conflicts.

To Mrs Robinson, her second marriage offered more potentialities for achieving a resolution of these conflicts than had her first. Her first husband seems to have represented the 'bad' sexual domineering side of her father to her, and many of her anxieties about this first marriage, her motivation for it and her role in it, arose from her feelings of guilt in relation to her parents and brother. Her anxieties about these feelings became later centred on her son Martin, to whom she had given her brother's name, and whom she saw as fruit of the 'poison' that her first husband had put into her.

Both to Mr and Mrs Robinson, Martin seemed to be expressing the 'bad' aspect of masculine and feminine sexuality, and their battle with the bad propensities within themselves was therefore fought out in their relationship with the boy. Besides these anxieties there was, however, very real concern about Martin and about their feelings towards him. When Martin's symptoms exposed some of the problems in their relationship, the couple were driven to seek help for their inner conflicts which the marriage had failed to solve. This striving towards better integration and a more satisfactory equilibrium in the family had been the most urgent concern for both partners, and the bickering expressed their frustration and disappointment that this had not been achieved.

Mr Robinson's inability to give in the sexual relationship was paralleled by the failure of all his efforts to please his wife—'If I buy her strawberries, it will be raspberries she wants.' His genuine wish for a loving relationship with her was constantly frustrated by his 'anger with womankind', and his wife's inability to accept love and gifts fitted into the patterns of his expectations and justified his anger and his withholding, time after time. Neither dared to show love and to accept dependence in the relationship because both feared that they would be rejected, exploited or destroyed. Neither could safely take control, because each was afraid of what he or she would do to the other if he was in his power, and each was equally afraid of the other's retaliation. Neither could allow himself or the other to take the 'appropriate' sexual role. Fear of the negative, and anxiety to safeguard the positive aspects of their sexuality prevented them from developing a relationship in which each could gratify his own or the other's needs. To acknowledge these needs in themselves, and to accept the goodness and the badness, the masculinity and femininity, the love and the hate in themselves, their parents, their marriage partner and in Martin, may be seen as the focus towards which the casework was directed.

For Mrs Robinson this move towards integration had apparently been helped by the client's experience in connection with Mrs B.'s holiday. At the session which followed it, she became aware of her angry feelings and yet gained reassurance that Mrs B. returned with the same concern for her. Having been able to tolerate both her positive and her negative feelings towards her caseworker and having felt that they were tolerated by her, she seemed to be able to integrate within herself her contradictory feelings towards her parents. Only after this experience was she able to tell the story of her mother's death. The fact that her relationship with Mrs B. was a temporary one, and that the latter, unlike her mother-in-law, was not trying to replace her own mother, may have contributed towards helping Mrs Robinson to 'bury' her dead mother so that she, herself, could live a fuller and a happier life, needing no longer to let her guilt about the past interfere with her present relationships. Inevitably this could not be worked through fully in nineteen interviews and the client's difficulty in returning for a follow-up meeting was probably an expression of the unresolved conflicts about her feelings for her caseworker. Her story, in the last interview, of the row with her husband, who was angry and unreasonable in spite of having been given more than he expected, seems to indicate this too.

In the work with Mr Robinson it was most striking, from the beginning, how quickly he was able to use the insight he gained from the casework contact, and how much work and thinking over he did between interviews. He really wanted to understand his part in the marriage and hardly an interview passed without Mr Robinson working out how he could use what he and Mrs A. had seen together to benefit the relationship with his wife.

Mrs A. did not work through with him his feelings of frustration towards his dead father nor explore very fully his anxieties and doubts about whether he could be a father himself. She rather tried, by her attitude, to help him feel that this was something with which he could cope himself. This was in keeping with the whole pattern of the relationship in which Mrs A. encouraged him to be an adult man in the casework situation, and to see herself less as one of the organizing and controlling women whom he had felt his mother and his wife to be. With Mrs A. he experienced a relationship in which his masculinity was acknowledged, yet in which his conflicting feelings about women and his role as a man and some of his anxieties connected with this could be expressed. This experience seemed to give him sufficient confidence to begin to seek his own way towards a more positive expression of his masculine drive.

Mr Robinson's move towards integration can be followed most easily through the sequence and timing of the material he brought. It was not until he could openly show his anger to Mrs A. and become aware himself of the value of experiencing his positive and negative feelings in his relationship with her that he was able to explore his feelings of anger, jealousy and love for his mother in the light of his childhood feelings about her relationship with his brother. Up to this point, too, his guilty feelings about his father's death seem to have been so frightening that they had become inaccessible to him. It is interesting that in the interview when he told Mrs A. of his change of feeling about his father he went straight on to speak of the improvement within the marriage, unconsciously connecting the two. It would appear that, with Mr Robinson as with his wife, it was not until the feelings of guilt towards the parent of the same sex had been lessened that it was possible for them to be free to seek a happier relationship with the marriage partner.

Although both clients brought material to their last interviews to show their caseworkers that their conflicts had not been resolved, they also showed that they had become much more aware of them, and were making conscious co-operative efforts to deal with them.

It will have become apparent that sexual conflicts and confusion about sexual roles are fundamental themes in marriage problems, and they have been highlighted in this last case. In the case which follows they will appear again, but in greater complexity, and the reader will be able to trace their gradual emergence in the material of successive interviews and the developing relationship between husband and wife and their caseworkers.

Mr and Mrs Cooper

This case seemed to lend itself to detailed exposition because it illustrates many of the common problems of adjustment in marriage and parenthood. The couple came for treatment after only one year of marriage; the wife became pregnant and had her first baby during the casework contact. The Coopers came from working-class families, were both of good intelligence, and their conflicts had not seriously interfered with their everyday working lives. They were genuine and conscientious people, very fond of one another, and our work with them, in particular that with Mrs Cooper, was not impeded by the intellectual defences which we meet in many of our clients.

The fact that Mr Cooper had had two and a half years' individual therapy before coming to the Bureau made the work with him in some respects different from that with other clients, but it probably enabled him to express explicitly many of the feelings that are only implicit in the material of others, thus contributing not only to a fuller understanding of his own personality and marriage problems but also to the understanding of many other clients and their marriages.

The case covers a period of two years. The material has been drastically cut, and much which did not seem relevant to the main themes has been omitted, yet it is inevitably a repetitious account, representing as it does the gradual working through of a few central themes and problems. Undoubtedly the reader will quite often feel that different comments could have been made, or that important aspects of the client's material have not been taken up. This is partly due to deliberate selection—and, besides, each worker will inevitably understand and use different facets of whatever her client brings.

Particularly in the early phases of the work, much of what the caseworker understands is not shared with the client. In this detailed case study this unverbalized understanding, as well as some of the questions present in the workers' mind, have been formulated in commentaries that follow the interview narrative; it will be noticed that these commentaries become less frequent as the work progresses.

For the purpose of this presentation, the casework has been divided into five phases:

In Phase I the two caseworkers get to know their clients and begin to understand why Mrs Cooper has such great difficulties in being a wife and is terrified at the thought of ever having a baby; and how the husband's problems in relation to women affect the marriage. They are also beginning to discover how their client's difficulties are related to their earlier relationships. At the end of the phase the caseworkers attempt a first assessment of this marriage.

In Phase II the couple's reaction to each other is beginning to change slightly, and this raises new anxieties and the questions What do they really want from each other? and What can each give to and take from his partner?

Phase III presents the most important part of the casework. By now both partners attend regularly at the Bureau and the work with them goes on with parallel developments and interaction in the four-person relationship. Husband and wife are re-experiencing, each in his own way, their ambivalent feelings towards their earlier love-objects, and are beginning to modify the conceptions they had of their parents, themselves and each other.

In Phase IV the central theme is Mrs Cooper's pregnancy, and both clients' struggle towards the new adjustment required of them by this situation.

By Phase V the baby has been born, though not without difficulties. Husband and wife are beginning to settle down to being a father and a mother and are weaning themselves from their caseworkers.

PHASE I

Mrs Cooper was referred to the Bureau by a psychiatrist who had been treating her husband for about two and a half years for hysterical symptoms, exhibitionist tendencies and a fear of relationships with women. Mr Cooper had been able to marry in the course of his treatment, but now, a year later, complained that his wife's coldness and her inhibited attitude towards sexuality made a proper marriage impossible, and that he felt increasingly frustrated and rejected by her.

At the time that Mrs Cooper came to see Mrs B. she was thirty-one. She was rather boyish-looking, with a round face, round, big, frightened eyes, clear-cut features, no make-up; she had short, straight dark hair and wore a high-buttoned coat with just a bit of white collar showing—looking like a choirboy. She was extremely nervous, yet from the beginning she showed confidence in Mrs B., saying that she knew that her husband had been helped in his treatment and so she hoped she might be helped too.

The problem as Mrs Cooper saw it was that she and her husband loved each other dearly and if they could only live like brother and sister without sexuality, all would be well. 'I love him all day,' she said, 'but at night I hate him.' Sexual intercourse was hateful, humiliating to a woman, and it gave her pain, because almost from the beginning of her marriage she had been suffering from vaginal irritation. A little puzzled, she added that she had often felt sexually aroused while they were engaged 'and couldn't go further'. But the difficulty was not only that she disliked sexual intercourse. She could not even be affectionate towards her husband, and he wanted that so very much. She did not like to kiss or to cuddle; she had always been like that, even as a child.

She told Mrs B. that she had met her husband at a dance. They had felt at once that they had much in common. They had 'the same ideas of right and wrong', were both from the North, both Roman Catholics, both youngest children and the only members of their families who had come South. After a year's courtship they had become engaged, and had married six months later, in London. They had had a very quiet wedding, with none of their relatives present. At the time of referral they had a flat in a friend's house, not ideal, but fairly adequate. Both were working: Mr Cooper in a secure clerical job in a retail firm; his wife, when she first came, full-time in a textile factory. They were able to save, lived quietly, had few friends or interests, never quarrelled, and 'could be so happy, if it weren't for sex'.

What are the problems that are interfering with the development of this marriage? Why is this girl not able, although she is so devotedly fond of her young husband, to manage a relationship with him in which she can express affection and allow herself to experience her sexuality? What must womanhood mean to her at unconscious levels that she has to remain a 'good child', looking innocent and undeveloped, and live with him in this brother-and-sister way, hating him for any expression of his manhood?

What problems in early life, or anxieties concerning herself and her relationships, have made the denial of sexuality so necessary to this client? What may she have felt unconsciously about her parents' marriage and what went on between them? What did love mean at home, and what anxieties did it arouse? What were the roles of father and mother? How has the pattern of their relationship affected her own capacity to develop as a woman and a wife; and how does it influence the development of her relationship with her caseworker, a middle-aged woman about her mother's age? She approaches Mrs B. as a good girl who tells mother her secrets, as far as she dares. And Mrs B. strongly feels her client's need to use her as a good competent person who will help her. That she is able to tell her worker in this first meeting so much of her deeper feelings is probably due to her confident expectation that she may be helped, since her husband had been helped by his therapist.

Although Mrs Cooper had told Mrs B. that her difficulty in showing her affection had started in childhood, she spoke at first only hesitatingly about her background. But slowly the picture of her parental family became clearer.

She had one brother three years her senior who was her 'closest friend'; she always preferred to be with him and his friends, rather than with girls. The brother was now married, with two little daughters, and his family shared the mother's house. They had an easy life; with a home ready made and mother there to help them. Mother had always done everything for the boy; all the money she could save had been spent on his education (he was a carpenter), so there had not been any left for the sister, who would have loved to train as a nurse. Instead, Mrs Cooper had had to go straight from school into service, and all she had learned was scrubbing and cleaning.

Her mother was nine years older than her father, whom she married when he was only twenty-one. The client spoke about this with great feeling. Father was so young and delicate, how could he cope with her mother, who was so competent and energetic? They were poor; mother had to work hard to keep the family, for father was always ill, with heart trouble and asthma. From the time that she remembered her father and brother had shared one bedroom and the client had slept in the double bed with her mother. As a child she had often wondered about this, feeling somehow that it was not quite right. She had worried too because mother was not patient enough with father, and did not show him enough sympathy. She herself would have liked to, especially when he had his choking attacks, but she never dared, because of 'what it might lead to'.

Mother was strict; she never had time for play or 'nonsense', and the little girl was a bit frightened of her. Father, who was shy and withdrawn, worshipped his daughter, but 'of course it was Mother who had the say'.

These were the things Mrs Cooper spoke of again and again to her worker, at first hesitatingly, then, as she felt Mrs B. valued what she told her about her childhood, with growing ease, as if she was gradually acquiring a realization of the deep importance these pictures and feelings had for her. Slowly her family came to life, as she spoke about them in her quiet earnest way. And always with the stories came shy, puzzled questions: 'Why am I so cold?' 'Why can't I show any affection when I have such a good husband, who is so affectionate himself, always friendly and helpful, and never angry with me?'

At one point, when Mrs B. commented on her anxiety that she and her husband were not as alike as she wanted them to be, she said that he was only different when he had sexual feelings, and then he got excited and breathless—'like Father in his asthma attacks', Mrs B. ventured. Mrs Cooper herself dreaded getting excited, and when asked what she feared would happen if she did, she said with great feeling: 'I would make a fool of myself, an exhibition, stand out in the crowd!'

Now we can begin to see what kind of relationships Mrs Cooper experienced in her childhood and can speculate about the feelings and phantasies which they aroused in her.

Her brother was her 'closest friend' but also her rival for the parents' love; the boy who was mother's favourite and who shared father's room. She dealt with her jealousy by a bond of companionship with him— being as good as a boy—denying her resentment and the fact that she was a girl. Later, in courtship and marriage, she lives out her desire to be the husband's equal and to sustain a safe adolescent relationship in which sexuality is prohibited and controlled.

Her mother was not able to give the little girl much time or affection; her infant need for a close exclusive relation with her remained unsatisfied. She tried to please by good behaviour and denial of her rivalry with mother in relation to father—though she sensed his needs and knew of his affection for her, to which she would have liked to respond. Would she have been a better wife to him? By unconscious denial of this wish she tried to keep the relationship with mother secure, and to keep hostility out of it.

What had happened to her father that made him choke and pant at night? Why did mother not want to share her bed with him? Had she, as the youngest-born, separated her parents? Her anxieties about the situation, and her guilt-laden wish to have things differently—to have one of them all to herself in the kind of intimacy that belongs to mothers and babies and husbands and wives may have been the cause of the little girl's continual tension and her inability to enjoy life and affection.

Her unconscious phantasies and anxieties about the relationships at home are carried over into her marriage, and the elements of sexual feeling in them intrude into the relationship with the husband. Her relationship with her mother, by whom she feels sexuality to be forbidden and denigrated—and who yet, by sharing her bed, stimulated the girl's phantasies—still prohibits her sexual response to her husband. If she has intercourse with him, does he become in phantasy the father, the man she must not have; and if she lets his excitement mount, will he too become ill like father? If she allows herself sexual feelings, and is excited by him, does it mean that she gets the penis from him and has intercourse with mother and becomes an exhibit, 'stands out in the crowd'? It is interesting to remember here that Mrs Cooper knew nothing of her husband's exhibitionist tendencies, for which he had sought treatment.

Although she cannot yet make any conscious connection between her earlier love relations and her marriage, she spontaneously associates feelings about her family with her difficulties in relation to her husband.

At the third meeting, even before she sat down, Mrs Cooper showed Mrs B. a scar on her neck. This, she said, was caused by a boy-friend who had attacked her with a razor when she was twenty-two. They were considering marriage—until she felt that he would not make a reliable husband, and suggested that they should just remain friends. The boy seemed to accept this, but soon after, when they were travelling home together, he suddenly attacked her in the train. She was badly injured; the train had to be stopped; afterwards she was in hospital for weeks. There was much gossip and publicity, and Court proceedings; however, she was greatly relieved when the boy got off unpunished. She could only explain this relief to Mrs B. by saying, 'I always think that when girls get attacked like that, it must be their fault.' Mrs B. said she seemed to feel that she had provoked this attack, and was frightened that there might be something attacking and violent inside herself. Perhaps when she felt excited she got these violent feelings, and perhaps that was why she was so afraid of excitement. The client did not respond to this suggestion. She insisted that the incident had had no effect on her; she hardly ever remembered it, and could not think why she had told Mrs B. about it. Then, immediately, she changed the subject and talked of her inability to relax and enjoy herself. Even dancing, which she used to love as a girl, she did not like now. She was relieved if it rained on a Sunday so she could remain indoors, for she hated sunshine and she would never sit on the grass for fear of spiders. She went on to talk about her constant worrying—although she had 'nothing to worry about'—and of her fear of accidents, especially accidents to her husband. Whenever he cleaned the windows she was afraid he would fall, and when he went out, that he would have a bus accident, or be run over. She was sure she could never have a baby, because she wouldn't have a quiet minute for fear that something might happen.

Mrs B. made very few comments; she accepted the client's anxiety, saying something from time to time about violent feelings, exciting attacking feelings that make people fear that things may get out of control and that anything may happen. Mrs Cooper became more and more silent, and Mrs B. went on to say that sometimes, when accidents happen, people feel that they are in some way responsible—

as if their own violent feelings had got outside them and done this, 'Just as you felt with your boy-friend.' Mrs Cooper seemed to struggle with this idea, saying nothing; and although she was still unable consciously to make links between her anxieties and her aggressive competitive sexuality, nevertheless, this interview, in which she had told Mrs B. 'the worst about myself', affected her deeply. After it, she gave up her full-time factory job, and took a part-time post in a maternity home, so that 'I can be home in time for my husband's tea'. She reported with surprise at the next meeting that her vaginal irritation had disappeared. She had her hair permed, began to dress in gay colours, and the choirboy look never came back.

In the new situation with her caseworker, Mrs Cooper can very soon tell the story of her first boy-friend's attack on her; and in her doubts as to whether she had, in fact, provoked that attack, her deep hostility to men and her fear of dangerous sexual feelings are revealed. Although as yet she is not aware of it, the order in which she speaks of her anxieties clearly shows the unconscious connection between these violently aggressive feelings towards men and her terror of accidents to them.

Mrs B.'s verbalized recognition of Mrs Cooper's aggressive feelings, although rejected in the interview, brought a tremendous relief. It is as if the client had at last found a mother who can tolerate her hostile feelings towards the brother, and can at the same time allow her her sexual wishes, and so let her grow up and become a woman.

We have seen how Mrs Cooper has in the past tried to solve her problems of hostility and jealousy towards her brother and husband by identifying with them as far as possible. Her lack of femininity reflected her confused feelings about a woman's role, and her doubts whether her mother valued femininity. Now that she feels femininity valued by her caseworker, she makes rapid moves towards it, and can begin to give up a little of the identification with her husband.

In the next meetings Mrs Cooper settled down to talk about her mother, saying how reliable she was, looking after everybody's needs. Mother did not have much patience with the sick father, but when he was really ill she nursed him well. She was a cook by profession—the client also cooked well, better than her mother-in-law. Her husband said she was 'altogether a very good wife in all but the one point'.

Each time the client had said something negative about her mother, she hurriedly said something nice and good, and when Mrs B. showed her how afraid she was of admitting anger with her mother, she became quite alarmed, saying it would have been unthinkable ever to be angry with mother. She quickly talked about other women; her brother's wife who did not look after him well; and her mother-in-law, who ignored her husband, who was deaf and withdrawn but might be able to participate much more if she would only take the trouble to make herself understood by him. Mrs B. said that it seemed safer to criticize these other women than her mother; and also that Mrs Cooper seemed to feel that not one of these women was really good to her husband. Perhaps she was wondering what sort of woman she was, and what she wanted to be like?

After this came a few meetings during which men were not mentioned at all, and the discussion centred on mothers and babies. Usually Mrs Cooper started by talking about the maternity hospital and telling Mrs B. about the pain endured by the mothers, and how some of them seemed not to love their babies at all, and deserted them; one woman did not want even to see her new-born baby and yet was very concerned about the dog she had left at home. Then she wondered what she herself would feel and what sort of a baby she would have? Could one ever have a quiet minute if one had a baby? Or had one to worry all the time about what would happen to it? Babies were so fragile, got ill so easily; were so ugly. And with great emphasis: she certainly would hate to have a little boy.

Mrs B. talked with the client about her fears of how damaging babies and mothers may sometimes seem to be to each other, and linked these fears with the client's anxieties about her feelings towards her own mother. At the same time she helped Mrs Cooper to recognize her more positive feelings which were shyly and hesitantly mingled with all the anxieties—feelings that mothers and babies were also good for each other and could love each other, just as the client loved, and knew herself to be loved, by her mother.

The recognition of these more positive feelings seemed to help Mrs Cooper in her struggle to believe that she could be a good mother and have a good baby.

During this period Mrs Cooper is making a dependent affectionate relationship with her worker, who allows herself to be seen as a 'good mother' who can tolerate angry feelings, and with whom the client can make her own discoveries. That means, though, that for the time being she finds it difficult to recognize her good feelings for her real mother, so that in her explorations of what sort of woman she wants to become she does not identify with her own mother.

She considers, in connection with the women she knows best, what it means to be a woman in relation to men. She can see no pattern of a good wife, or a woman who can love men and not harm them. Love seems to be so much safer between women.

In the daughter-like intimacy with her worker, the client can safely explore her feelings about mothers and babies. In this setting, in which no men intrude, she begins to feel that a loving relationship between mother and child should be possible, and that she herself could be a good mother—although the thought of a boy baby still makes her anxious.

Soon the stories about the maternity hospital changed in character. Even the newest new-born baby began to look 'pretty' and 'sweet'. Mrs Cooper seemed to see more mothers now who had their babies without or almost without pain, and who were thrilled to have them and did not seem frightened to handle them. One day she said with feelings of great relief: 'It seems that *all* babies cry, even quite healthy and normal ones.'

After three or four repetitious sessions in which the material became more and more positive, Mrs B. asked the client about her husband, pointing out that they seemed to have avoided talking about him. Mrs Cooper responded at once with extreme anxiety and agitation, and spoke about her 'violent anger' and 'blind fury' with her husband whenever he attempted intercourse. She felt she could kill him; wanted to hurt him. 'I have to clench my fists and shut my eyes not to hit him.' She said she made herself cold and stiff for fear what she would do; and again expressed, with very great feeling, her disgust with her husband 'when he feels sexual', and her resentment that women were 'inferior'.

Mrs B. took up this violent expression of her anger with, and jealousy of, men and her fear of attacking her husband in this battle, relating it to what the client had told her in earlier sessions about her father, brother, boy-friend and husband. Of all these, the brother seemed at this moment the most important, and the client recalled, very vividly, a childhood quarrel in which he had chased her and she had squeezed his head in the door—and was severely punished by mother. She went on to tell Mrs B. how shocked she was when her husband first made love to her. She had expected sex to be 'just the act'; to be caressed by him so intimately was most alarming. Mrs B. again asked why she felt that sex had to be something punishing and hurtful. Was she afraid of her own warm feelings?

For a few weeks after this meeting, Mrs Cooper was very unhappy, feeling herself to be 'awful', wondering whether she could ever change. She would be quite all right if only her husband did not need 'this'; but, as he seemed to need it, it must be so bad for him when she could not let him have it. He really had a right to be angry— yet he never showed it; he was always kind and considerate. But why had *she* to change—and with great anxiety: what would she be like if she did? Mrs B. went along with her in these explorations about her love and hate, which were so alarming that she had to keep herself 'cold and stiff' in order not to feel either, for both seemed so mixed up, and so powerful.

At this, the client said with great relief that a priest too had once said to her that it was not true that she had no feelings—rather that she had very strong feelings, stronger than many other people's.

When Mrs B. shows her client how she is keeping her husband out of their interviews, Mrs Cooper reveals the intensity of her ambivalence to him. She tells her worker of her almost uncontrollable fury with him when he attempts intercourse; how she becomes intensely anxious and, instead of being able to experience a climax of genital sexual feeling, has a climax of fury and terror—'goes stiff'—and stops anything happening that would show that he is a man and she is a woman—that might make her acknowledge that he has the penis and she has not.

She associates her feelings of fury with quarrels with her brother, and with having hurt his head; earlier she had told her worker that if she had a boy baby she would be afraid of hurting him, and had talked of the boy-friend's attack, and of her constant anxiety about accidents that might befall her husband: her unconscious phantasy must be of sexuality as violent and attacking. Her husband's love-making represents violation of the family taboos; caresses are forbidden and horrify her. To accept his masculinity, to allow herself a sexual response, may also mean to lose her mother's approval and love. Nevertheless, she feels guilty about the refusal of her 'duty', which may be affecting her husband; and anxious about the anger that he may be hiding, now that she has become more aware of her own hidden anger with him. She senses the risk in altering the safe but 'phoney' relationship they have built up, in which he is so nice and they never quarrel, and is angry with the husband for insisting on the sexual 'difference' which demands change from her.

After three interviews in which she spoke of her anger with her husband, Mrs Cooper told Mrs B. that this had disappeared and she was no longer worried about intercourse. She had no pain during coitus and now did not mind showing herself without clothes to her husband. Her change of attitude, although mentioned with the pride of achievement, was described in a rather subdued way, and Mrs B. was still wondering why this was so when the client said that the vaginal irritation had returned and that in fact it had been particularly bad this morning just before she came to the Bureau. Mrs B. said she evidently felt that the irritation had something to do with the interviews, as well as with the improved relationship at home. The client replied that it seemed that she had either to be angry or to have the irritation. When Mrs B. talked round the feelings that appeared to cause both and which resulted in the same thing—her rejection of the husband's penis—the client again became anxious and insisted that the irritation must have physical causes, and that she ought to consult a gynaecologist. Mrs B. agreed that this might be a good thing, but at the same time pointed out how painful it was to the client to accept the connection between the vaginal irritation and her angry feelings with the husband who had the penis, and with Mrs B. who expected her to share it with him. From this the link was made with childhood difficulties in sharing mother with brother, father with mother, and then with the client's attempts to keep her husband out of the talks at the Bureau.

At this point Mrs B. suggested that the husband (whose individual therapy had by then been terminated) should come to the Bureau too; she would not see him herself but would arrange for a colleague, Mrs A., to give him an appointment. She explained that while the Bureau's aim was to help the marriage, *her* main concern would always be with her client, and though she would naturally have discussions with her colleague, nothing Mrs Cooper told her would be repeated to the husband.

The discovery that the revelation of her 'bad' violent feelings did not mean the end of Mrs B.'s concern for her has to some extent enabled the client to accept 'permission' to have sexual intercourse. But her deeper resentments are not yet resolved and find expression in a return of her vaginal irritation. This way of dealing with her aggression by converting it into a physical symptom seems similar to her father's, whose asthma may also suggest repressed aggressive feelings.

That the irritation is particularly troublesome on the day of Mrs Cooper's interview may mean that she is angry with Mrs B., who talks about her husband's sexuality as something good that she ought to value and accept, apparently disregarding the intense conflict that the client still feels about it.

It may also mean that a close exclusive relationship with her worker (as with her mother) makes the client anxious: but so does the prospect of having to give it up; her feeling that Mrs B. now wishes her to share the Bureau with her husband is confirmed at this meeting.

The client is alarmed by the recurrence of the vaginal irritation at this point, and by the 'insight' that it almost forces upon her. Mrs B. makes few interpretations; instead, she gives the client permission to seek medical advice and explains in great detail the procedure at the Bureau when the husband attends. In all she says and in her attitude, she aims to convey to the client that they are both aware of the connection between the irritation and these two most important relationships—the one at the Bureau, which evokes her feelings for mother, and that with her husband.

During the three weeks that preceded the husband's first interview, Mrs Cooper became more depressed. Her depression centred on the question whether it was a good thing to want to be a woman. She had consulted a gynaecologist, who had reassured her—so her body was all right; therefore she must be wrong as a person and needed to change. She talked about this 'change' in herself as if it were something violent like an operation or an attack. She would no longer be herself. What would she be like afterwards?

It was clear from what she told Mrs B. about her day-to-day doings that she continued to make moves towards femininity, but when talking about them in the interview she devalued and questioned them. There was, for example, the new relationship with the baby boy downstairs. She had been afraid to be alone with him in the past, now she often had little games with him by herself and liked to have him about. But recently, when she had the little boy on her arm, he punched her, 'so surely he must hate me', and it would be better for her not to care about him. Then there was a story about her own trusted doctor, with whom she had always got on amiably, and who got so very angry when she wanted to see the gynaecologist. They almost had a row; she never thought that such a thing could be possible with a doctor. And it all culminated in the story of the coalman who had emptied sacks of coal outside the Frencñ window during her absence; when she came home, the new chair-covers of which she had been so proud, the first ones she had ever made herself, were soiled. In all this was the anxious question, 'Is there any point in trying to become a better woman when it all turns out so badly?'

Stories like this continued after the husband's first meeting with Mrs A., and now they were mixed with another anxiety: 'What should one tell and what should one keep secret?' She talked about the inquisitiveness of the people downstairs who seemed to want to find things out about her. Then more directly: 'What would the husband tell Mrs A. and would, through her, some of the things she had told her worker be told back to her husband?'

Mrs B. explained again that nothing that Mrs Cooper had told would ever go back to her husband; then she went on to show the client that her husband's coming to the Bureau may have stirred up old feelings about her mother siding with her brother. Perhaps she felt that this situation would be repeated, and felt angry with her worker? Her reply was: 'I am not a bit angry with you, but I am very angry with my husband because it is for his sake that I come here.' Mrs B. said that the husband's coming had made his wife so anxious that she could be aware only of her negative feelings; she seemed right back in her childhood, where anger with brother was punished by mother, and so it was better to stay away from mother. But both she and Mrs B. knew that, quite often, she enjoyed coming to the Bureau and also that she loved her husband. This brought very agitated material about why she was unable to be affectionate: 'All my affection is locked behind doors and I have lost the key.' There was great pressure to find the key and also *not* to find it, when she said: 'What would happen if I could show affection? Would I become different? What would I be like? What would *they* find out about me?' And again Mrs B. talked with her about her fear that her love and hate were all mixed up 'behind the locked doors' and, if she found the key, the hate might come out with a bang and do something destructive, or the love would be rejected or soiled. Either way she feared she would be hurt and quite unable to control these locked-away feelings.

This interview ends, as it began, with the client's most pressing anxiety; what will it mean to change, and what threat will change represent to the defences she has built up throughout her childhood and incorporated in her marriage to protect herself and her husband from the intensity of her deeper feelings—fierce and sensitive affection and the destructive anger and jealousy that shadow it? She has not yet been able to feel that she might reconcile these contradictory feelings within herself, and that her caseworker's permission to change implies her confidence that this may become possible.

Mrs Cooper's story about the coalman vividly expresses her feeling that male sexuality is dirty and damaging—how was it possible to be clean and good if her 'house' has to be open to such soiling? The baby boy downstairs seems to return her newly won ability to show affection only with hate; the trusted doctor is hostile when she cares about her female organs. How can she love a man when all men seem to want to hurt and soil and attack her? What use is it to try to be a good woman when men turn it all bad? So, if women are cold and hard and unloving, it is really all the men's fault—and if her husband expects her to change for his sake, she has surely the right to be angry with him! Especially as he now threatens to interfere with the support she has found with her worker at the Bureau—and this time Mrs B. links her client's fear of losing her with her relationships with her mother and brother, as if somehow again she might have to cede her place in the mother's affection, and be faced with the frightening anger that is the alternative to her love for her.

*   *   *

When Mr Cooper started coming to the Bureau to see Mrs A. he was a slight, neat, pale, bespectacled man of indeterminate age, though in fact he was thirty. Later, it emerged that he was blind in one eye and was suffering from a form of progressive deafness. Though he still heard well, he tended to speak quickly in a quiet, monotonous way with a strong accent which sometimes made him difficult to follow. When he came in, and again when he left, his intense shyness was most striking—but as soon as he took his coat off he warmed up, and in the interview talked easily with much insight, though in a somewhat intellectual manner. It immediately became evident that he felt safe and at home in the two-person interview situation, and that his earlier experience of therapy would considerably affect the course of the interviews, particularly at the beginning.

He at once began to talk of his wife; she was always tense, never able to relax, and terrified of any show of affection. This, together with her refusal to have intercourse, was, he said, taking him back to his old problem of feeling rejected by his mother and of being compelled always to return to her for proof of her love. With his wife he dealt with this fear of rejection by pretending that all this did not matter and was of no importance whatsoever. He did this because if his wife felt anything was important she immediately became tense and anxious. One evening she refused intercourse, and he assured her that it did not matter; during the night, however, he took her by surprise 'before she had time to put up her defences'.

Except for her aversion to sex he considered his wife a conscientious housewife, very eager to do her duty. Since coming to the Bureau she had become less shy; she was able to undress in front of him now, but in intercourse she was still quite rigid and it seemed 'just like raping her'. She never really relaxed except in the darkness of the cinema, and this was the only form of pleasure they could enjoy together. She set very high standards for herself, and his dinner was always on the table the moment he came in at the front door. She looked after all his essential needs, but never gave him any extras, such as a packet of cigarettes. With some feeling he added: 'It is like giving a child slippers for a Christmas present.'

He had always been terrified of women, and if a girl refused to dance with him it was a major disaster. His wife had been 'different', the first girl with whom he felt 'safe' and whom he felt to be dependable; someone who would not let him down or despise him. But when he became rather ardent towards the end of their courtship, she had been very frightened and rebuffed him; he should have taken his warning then.

Mrs A. said little, but her concern about Mr Cooper's lack of involvement in his wife's problems seemed to reach him, for he expressed some of his hurt and despair, saying that he did not usually keep on at a problem if he found he could not solve it. His wife's rejecting attitude had begun to drive something of a wedge between them. 'She expects me to be a hundred-per-cent man, to give her orders, but never to show her any feeling. I am overflowing with love and affection, but have no one to give it to.'

Mr Cooper impresses his worker as being very withdrawn in his ordinary contacts, but it is clear that he feels at home in a therapeutic relationship and can, as it were, continue his conversations about his inner life almost as if he were still with his former therapist. His previous psychological treatment has relieved him of his most disturbing symptoms and undoubtedly contributed much to his capacity to make a quick and intense relationship with Mrs A. From the beginning she is aware of his need to have an intense relationship with her, sealing himself and her off from life outside as it were. The change from a male to a female therapist is, as we shall see, of immediate significance.

He makes no attempt to be objective, but brings his feelings as the most important aspect of his experience and, throughout the early contact with Mrs A., he hardly ever brings factual material that might threaten the phantasy intimacy of this new relationship with a woman. Although he reveals so much about himself, he keeps up a pretence of coming to the Bureau on behalf of his wife and talks about her rather like a parent who has come to discuss a child's symptoms with a doctor. It is as if he must not make demands for himself, or ask for 'extras' that he must not expect, and he withdraws the moment the hour is up. His attitude leaves Mrs A. frustrated, feeling as if she has been kept out and has not been able to participate in the interview. The frustration that the client had been unable to deal with in relation to his mother has determined the pattern for his subsequent relations with women. He is intensely afraid of rejection but, perhaps, in spite of his protestations, equally afraid of letting himself love or be loved, so he pretends that nothing matters. His wife comes near to offering him a 'safe' relationship in which deep and disturbing feelings can be avoided and controlled and in which giving and taking can be restricted to 'essentials'. The theme of their mutual frustration in giving and accepting presents, which he introduces in his first interview, recurs in innumerable guises throughout the whole casework contact.

The change in Mr Cooper the following week was quite dramatic. Once inside the room he was more assertive, almost defiant, and evidently resentful and angry. Nevertheless, he began by saying that his wife had been a little better, had shown 'a bit more life and sparkle.' For example, one night when he made a sexual approach, she had said emphatically 'No'. Once again he had tried to convince himself that this did not matter to him, but had said to her: 'You won't be able to say that much longer'; to which she had replied:

'Are you threatening me?' They then turned over and went to sleep.

Mrs A. took up the matter of his anger with his wife, and with herself for making him recognize his own involvement in the marriage problem. She said it felt as if his fury with women was sometimes quite overwhelming. He smiled and said: 'That night I could have wiped them all off the face of the earth'. He added somewhat grimly that all next day he was furious, hating all women, regretting his marriage, feeling that nobody wanted his masculinity. Mrs A. then discussed with him his difficulty in showing his frustration to his wife because of his fear of the terrible things he might do in anger. He said it was inconceivable to convey to his wife any of his feelings of rejection and fury, just as it had been impossible to show them to his mother as a boy because he might then lose the 'last little bit of her love'. With his wife, he felt it would be like 'blackmail' to try to get her to respond by appealing to her through his injured feelings.

Mrs A. wondered why he doubted his right to her love. Did he, somewhere inside, want her to remain rejecting? Had he perhaps chosen a wife who, like his mother, apparently did not want his sexuality? Mr Cooper's response was to say he was beginning to realize how much he had to do with his wife's problem, and then to ask Mrs A. whether she thought he was the real boss in the home, appealing for reassurance on this point. When she merely smiled, he said he had in fact brought his wife to town with him and she was waiting for him in a nearby café. As he left he said, 'So you think I should share my feelings more with my wife. I suppose there will be an outcry.'

The previous interview must have stimulated in Mr Cooper both his needs and his frustration, for he now no longer comes on his wife's behalf, but brings himself.

Although he could not risk expressing his hurt and anger with his wife directly when she again refused his sexual approach, he does bring to his worker his feelings of unhappiness and anger, not only with his wife but with 'all women', and his savage phantasies. At the same time he is experiencing his anger as something that Mrs A. can accept, that cannot, therefore, be as destructive as he has imagined.

We have seen how the wife needs to identify with her husband, pretending that they are both alike, that there are no differences. Now

*that we are beginning to know him, we must ask ourselves: what is his
part in this denial?*

*It seems that the couple are alike in their feeling that sexuality is
aggressive and dangerous and must be denied or controlled, and also
that neither must risk showing love or asking for it. In the new therapeutic situation, in which both husband and wife are given support,
it is becoming safe to show some feeling, and Mr Cooper has warned
his wife that things must change. He feels that his worker is telling
him that he will have to risk expressing his demands and frustration
directly to his wife. His misgivings are linked with his phantasies of his
mother who would not tolerate angry feelings. That he brought his wife
with him on this occasion when he was particularly angry with her
indicates his need to reassure himself that he has not damaged her, to
make up for his anger by offering her a treat, and, perhaps also, to
include her in the safety which he feels that Mrs A. is offering.*

A week later Mr Cooper reported that he had tried to tell his wife
of his feelings when she again refused him. To this she had responded
with silence and he had said no more. For the next few days he was
stern and severe with her, not helping her in the house or relating
to her anything of his day's doings. As a result he felt very remote
from her and empty of feeling, but, nevertheless, he had to satisfy
his overwhelming desire to punish her by withdrawing his love and
affection. He then wondered whether he did the same when making
love to his wife. This never happened because he felt sexually roused
or loving, but because he insisted on his due as a husband. He went
on with Mrs A. to explore what sexuality really meant to him, and
brought the following incident.

A few nights after he had told his wife of his anger, she allowed
him to have intercourse, but he was left feeling resentful and distant
because he had only been given his due rather grudgingly and with
no warmth whatsoever. Then came Saturday night; they went to a
party together at which towards the end of the evening a lot of
balloons were showered from the ceiling. His wife got into 'a
destructive frenzy', bursting every balloon she could lay hands on,
and upsetting some children who wanted to save theirs. Mr Cooper
was absolutely horrified by this display of 'vindictiveness', but that
night the couple had intercourse that gave him satisfaction. The next
day they had childlike playful fights in which they tried out their
physical strength on each other. They both showed a great deal of

fight and neither would give in to the other. As he put it, 'Underneath our playfulness we were in deadly earnest.'

When Mrs A. remarked that the playful fights seemed a fairly safe way of sharing angry feelings, he said it was so much easier to talk to her than to his wife and felt so much safer. He followed this by a story of women at work who were constantly 'chasing' him and who seemed to be out to seduce him. He said with feeling: 'If only my wife would tempt me like that!' He also spoke of a row he had had at work in which he had been able to say what he really felt without any terrible consequences. If only this were possible with his wife too!

With the support of his worker, he has risked showing his displeasure at his wife's rejections of his sexual approach by a characteristic withdrawal from her. He seems to feel that his mechanical performance of the sexual act punishes her for her coldness. But he is no longer satisfied with her passive participation, though not many days earlier he would have been content with this, finding ever new excuses why it could not be otherwise. Now he can let himself become aware of his need to experience intercourse with his emotions as well as his will power, but still shifts the responsibility on to the woman. Why can't his wife be as understanding as Mrs A., as seductive as the girl at work, as robust as his workmates? Can she ever give him what he really wants—it seems that whatever she has to give may not be enough for him.

The episode of the balloons is an indication of the change in their relationship. Many weeks later we hear from Mrs B. that Mrs Cooper had submitted to her husband's pressure to go to the dance—and had then felt free to act out her aggressive protest. He does not mention his victory, but only her 'vindictiveness'—which seems to have made it safe for him to get really close to her without fear of destroying her. When she can be more freely aggressive and he can respond, and they can join in playful but 'deadly earnest' conflict, it seems possible that they both can drop their armour of indifference and distant helpfulness and allow themselves to experience their love as well as their anger in the shared relationship.

After saying that 'nothing much' had happened, Mr Cooper told Mrs A. at the next meeting how, when the woman from downstairs and her father had come to dinner on Sunday, his wife had given him only a very small helping and he had complained about it in the evening. Mrs A. suggested that this must have reminded him of occasions at home when his mother had given him small helpings, favouring his father or sister. Mr Cooper ignored these remarks, saying that he only complained in order to stand his ground, and not to be 'browbeaten by a mere woman'. He had really hoped his wife would 'blow up'—in a way he had tried to provoke this to see whether he could hold his own when she was roused.

After this incident, just as after her 'vindictive' bursting of balloons, he had approached his wife for intercourse. She submitted without protest, but again he felt dissatisfied because she did not seem to enjoy it. This made him feel like a naughty boy, and his wife felt to him like his mother disapproving of his naughtiness. He added: 'Though she reminds me a lot of my mother, she is much more dependable and predictable and less liable to blow up at you.' After a pause he said: 'If I make her feel I am a naughty boy, I will also make her feel that her sex is something naughty.' Mrs A. suggested that he really knew how his need to experience his wife as if she were his mother affected her sexual response. But as he also knew that she was very different, could he perhaps begin to approach her differently? In reply Mr Cooper spoke about the seductive girl at work and how dangerous she felt to him. When Mrs A. wondered why sexuality felt so dangerous to him, he talked about his wife's lack of sexual response; the vaginal irritation which could not be so bad, since it was he who always had to remind her to get her ointment; and her complaints that intercourse hurt her, although she often did not know whether he had penetrated or not. He was puzzled whether it was he who hurt her or whether her complaint was like his own headaches, which came when he tried to reason rather than use his feelings: 'As a matter of fact I have got one today.'

Mr Cooper brings another instance of his feeling that his wife (like his mother) never gives him his fill and leaves him unsatisfied. When he shows his anger he pretends that he wants to provoke hers, but at the same time he tests out his phantasies about what might happen 'if she gets roused'. Can he stand up to her and be strong and manly? This is a wish which, at the moment, he needs to try out both at home and at work. His association of frustration with anger, getting 'blown up', sexual assault, and punishing women is revealed.

Unconsciously he must have felt his sexuality·as being so dangerous and dirty that he chose an unresponsive wife; in his approach he unconsciously ensures that she remains so—so that he still feels as if he were under his mother's disapproving eye. He must remain ineffective and harmless because sexuality and hurt seem inseparable to him. He wonders how much he damages his wife. That she seems unaware of his penis, refuses to give him even this proof of his potency, also means that she has no cause for revenge, and this is a source both of relief and of regret to him.

A week later Mr Cooper seemed to feel more secure. He had had an upset at work and once again had lost his temper, but had been able to cope with his anger.

Then he told Mrs A. that his wife was becoming more affectionate and spontaneous. One night she had put out her hand towards him in bed, and he had ignored it. When Mrs A. remarked that he seemed to be at great pains to hide the fact that he had noticed it, he was busy making excuses about why this change in his wife could not possibly mean anything, but he readily accepted Mrs A.'s interpretation that he was afraid of his wife's affection as yet, and needed to deny and control it.

He then spoke of an argument in which he had been aware only of putting his own 'manly point of view' and of his need to prove his 'overbearing manhood' to her, so that he had been totally unaware of *her* feelings on the subject. He said that exactly the same thing happened in their sexual relations, where he used her to prove himself a man and became quite unaware of her as a person. She became 'any woman to me, almost as if she were a prostitute', and he became 'just any man'. To him it is just as if he had split off sex from the rest of their relationship, and he described this with much feeling as 'I have made her feel that I do not want her *sex*'. Mrs A. suggested that it felt to him as if all the chaotic and powerful feelings associated with sex might destroy something of their otherwise good relationship, which he was at great pains to keep intact.

Mr Cooper reports an instance of his increasing aggression at work, almost as a present to his caseworker, a sign of progress. He needs reassurance about this because what is happening at home is confusing to him. His wife's more open affection threatens him so much that he has to deny it and make a feeling contact between them impossible by imagin-

ing himself a strong relentless 'he-man' having intercourse with an anonymous prostitute. To allow feelings in sexual intercourse threatens his control of the situation. The only alternative seems to be a brother-and-sister relationship without sexuality.

So far—this is his fifth meeting—he has hardly talked about his parental family. We knew from Mrs Cooper that he has two elder sisters and one elder brother, but neither they nor his father have been mentioned by him. When he talks about his mother it is always just about her and himself as though nobody else existed. He cannot give up his phantasy of an omnipotent exclusive infant-relationship with his mother, and attempts to perpetuate this with his worker. He dreams of such a relationship with his wife, yet makes it impossible for her to come close to him by his lack of participation and his denial of feeling.

* * *

Some Questions and Comments on the Coopers' Marriage

Since Mr Cooper had been coming to the Bureau, the two caseworkers had frequently consulted with each other, and after a
month or so they felt they knew their clients sufficiently well to
attempt a joint understanding of this marriage.

The first questions here, as in all marital cases, are: Why did these
two people choose each other? What were the conscious and
unconscious motives that brought them together? What satisfactions
did they expect and hope to receive from each other?

In the first interview, Mrs Cooper said: 'We are so much alike'
and he: 'I feel safe with her—she will never despise me'. These
remarks indicate a surprising awareness in both partners of the
nature of their motives. We have already seen that Mrs Cooper's
need to be like her husband is her way of coping with her anxieties
about the difference in the sexes, her feeling that men are superior,
and her anger about it. Mr Cooper's initial request to the Bureau is
to make his wife into a sexual woman. Yet his anxieties about his
own sexuality are soon revealed. It seems that he chose his wife just
because her lack of sexual response makes it possible for him not to
put himself to the proof as a sexual man. The caseworker's 'hunch'
that he will feel less 'safe' with his wife if she becomes more of a
woman is soon to be confirmed. It seems, therefore, that the couple
have been in unconscious agreement that their sexual feelings are
aggressive and dangerous and must be denied and controlled.

We must now ask ourselves how the needs and expectations in the
marriage are related to the two partners' experiences in their parental
families. What unresolved conflicts, stemming from these earlier
relationships, are they trying to solve in their marriage?

Mr Cooper has so far hardly talked about his family; it may be
particularly significant that his father has, as yet, not been mentioned
at all. We know that his wife reminds him of his mother, and that he
is still so preoccupied with love and hate for his mother that, in his
relationship to his wife, these conflicting feelings for his mother are
always with him.

For Mrs Cooper, the most vital thing seems to be to hold on to her
mother's love. In childhood she tried to achieve this by being as

much as possible like her brother, who seemed to have everything that mother valued. In her marriage she attempts to continue this pattern of identifying with the envied male, unconsciously seeking to avoid angry feelings towards her husband in this way. But all the men in her life, the brother, the gentle suffering father and the helpful considerate husband, are shadowy figures compared with her mother, who appears to be her most important person, and who seems to provide the most powerful motives for Mrs Cooper's denial of her own femininity.

This husband and wife consciously feel themselves to be very well suited, and each has, in fact, found in the other a dependable and conscientious partner. They care for each other and help each other to maintain a restricted but safe way of life in which both can avoid strong feelings of love and hate, and the guilt that these arouse in them both.

Why, then, did they find adjustment so difficult after marriage that they had to seek outside help? What sort of unsuspected and unforseen obstacles arose in their marriage?

It is the sexual relationship that makes for strain between them and brings them to the Bureau, for it is in this sphere that they can no longer deny their differences and have to accept that each has a need which can only be fulfilled by the opposite sex. This arouses such angry feelings that love and good companionship are threatened.

Their seeking help with this problem indicates the strength of their conflicting feelings: wanting to grow up and achieve a husband-wife relationship, but also dreading any change and wanting to fulfil, in their marriage, their phantasy of a close exclusive parent-child relationship.

What then is the caseworkers' aim in this marriage? How can they help their clients to overcome the obstacles which stop them from growing up and to reconcile their conscious and their unconscious needs sufficiently to make a more gratifying and realistic marriage-relationship possible?

The aim is to enable these people to give up the rigid conceptions of themselves and their partners and become free and flexible enough to test out their feelings, and their needs and demands in a relationship of partial and more mature dependence on each other. This they may be helped to achieve if they are given the opportunity to explore, in the security of a continuous contact with their caseworkers, the phantasies about their relationships with their parents and experience for themselves how these phantasies intrude into their present relationships, in particular with the marriage partner. In this first phase of casework, both husband and wife have made the beginnings of good and trusting relationships with their workers. This may help them to test out and gain some reassurance of those aspects of themselves which they have hitherto felt to be so frighteningly destructive.

This first assessment will have to be reviewed again and again, in the light of new understanding of the needs of these two people and their marriage, the developing relationships with their caseworkers, and the movement of the case within the four-person relationship in the Bureau. All assessments will be based not only on the shared experience of Mrs A. and Mrs B. but also on the clarification that results from discussing the case in case conferences.

PHASE II

When Mrs Cooper had been coming to the Bureau for six months and her husband for about four weeks, there were indications of the beginning of a change in the marriage, and of a new ease in the relationship between the couple. Mrs Cooper no longer mentioned either sexual difficulties or the vaginal irritation; yet in a number of interviews she talked of her intense envy of her husband, for instance, when he laughed wholeheartedly or sang. When Mrs B. tried to discover with her client what it really was that she was so envious about, Mrs Cooper would say: 'Well, the things men have got— more freedom, more abilities!' And that was how it was left at this stage.

She went on to compare herself with the depressed woman who lived downstairs—would she get like this with her constant worrying? Why couldn't she enjoy things? Then, after a pause, she added suddenly with a twinkle and a laugh that her husband had 'made' her go to a dance, and in spite of herself she had enjoyed it tremendously. But she was not going to tell him so. When Mrs B. wondered why she could not let him know that he had given her pleasure, Mrs Cooper said she did not like it if he felt 'right'. Attempts to find out what this meant brought a great deal of anxiety; if he is 'right', it must mean that she is 'wrong'. This was linked by Mrs B. with earlier remarks all revealing the client's feeling that women are inferior, her envy of her husband, and her insistence that she must be the same as him. Mrs Cooper, who had quietly listened, said with great feeling: 'I don't want to change. I couldn't bear it if my husband said "I told you so".' What his victory would be about she did not know; Mrs B. put it to her that it would be that she was a woman, just as he was a man, and that it was just that that was 'right'.

Next week Mrs Cooper arrived very pleased. Usually she fussed and worried about the journey to the Bureau, but on this occasion she had 'just got on to a bus and it got me here at the right time'.

Then, talking about the maternity hospital, she spoke of a new-born baby girl she had seen. The mother had had hardly any pain, and the baby was lovely. Perhaps she could have a baby girl like that one day—but then, she pondered; would she still care for her husband or would she 'want a baby really only to get the better of him?' Mrs B. wondered why she felt she needed to get the better of her husband. If she had a baby it might prove to herself that she had something important that he had not—and perhaps then she need not envy what he had got. Mrs Cooper replied quickly: 'It really is funny, I like his advice, need him to be stronger in every way, but in bed I cannot bear it,' and banging the arm of her chair she said with great emphasis, 'and if I say NO, then I am the stronger one'. Mrs B. said that perhaps she might one day begin to feel strong not merely by controlling his sexuality, but by becoming aware of her own creativeness. At first this seemed to give her relief, but soon she began to be confused, talking of her husband as 'such a silly baby who wants to be loved by me as though I were his mother'. Mrs B. agreed with her that her husband's needs were as contradictory as her own.

Mrs Cooper went on to talk about her mother, who used to be so undemonstrative but was now quite emotional and always cried when the client left her after a holiday. She too felt like crying, but never did for fear of hurting her mother—but then, she added, perhaps not showing her feelings hurt her mother much more.

The client and Mrs B. talked about these confusing situations and conflicting needs in her important relationships: the question of who is in control; and whether one really has to be either right or wrong, strong or weak, or whether each could give the other something, so that each in turn could be 'weak' and 'strong'; sometimes the one, sometimes the other.

At this time Mrs Cooper is becoming aware both of her own and of her husband's conflicting wishes in the sexual relationship. She competes with him both in her need to have control of his sexuality and in her need to be the loved, protected baby, and cannot tolerate him either as a 'silly baby'—a little boy who possesses a penis and asks for love as well—or as a man who asserts his strength and potency in bed.

Her anxiety about yielding in an emotional situation is also expressed in relation to her mother, who was so controlling and so much stronger than father, but who now cries when her daughter leaves her, and makes her feel that she must be the stronger one. Here, too, she has hitherto been unable to manage to give and take, or to solve the problems of dependence and control.

Mrs Cooper's opening comment about having trusted herself safely to the bus may be an indication that she can now relinquish some of her anxious control in the relationship with her worker. This seems to help

*her to face and experience her conflicts in her other relationships and
to risk becoming aware of the other side of the picture that she has of
herself, her husband, and her parents.*

In the next few interviews Mrs Cooper continued to express her
confused feelings about what her husband wanted from her. Did he
really want sexual intercourse or did he only think he wanted it?
When she did not respond to him she felt awful for rejecting him,
but when she said 'yes', he was not happy either, and confessed he
felt as if he had raped her. She was extremely confused, saying
repeatedly: 'I don't know what to do.' At about the same time she
began to talk quite angrily about her husband. So far he had always
been described as helpful, affectionate and considerate, but now she
said he was mean with money, which made her feel dreadful since
Christmas was approaching and she wanted to plan presents. He
even expected her to pay her own money into the joint account and
never to have anything for herself. With Mrs B.'s help she linked the
holding back of money with the holding back of feelings, especially
sexual feelings, and was able to see the connection with the difficulties
they both experienced in sharing.

Then she said that she wanted him to *be* happy, but did not want
to *make* him happy. She grew very anxious, saying that these seemed
to be very different things, because 'wanting to make him happy
seems like wanting something for myself'. When Mrs B. tried to find
out why she was so frightened of having something for herself, it
seemed to feel to her that what she wanted for herself she had to
take from her husband. Was not what she wanted really what she
could not have? Did not wanting something for herself always
lead up to what was so frightening in sexuality?

*Mrs Cooper continues to talk of her confusion, this time directly
in relation to sexuality. What does her husband really want from her?
Which of them is it who does not want intercourse and feels it is a
damaging rape—he or she? Will it be more hurtful to respond than to
withhold? She wants him to be happy, but not through her responding
to his masculine needs. For this would mean wanting to get something
for herself—and she has learned to recognize her aggressive wish for
the penis. It would also mean letting him feel that he has got it. Does
intercourse arouse her fears that she would rob her husband of this
precious possession or be for ever robbed herself of the phantasy that*

*she might yet obtain it? If only he could be happy by himself, and let
her remain 'right' by herself!*

*In the relationship with Mrs B. the situation is different. There it
seems quite safe to ask for something for herself, and whatever she
gives will be given back to her without damaging Mrs B.*

Having understood his need to avoid an emotional relationship
with his wife, Mr Cooper went home intending to convince her now
that he wanted *'all of her,* including her sex'. He soon found an
opportunity of having a talk with her in which he told her just this,
adding that the problem between them could not be only a sexual
one, because if it were he could easily go elsewhere for sex. His wife's
spontaneous reply was that she loved 'ninety-five per cent' of him,
all except his sexual organs. Nevertheless, she was evidently moved
by her husband's declaration of love, because the following evening,
when he returned from work, she was dressed in her prettiest and
most feminine clothes, looking as seductive as she knew how. He
noticed none of this until she drew his attention to it, and then
apologized profusely for being so unobservant. It was something
of a shock to him to realize that he had to remain so blind to her
attractions as a woman. The next evening she tried herself out on
him again by suddenly putting her arms round him—something she
had never done before. This really frightened him. He told Mrs A.
that this was a long way from his idea of love between grown-ups,
and was more like 'a child's longing for affection'. How was it
possible, he asked her, to reconcile 'childish affection' with the new
'he-man' he was trying to become?

Mrs A. had been aware of his remoteness and detachment during
this interview, and it then became clear that he was very angry with
her. She took up with him his feeling that she had undermined his
newly acquired manhood by having made him aware of his suppres-
sed longing for affection that he had relegated to childhood. He
replied that this need in him 'to be loved like a child' by his wife, and
his worker, had become so strong in him in the course of the week
that he had been able to cope with it, as of old, only by convincing
himself that it did not matter at all.

As might be expected, he had had a strained and unhappy week
in which he felt himself drawn back into the problem with his
mother. He said he had always been terrified of being hurt; therefore
if he gave up being a 'he-man from top to toe', he would become

once again 'the little boy who is weak and exposed'. His wife would then 'dominate and despise' him as his mother had done. He had therefore aimed at becoming a 'kind of Colonel Nasser', invulnerable and strong. In becoming aware of a 'desperate need to be loved and cuddled and spoiled like a baby' by his wife, could he ever let her know how insecure he was on his pedestal?

The dilemma of having to be either the dictator in complete control, or the baby whose very helplessness makes him feel sometimes omnipotent and sometimes utterly annihilated, was discussed with him in relation to the casework in which he could never be quite the one or the other.

He returned the following week in a state of crisis provoked by a story of his wife's from the days when she had worked in a hospital. She told him how they used to have to help the male patients to urinate by putting their penises into the bottle for them, and how the nurses would joke about it. At this Mr Cooper got into an almost uncontrollable state of rage and embarrassment, and was 'nearly bursting with confusion'. All the next day he felt 'so intensely angry with all women' that he could have 'killed off the lot of them'. He wanted to separate from his wife and never see Mrs A. again. His wife had sensed his intense emotion, and wavered between keeping her distance and showing her sympathy. She compromised by doing many little labours of love for him, such as shining his shoes and cooking his favourite dishes.

Mrs A. helped him to see that it was in the course of this painful experience that he and his wife were able, for the first time, to become aware of each other's problems and to respond with feeling. He then said that the hospital anecdote had reminded him of an agonizing childhood experience when he himself had felt utterly ridiculed by a woman, and overcome by embarrassment and rage. It was when he was fourteen or fifteen and his mother came into his room to wake him up, pulling his bedclothes off. Just then he was naked and having an erection; he felt exposed, ashamed, wretched, and cried all that day. When his sister asked what was wrong, his mother told her 'sneeringly' what had happened. 'I could have killed her for that,' he said. She seemed to him to be hating all men and to be taking this opportunity 'of getting her own back'.

If only he could surround himself by a 'thick armour' so that he need not feel anything!

This phase brings evidence of some work and growth in the marriage. There is a to-and-fro of approach and withdrawal, as each attempt by husband or wife to explore or express newly found feelings makes the other feel threatened.

When his wife becomes more feminine and spontaneous, Mr Cooper is alarmed. He cannot relate to her in a free give-and-take, for he can only relate to women in two alternative conceptions of himself; either he has to be like his father (as he saw him at this stage) a strong he-man, withdrawn, undemanding, and therefore invulnerable, or he has to be a demanding baby who can satisfy through mother all his longing for absolute dependence. It is the latter he really longs to be with his wife and with his worker, but is frightened of being rejected, ridiculed, hurt, castrated. This rigidity in his perception of both himself and the woman makes him cling for a long time to these unrealistic alternative roles, which remain a major theme in his interviews.

Mrs Cooper is anxious about making an active response to her husband; and he, too, is anxious about what her sexual participation will mean for him. To enter fully into a relationship is equally disturbing to both—for both are frightened about their own and each other's destructive demands.

When Mr Cooper came again he was calmer, and told Mrs A. that the attractive girl at work had been inviting him to visit her in her flat, and this had produced in him 'delicious phantasies' of being 'naughty' with her. She seemed to him so relaxed, so attractive—he would be able to let himself go for once, and she would never say, like his wife, 'Don't do that.' But, alas, he had come to realize that if he were married to her things would be just the same as with his wife; she too would take on for him the forbidding aspects of his mother. It was as if mother were always there, watching to see he did 'nothing naughty'.

Mrs A. said perhaps that was what he was beginning to want—mother watching him doing something naughty and disapproving of it, and he not being put off by her any longer.

He then spoke about his constant yearning to be 'gay and light-hearted' instead of always 'heavy and aching'. He always felt as if he were carrying a heavy burden on his back. This burden, he said, was his father, whom he felt he had to carry around bodily with him everywhere. He then described him as always strong, detached, undemanding, invulnerable. He remembered how impossible it was for anyone ever to upset or hurt his father; he had the power 'to shut anyone up with one stunning word'. How much he wished to be like his father! When Mrs A. said that perhaps now he felt he wanted to be more himself, he replied: 'that would be a great release, but too dangerous'. He might be quite overcome by his feelings, 'sob or laugh hysterically—or even wet or soil' himself. Mrs B. suggested that he had to stay like father because he could not possibly believe that he could be loved with his aggressiveness and dirtiness.

After this interview he felt more lighthearted, and found himself kissing a girl at work on the forehead, just in fun, and quite spontaneously. He said the reason for his lightheartedness was that he now felt sure of getting help. In fact, he said he had freed himself of something that had long oppressed him; he had come to realize that the burden on his back was not his father but the weight of his father's love for him. In his father's eyes, he said, he could do no wrong: 'It was as if the sun shone out of me.' This had frightened him always, because he could never be a 'real boy' and do as he liked. In addition, there had seemed to be something 'physical' in his father's feeling for him, 'something that should have gone to my mother', and which he feared would 'pervert' him and make him into a girl. He recollected two episodes with his father at a swimming-bath that had been in the nature of homosexual experiences for him. These had made him very anxious and he had run to his mother 'for reassurance that I was still a real boy'. This he did not get, and Mrs A. showed him that she understood how he needed it now from her.

That his experience of love with his father had contained an element of 'perversion' was, he thought, also a barrier between him and his wife. Perhaps she sensed that he was not quite 'normal' in his sexual practices; perhaps now he was afraid of perverting her as his father had perverted him. This was why he kissed and cuddled her 'mechanically and without feeling'. By withholding affection from her, had he made her feel, he asked, that it was a bad thing?

Mrs A. had the feeling that her participation was not invited, and that the client needed to use this meeting like a confession. She was wondering how best to take this up with him when he suddenly said: 'I now feel quite differently about my mother. I have always resented her because she did not restore to me my manhood which my father had taken from me, but really she was quite a capable woman to

have coped with everything.' Then he beamed and said: 'I feel as if
a great weight has been lifted off me.'

*In the growing security of the relationships with their caseworkers
this couple have been able to look at themselves and each other more
realistically, and have been able to be slightly more flexible in their
behaviour. Their new awareness of the ambivalence of their feelings
and of their conflicting needs and wishes is an essential step towards
maturity, but it is also bewildering and alarming. We cannot attempt
to reproduce all the ups and downs, the hopes and despairs, that*
*inevitably accompany such a readjustment and have to be experienced
both in the clients' lives and in the therapeutic situation. However, with
the support of the caseworkers who help them to express these feelings,
and who can take, or at least know about the dependence and aggression
that they have needed to keep hidden, both clients slowly learn to
tolerate the strain of these painful conflicts and uncertainties. The
fact that each knows that the other, too, has his supporting relationship
at the Bureau, decreases his anxiety about having more than his share,
about giving and taking, and about whether he can face the uncertainties of change.*

*This phase of therapy represents a move, however slight, towards
independence and growth. Both partners now want to work through
some of their problems in relation to their parents and to their own
development as individuals, and use the therapeutic situation at the
Bureau to test out how much feeling can be safely brought into the
marriage.*

PHASE III

After a break of two weeks Mrs Cooper arrived looking depressed and lifeless. She dutifully reported on their Christmas holiday, which sounded very dull. Yet she said sadly, 'Now there is nothing to look forward to until we go home next summer.' Mrs B. wondered why she felt that only such a few pleasures were allowed to her, and only those connected with her home or her religion? Were only those sanctioned by her mother? Or did she not dare to allow herself pleasure because if that made her feel excited, there was always the worry about what excitement would 'lead to'. The client was listening intently, nodding at every sentence. When Mrs B. added: 'Can't you trust your pleasure to be good?' she said eagerly: 'But can't you see that I am striving for something?'

Later she talked angrily about her husband's meanness with money; he would not even let her buy Premium Bonds in her own name with her own earnings. Mrs B. remarked that the husband, like her mother, made Mrs Cooper feel that it was wrong for her to have anything for herself. To this the client said with great feeling: 'I know he needs to feel the big man, the head of the house—and I don't really mind.' Then, after a silence: 'Perhaps I will tell him that he cannot have it all, that I want a bit too.' Again a silence, then with relief: 'Then the money would not worry us any more.'

Mrs Cooper had taken this step for herself, and now Mrs B. supported it by saying that the client seemed to feel that it might be possible to share money and pleasure and many other things with her husband. If they could manage that she would feel less worried about what she might do, or what might happen, and then they could both perhaps really enjoy life.

*   *   *

When Mr Cooper was seen after the fortnight's Christmas holiday it soon became evident that even this short break in the interviews had been difficult for him. He was rather withdrawn, and very negative towards Mrs A., giving her to understand that he felt himself back where he started, as if nothing had been achieved.

When these feelings in him had been discussed and linked with the longer break, it became possible to get back to his relationship with his wife who, he thought, needed to keep him on his 'pedestal'. Half of him wanted to come down, half of him was 'terrified'. The bit of him that wanted to come down longed to go home to her as a child, and be told by her: 'I love you like that and don't want you to be the big strong man any more.' But it was impossible to risk this because, if she were to reject him, he would have to become 'cold, withdrawn, and remote for evermore'.

When Mrs A. said she thought that he was feeling the same about her on this occasion, he said if he were to let himself go at that moment he would cry, 'and that would be terrible.' He still felt doubtful whether any woman could accept him with the messiness that he felt belonged to being a child; therefore the alternative was to become like his father—the strong man.

At this point he allowed himself one of his few expressions of feeling, saying: 'How I long to be myself—something I have never really experienced!' In his marriage, he said, it felt as if both he and his wife were in a 'straitjacket', which restrained them from coming really close to each other. Money had formerly been a source of 'power and safety' to him, but now it had ceased to carry this meaning. Somehow the old ways of asserting himself over her no longer seemed to work.

After the Christmas holiday—the first interruption in treatment for both—Mr and Mrs Cooper came depressed and negative to their caseworkers. Mr Cooper responds with anger and withdrawal to the break, which he feels as a rejection.

The caseworkers are aware that any change in the routine of meetings may be disturbing to their clients. This has to be worked through before and after each break and it can often be useful in helping the client to become aware of his reactions. Although this had been a public holiday and a short and expected break. Christmas, the festival of love, carries with it its own emotional strain, and is often particularly disturbing for people who have problems about sharing, giving and taking.

The material brought by both clients shows striking similarities, yet there is a very different feeling about their interviews. For Mrs A. and Mrs B. respond not so much to what their clients say as to their different emotional demands.

Mrs Cooper demands from Mrs B. that she shall be a strong, competent person, like her mother, and she makes her fight her depression for her by underlining the positive side of her feelings. More by implication than by words, Mrs B. shows her client that she sees her as a loving person who does value her mother, her home, her

*Church, the meetings with Mrs B., and her husband's masculinity,
even though she is depressed and angry because these valued things
are not always within her control.*

*Mr Cooper, who finds it intolerable that his wife needs him to be a
strong positive person, tries to be accepted by Mrs A. with his weakness,
dependence and anger. By helping him to see the real implications of
his demands she helps him to look at and to appreciate his childish
needs.*

*Both clients and both caseworkers have learned what they can expect
from each other, and have become aware of the impact on the situation
of the other partner and the other caseworker. Now that the Coopers
really work as a couple and the 'foursome' is established the co-
operation between the two caseworkers becomes more dynamic. In
addition to the experience with their own clients, the two caseworkers
can begin to see what is happening between the four of them; by now
they each have formed a clearer picture of their client's partner and the
interactions between the couple. For example, when Mrs A. discusses
with Mrs B. the closeness and dependence demanded by Mr Cooper
in their interviews as contrasted with her feeling of exclusion and his
verbal rejection of her, Mrs B. checks this in her mind with the picture
Mrs Cooper has of her husband as needing to be so dependent, all-
powerful and depriving. Or when Mrs B. talks to Mrs A. about Mrs
Cooper's demand on her to be always such a strong and confident
person, Mrs A. can understand Mr Cooper's conception of his wife as
constantly rejecting his childish needs and tolerating him only when he
is strong.*

*Although both caseworkers accept their clients' projections and
dependence, their anger and resentment, they imply by their attitude
that they should each work things out for themselves and with one
another, thus emphasizing their belief in their clients' ability to grow
and to mature. It is within this new experience of finding themselves
accepted as they are that it becomes possible for the Coopers to express
their need to change. He 'longs to be himself'; she is 'striving towards
something'—towards more freedom and reality, perhaps, and both
seek to get away from the rigid conception of themselves and their
partners, from 'the straitjacket' of control and anxiety in which they
are held by their childish phantasies.*

A week later Mrs Cooper came looking very cheerful, saying she
had enjoyed the whole of the previous week as though it had been a

holiday. Last week's talk had shown her how silly she was to worry. She had looked round and found that 'even quite elderly people look happy, so why shouldn't I?' When Mrs B. related this to herself, she laughed and said, 'Yes, and my husband feels just the same about Mrs A.' He said, 'Lucky the man who has such an understanding wife.' Mrs B. wondered what she felt about this. Did she not resent her husband's feeling for another woman? She replied: 'I know that I cannot be perfect, but I am much better, and I almost enjoy intercourse.' Then she went on to talk about new friends—a young couple who live around the corner and who they had met at church. This couple have two small children and are happy and easy. The wife did not worry at all when the Coopers called on her unexpectedly; perhaps she herself need not worry so much about unexpected callers. What did it matter 'if they see my face as it is'? Repeating earlier remarks of Mrs Cooper's which indicated her fear of exposing herself, Mrs B. welcomed her client's newly expressed belief that whatever might be seen of her might be acceptable after all.

Mrs Cooper, disregarding all this, went on with her own theme: her priest had often advised her to have a really good friend. Last year she had found such a friend (clearly Mrs B.) and had realized what a difference it had made. Did Mrs B. agree that she should now make a friend of her own age, someone who lived near her? When Mrs B. warmly gave her the permission for which she was asking, to have a friend she could identify with in reality, the client went on: 'My mother never understood my striving.' And then, angrily and rapidly, she again told the story of how much she had wanted to train as a nurse and to have a better education, but the little money that could be saved had to be spent on the brother, so she had never learned anything but cleaning and had spent five years in service after leaving school.

Mrs B. did not take up the client's feelings of jealousy towards Mrs A. and towards the husband in the situation at the Bureau, and talked only about her anger with her mother and brother and the nagging feeling that boys are always favoured. Mrs Cooper relaxed and began talking happily about her present job in a nice nursing home, 'the best one in London, so spotlessly clean, such an excellent place for patients, with carefully selected staff'. Mrs B. said that perhaps it was almost as good as being a nurse herself, and that she need not be so angry with mother and brother after all. Her reply was that after the last meeting she had talked to her husband about his meanness with money, and he had at once agreed that he was unreasonable. He himself could not understand why he had been so greedy when she was so generous. After that they had had a very happy time. Getting up and buttoning her coat, she said: 'I've really enjoyed myself today.'

*   *   *

Mr Cooper came back cheerful and relaxed; he, too, had had a good week. He had been considerably freer with his wife. This he connected with a dream he had had in which he was standing outside the house where he had lived to the age of four, watching it burn down. Both while dreaming and on waking, he was overcome by a sense of relief, and Mrs B. discussed with him what this relief might be about.

Still in an elated and generous mood, he told Mrs A. how much his wife had changed for the better since Christmas, and how much she was benefiting from seeing Mrs B. Nevertheless, he could not really let his wife get near him because he had only just realized how hard and ungiving she was and how unable to treat him like a child, which was what he longed for. On being asked whether, perhaps, he felt that Mrs A. too was expecting too much of him, he replied: 'I cannot come out with anything really important because I am hating you. You take everything from me and give me nothing in exchange.' He went on to describe Mrs A. as 'a vampire who sucks you dry and then leaves you to rot'. All women, including his wife, were like that. Mrs A. suggested that he needed to feel women were like that because he was so frightened of what he might do to them with his own demands if they were loving and giving. Perhaps he would then suck them dry and leave them to rot. He then said that for a long time he had wanted a motor-bike and a T.V. set, but his 'reason' had always told him that it was more important to save up for a house. But had his wife said to him, 'Do have these things which you want so much', *then* he could have been happy. She was, however, not likely to say that, and he looked like having to go without them.

The Coopers have had a happy week—both have taken away from their interviews the permission to be freer with each other. But this new freedom immediately raises new anxieties, and doubts and hostility about the other partner's worker, who is seen both as good and helpful and as threatening.

Mrs Cooper, who has needed to identify with her worker, is now confused about her husband's relationship with Mrs A., with whom she feels unable to compete. Is there also the fear that Mrs B. might come to prefer him to her? And what about the bond between Mrs A. and Mrs B., from which she feels excluded? All these questions are in her mind when she expresses the wish to have a friend of her own age who lives near and is a happy wife and mother. At the same time, this is a real indication of growth and independence.

Mr Cooper connects his sense of relief with the dream in which he experiences a new freedom from his childhood ties. Mrs A. makes no attempt to interpret the dream for him but talks with the client of his own speculations and feelings about it. In spite of a sense of relief at the burning down of his parents' home, Mr Cooper is not free to build his own home with his wife, because he dare not yet get close to a woman in an adult relationship. That Mrs B. makes his wife better, makes her more into a woman, is therefore felt as dangerous, and presents a real threat to him. He tests out with his worker his anxiety about what he will do to women, and what women will do to him as well as his hope that he will be given what he wants so much—by magic, without risking a real involvement.

His worker once again accepts his frustration and anger and survives it, disproving his unconscious anxiety that it will destroy his relationship with the 'good mother'. Nevertheless, she does not treat this like a child's outburst that will pass over, but relates it to his adult situation and helps him to deal with it there. She shows him that he still needs and uses his wife to help him to control his own omnipotent demands, and yet hopes that she may make them safe for him.

Mrs Cooper began her next interview by saying that she and her husband had had a 'bit of a tiff' because he wanted a television set and she felt that they ought to save for a flat.

Mrs B. linked this with her anger the previous week because all the available money at home had been given to her brother, to which she replied: 'Of course, he didn't have to worry about a flat; he just walked into mother's home and settled down. He didn't even have to buy furniture, and his wife can have as many babies as she likes because there's always mother to look after them.' So Mrs B. returned to the subject of her love for the mother with whom she was also angry, and her jealousy of the brother; and about what that meant now in relation to her caseworker and her husband. Again Mrs

Cooper seemed to accept all Mrs B. said and to feel a good deal easier. After a while, she laughed and said: 'All right, he can have his television set; I think you are on his side.' Then she went on to talk about the television set, planning where they would put it, how they would pay for it, and saying how much she too would enjoy it.

However, there followed quite a long silence, which she broke by saying in a depressed voice: 'I wish my mother were here.' Mrs B. showed Mrs Cooper how angry she was with her at the thought that she was taking sides with the husband, just as her mother had sided with her brother; and how anxious she was about these angry feelings she had expressed, and how she felt she needed her mother's presence to reassure her.

As usual the client accepted this, nodding her head, relaxing and saying 'That's how it is.' As she left, she mentioned that Friday was her husband's birthday. She never knew what he wanted so she would probably give him some money towards the television set. At the doorway she added, 'But whatever the outcome, I'm not going to let this spoil my pleasure'—a remark that greatly puzzled Mrs B.

* * *

Mr Cooper continued from where he had left off: his wife was trying to come even nearer to him, but he had to keep her at a distance, as he did his worker. Mrs A. replied that although he apparently needed to feel he was keeping her off, her own experience of recent interviews was quite different; she did not feel herself being kept at a distance at all. Thereupon Mr Cooper said that his wife had specially hurried home for him that day, which had greatly pleased him, and had made him feel so close to her that he would have liked to have stayed at home with her. She was even 'coming round' about the television set, but that did not matter to him so much any more. He really only wanted a proof of 'her motherly self-sacrifice and devotion'.

This led to the theme of why all love from a woman had to be 'motherly'. How afraid was the client of the sexual, feminine, seductive woman? He by-passed this consideration and complained that a woman made you dependent on her by 'mothering' you, but simultaneously expected you to be a 'real man', a kind of superman made of stone, and would despise and ridicule your weaknesses. If only his wife could love and respect him *with* his weaknesses; if only she could love the whole of him! The worker pointed out to him how difficult he too found it to love the whole of his wife, and how he needed to see only her mothering possibilities. He agreed that he could not let himself experience her as anything but his mother, and added, with much emphasis: '*I must first really have my mother before I can get to the rest of my wife!*'

Is coming closer to each other, being a sexual man and a sexual woman, giving and taking, permissible? These seem to be the questions which raise the couple's anxieties because both experience their own demands, and those of their partner, as so excessive that they must destroy, or be destroyed by the loved one. In these interviews both express their doubts about their mother's and their worker's sanction of their 'new' sexuality, which will mean growing away from both. Is it safe to love each other as husband and wife without mother's blessing and permission? They are striving to free themselves from dependence on the mother, but dread losing her or hurting her by this rejection.

For Mrs Cooper, the situation at the Bureau now rekindles her feelings about her brother's favoured position with mother. Her worker seemed to understand her need to become an adult woman, yet now appears to side with husband (brother). This revives the client's anxious ambivalence which makes her long for her real mother, or, rather, for her phantasy of the entirely 'good' mother who will give her everything that has been denied to her, and thus will make her feel loving and good. But she has now discovered a little of the positive aspect of femininity within herself and 'whatever the outcome' she is not going to let it spoil that pleasure.

Mr Cooper is equally aware of the destructive, dangerous aspect of love and finds it difficult to let his wife—or his worker—'come near him'. He takes permission from his worker to love his wife—but how can he love her without conjuring up the image of mother, the forbidden sexual object, whom he wants to have first. The only way out of this is to become like father, a strong unfeeling superman. Unless—and this is his first expression of hope—his wife could 'accept the whole of him', a hope which he is testing out with his worker.

We have seen that this couple managed successful intercourse on several occasions after a quarrel, or after the wife had been, in the husband's eyes, an aggressive, vindictive, threatening woman—as far removed as possible from being the loving, good mother. And we shall see soon how they can love each other when he is ill and like a helpless child again. But they are not yet free 'to love the whole of each other',

with the needs and demands, the tenderness and aggression which
belong to their own unique adult relationship.

When Mrs Cooper came next time she was rather depressed. She
had told her husband that he could have the television set, and now
he didn't want it. He asked her what Mrs B. had said about having
one; she made him guess, and he said, quite alarmed: 'surely she
didn't take sides?' Mrs B. said that her client had felt that she had
in fact taken sides, just as her mother with the brother, and now
that she had done what she felt was expected of her, her husband
had rejected her offer. She must be very angry with Mrs B., as
angry as she had been when talking of her mother last week. This
was denied, and the client started to talk in a very lively and emphatic
way about her husband, saying he was kind and considerate and did
not really want anything for himself. Mrs B. said they both seemed
to feel so guilty about wanting something for themselves; almost as
if they had to rob each other to get it. The client, much more at ease
now, went on repeating: 'That is it, that feeling guilty.' Mrs B.
continued to talk of their anxiety about having things for themselves,
accepting things from one another, and giving to one another. The
client, still nodding and repeating at intervals: 'That is true, that
feeling of guilt', said after a while, 'I think now I would really enjoy
the television set.'

She said this with so much feeling that Mrs B. linked it with last
week's statement that she 'now almost enjoyed intercourse', adding
that perhaps now she did not mind her husband having something
which she did not have, because she felt she might share it and get
pleasure out of it. Her immediate response was: 'If I had a baby it
would belong to both of us.' Mrs B. felt that in talking about the
television set the client had become aware of the underlying meaning
of shared sexuality, and repeated what she had said earlier, emphasizing that sharing concerned both of them—that both had something
to give, and could safely take from one another. The client, sitting
relaxed in her chair, and making accepting little murmurs, said,
apparently quite unconnectedly: 'I am no longer worried about my
mother', and then, bending forward and looking intently at her
caseworker: 'Can you see any visible change in me?' Mrs B., at
a loss what this meant but aware that something important had
happened to the client, asked smilingly: 'What do you want me to
see?' At first there was no reply, but the silence was a comfortable

one, broken by Mrs Cooper with a sigh of relief, and: 'This has been very helpful to-day.'

At the end of this interview Mrs Cooper said that her husband had decided to have a 'small ear operation' and was going into hospital soon. She hesitated to fix a date which might interfere with necessary arrangements for him and a tentative appointment was made for two weeks later.

* * *

Mr Cooper returned with the news that his wife had been 'more relaxed, more maternal and more accepting'. Sex between them was much improved, and he now felt the trouble to be mostly in *him*. 'As she gets better, I get worse,' he added. If only they could be like children together, and yet remain man and woman! Then came an afterthought: 'If sex were to come right with us I would be jumping the queue, and I haven't got there yet.'

To illustrate this he related a story his wife had told him during the week which had aroused much emotion in him. When she was working in a hospital she used to take a short-cut along a dark lane. On several occasions a man had exhibited himself there at a lighted window. The nurses complained to the police, and his wife was questioned by a policeman as to whether the man at the window had had an erection. Mr Cooper then said how much he wished he had been that man; in a way he felt as if he were! Why couldn't the police have said that to display one's genitals was something 'nice and fine, instead of turning it into something dirty and shameful' as his mother had always done.

Mrs A. said it seemed as if he were looking for reassurance from her that his sexuality was desirable and something 'nice and fine' much as a small boy looked to his mother for approval, but such reassurance would not help him. He must feel for himself that his sexuality is something 'good'. His answer was that: 'Unless women accept and welcome my manhood it feels as if they are taking it away.' If only it weren't for sex he would get on perfectly well with his wife. 'If only I could do without sex!'

Both now express quite openly their fundamental anxiety about sharing, giving and taking, in terms of their sexuality.

Mrs Cooper has been able to make positive moves—she has 'offered' and is beginning to feel the pleasure of becoming a giving and accepting woman. She has been afraid to acknowledge her wishes for 'something for herself'—her husband's love and share of his sexuality, and a baby of her own—for fear of upsetting her relationship with her mother whom she has experienced as forbidding, and who may not tolerate her daughter's 'unfaithfulness'. She feels guilty, both about wanting something for herself and about her anger with the rejecting mother, but the caseworker's acceptance of her wishes as well as her anger seems to have helped her to feel less worried about her mother's disapproval and her own guilt about moving away from her. Her sense of inner change is expressed in the eager question: 'Can you see any visible change in me?'

To Mr Cooper his wife's new femininity is frightening: 'I get worse as she gets better.' It is now he who wishes they could be like children together and do without sex. Just as in the Clarke case the whole situation now seems to be standing on its head. Mr Cooper had sent his wife to the Bureau because of her coldness in sexual intercourse; now it becomes clear how much he—because of his own sexual inhibitions— has needed her to play this part although consciously he was frustrated by it. Through his stories he exhibits himself to his caseworker pleading for her acceptance and reassurance that his masculine sexuality is valued; yet in his remark that he must not 'jump the queue' he reveals his need to continue his infantile introverted sexuality. Mrs A. is aware of this conflict and conveys her belief in his potentialities as a man, no longer dependent on his mother's appraisal of his sexuality, who can test it out in an adult relationship with his wife, and so find reassurance within himself.

As usual Mrs Cooper began the next meeting by telling Mrs B. something that would please her: she brought a number of incidents to show that she had continued to make progress in her marriage and in her life. But now there was a new problem. Each Thursday when the husband came home after seeing Mrs A. he seemed worried, and was cross with his wife. She was puzzled about this: 'There must be something worrying him with Mrs A. which he lets out on me', and when exploring with the worker what she felt this something might be, she said: 'My husband seems now to be so frightened that I might hurt him, almost as if he was afraid that I might attack him physically.' Mrs B. then talked quite openly with her about men's fear that women would not let them have their penis and would take it away from them; and how her husband may always have had this feeling about women, and she may have confirmed it, because of her jealousy of her brother and the resulting envy of men, which had caused such alarming feelings in the sexual relationship. She listened intently, and when Mrs B. asked whether all this sounded a bit strange, she looked surprised and said: 'Oh no, it feels quite natural.'

Then she went on to talk about her growing sense of safety and how that must help her husband to feel safe with her, too. She was very pleased with herself, she felt more energetic, more able to enjoy life, and much less worried and anxious and embarrassed. She described how she had watched television in a friend's house with three men and no other woman present. The film shown was of the birth of a baby. She could never have sat through this a few months ago with all the men there—now it did not bother her at all. It was her husband who got anxious and embarrassed. But afterwards they talked about what having a baby would mean to them both, and she told him how much she would want him to be present during her confinement.

*   *   *

At the next meeting Mr Cooper looked gayer, younger and happier but nevertheless described himself as 'feeling terribly inadequate all week as if all of me is a fraud'. He said he came to be cured of something, but there was nothing in him worth curing. When Mrs A. asked why he was feeling like that, he replied: 'I would so like to reach out to you but stop myself in case you want to throw it all back at me.' Mrs A. said that perhaps it made him feel safer if he kept a barrier between himself and her. Yes, he said, he had constantly been aware of this problem with his first therapist—'the feeling of holding something vital back'. He was always aware of this with his wife too; and with his mother who also did not want his sexuality. His worker certainly did not want his 'messy, dirty, angry bits' because she was 'too good'.

Having said this, he proceeded to tell her a series of 'dirty' jokes to test out her reactions. He then said he would like to invite his wife to enjoy his 'dirty sexuality' with him and then to say she forgave him.

Having done precisely this with Mrs A., he proceeded to tell her that she was the 'ideal person to be married to', but of course she was not for him. Mrs A. then discussed with him the situation at the

Bureau where he accepted a good deal from her without all the anguish, the frustration, the anger which seemed to him so inseparable from any relationship with a woman. He could not 'have' Mrs A. any more than he could 'have' his mother entirely for himself, and perhaps it was just that which made them both feel so desirable, and in a sense so 'safe'.

He became visibly happier, and went off saying: 'At least I can have my wife to myself.'

*　　*　　*

As might be expected, this interview was followed by a good week for Mr Cooper, but he said he had felt tense and unhappy as the next meeting came near, because he had always to 'test' himself with his worker, hoping for 'forgiveness for my dirtiness'.

At this point, feeling some uneasiness about the intensity of the transference, Mrs A. deliberately brought his wife into the conversation. Mr Cooper then told her he had reported some of last week's session to his wife, who had criticized him. This made him 'wild', and yet he knew that as long as he excluded her from his inner life she would be unlikely to want to share intercourse with him.

He then talked of a letter he had received during the week. It seemed to him that the sender had misused his confidence, and he had felt very 'affronted'. 'I feel myself to be someone special, and am humiliated by this kind of thing.' He added that he had come to realize that he must sometimes 'come down from my pedestal, and be prepared to put up with a little embarrassment and humiliation without feeling annihilated by it'. In the interview it became clear that he had already tried this in his sexual relationship, where his need to be the he-man had become much less, and where the couple were allowing themselves a good deal of love play which did not always lead to intercourse. He said he no longer felt in danger of being 'despised' by his wife.

Towards the end of the meeting Mr Cooper asked if he could come on a different evening as their television set was to be delivered next week on his usual day, and he and his wife 'would like a quiet evening looking in together'. When Mrs A. replied that she could not change his appointment, he quickly insisted that in that case he would come as usual as he did not want to miss it. Mrs A. then said he appeared to be looking for permission to share this new pleasure with his wife, and what a good idea this was. She thought he was quite ready to let the occasional interview go. At this he was much relieved, saying he felt he had got a lot further this week, and that he and his wife were 'much more relaxed and closer to one another'.

As he left, he said that he would probably be going into hospital for an ear operation in a few weeks.

Mrs Cooper is aware of the husband's relationship with Mrs A., and his difficulty in returning from this safe intimacy, in which he need not test out his sexuality, is keenly felt by her. She intuitively links this with his fear of being castrated by her—now that she is no longer stiffly withholding herself and he feels threatened by her increased vitality.

It is interesting how this simple inhibited girl (who has never read or heard about 'penis envy' and 'castration anxieties') finds Mrs B.'s comments 'quite natural', and can take them up in her own material without undue anxiety. Does she feel that her husband could be safer with her now that she, watching with him the birth of a baby on television, feels more reconciled to being a woman who has no penis, but can have a baby?

What does the television set—the 'looking in'—mean to these two, who have been so bothered about showing—exhibiting—themselves and so puzzled about their own and their parents' sexuality? It is as if television has become a safe way to watch what seemed forbidden. In the past they could relax together only in the dark cinema. It is as if in 'watching' together they can share some of their phantasies.

Although this prospect is very tempting to Mr Cooper, he is unwilling to give up any of his intimacy with Mrs A., and asks her to make both possible by seeing him on another evening. The worker, aware of his ambivalent wishes, deliberately refuses to be used as mother who stands between him and his wife, and encourages him to share his newly acquired pleasurable possession with his wife. This provokes one of his rare spontaneous positive comments and evident feelings of relief—but also stirs up his feelings of anxiety about being abandoned by her and he mentions for the first time the proposed ear operation which will mean a separation from his caseworker, as well as exposing himself to the handling of women/nurses who have hitherto felt so castrating to him.

Mrs Cooper came looking pretty and cheerful. Life was easy now, she said, because her husband was waiting for his ear operation. He had no pain, but nevertheless she could treat him like a patient and fuss and mother him. There were no conflicts now—'I know what he wants and can give him what he needs.'

When Mrs B. said that she seemed relieved because now her husband clearly needed her as the stronger one, and sexuality had become unimportant, the client began to reveal anxieties. She recalled that her father's bad heart was only discovered, and perhaps brought on, when he went into hospital for a minor operation. She also mentioned for the first time that her husband was blind in one eye as a result of a childhood accident during play, and that he was a little deaf, and had decided on this prophylactic operation to prevent him from becoming as deaf as his father.

Mrs B. commented on her anxiety that both these men seemed to be so vulnerable, but Mrs Cooper reassured her. Now she knew what her husband expected of her, and felt how much he needed her, she could love him so much better, give him *all* he needed (with great emphasis), and was happy 'to make him happy'. She went on to talk with Mrs B. about this new feeling, that being a woman wasn't humiliating after all—far from it, it made one feel almost superior!

*　　*　　*

For Mr Cooper the longer break, however, was not wholly successful. He had coped for one week, but then had felt tense again. Waiting for Mrs A. in the waiting-room he had felt 'embarrassed and ridiculous', and that was how he was feeling about everything. Evidently it seemed to him as if Mrs A. had rejected him by letting him stay away for a week, and this she pointed out to him. He then went on to say how he needed to keep his wife 'in her place'. He never told her about his life outside the home: 'I keep her out, pretend to be remote.' Intercourse always hurt her, and though he pretended to forget about that he really thought, 'she is only getting what she deserves'. 'All women should be hurt so as to get one's own back on them.' He must keep her in her place, 'treat her like a piece of furniture', so as to keep his power over her, and so that she could not do anything to hurt him. Mrs A. asked why he was so un-certain of his own power, and felt it was no match for the woman's? Mr Cooper replied that he wanted his wife to accept him with all his weaknesses and imperfections. That week, he had 'messed up' a fireguard he had been trying to make, and this 'did not worry her one way or the other'. The chaps at work, however, 'really had a good laugh and enjoyed the mess'.

He went on to say that he felt there must come a point in his relationship with his wife when he would make a fool of himself, and she would say: 'Never mind, we all do that'. On being asked how he would be making a fool of himself, he said: 'I don't really know, except by being my most messiest. We can never become one until this has happened between us.' His worker pointed out to him his need to try his 'messiness' out, and he replied: 'Yes, I try it out with you. The more I progress with you, the more I progress in my marriage.' His mother, on the other hand, had responded to his attempt at messiness by 'getting away' from him, 'dangling him on a string', 'playing a game' with his emotions. 'That is what any woman will do if you give her half a chance, and that is why you have to get in first by hurting her!'

When Mr Cooper is a patient, his wife can love him and want to make him happy. There is both triumph and guilt in taking this new role which is so much like her mother's. Can she love him without conflict only as a sick man, or can she feel proud of her womanhood without damaging him and 'give him all he needs' including sexuality? These are the questions which must be faced.

The same questions are reflected in Mr Cooper's meeting with Mrs A. He seems to feel threatened by his wife's mothering and by the sense of being in her power, and swings between wanting 'to keep her in her place', 'to hurt her first', and surrendering to her completely, sharing his 'messiest messiness' with her and being loved for it. This longing to recapture an omnipotent union with the mother, and, at the same time, the terror of being helpless in her hands, is at the core of his problems, and still makes a close loving relationship with his wife impossible for him. At the Bureau he has the experience of a close relationship with Mrs A. in which he is neither omnipotent nor helpless. If he can achieve this here, it may become possible in his marriage too. But as soon as he verbalizes this hope, he also expresses the feeling that his early experience with his mother will make it impossible to risk this as yet in his marriage.

As usual, he ends the interview on a note of despair. From his wife's material it is clear that he shows a great deal of love and co-operation in the marriage, but to his worker he brings his most infantile feelings in a desperate attempt to keep her as a mother who will still love him if he shows himself as a helpless child. The wife does almost the opposite. She needs to be a good girl; brings her achievements first in

order to please 'mother', expressing her anxieties almost guiltily as if
she does not feel entitled to bring them to her worker, and always ends
on a positive note.

A week later Mr Cooper began by saying he had felt happy about
coming, but again began to 'feel tense and indifferent while waiting
outside'. He had seen Mrs A.'s previous client leave and she suggested he got angry on seeing a rival, but was afraid to disturb his
good relationship with her. He readily agreed with this, and then
related how on returning home the night before he had found his wife
'glued to the television set', hardly noticing him, and how resentful
and frustrated this had made him feel. To crown it all his potatoes
had got burnt, but he had concealed his anger and resentment from
her and had thus forced her into feeling guilty and having to apolo-
gize profusely. He agreed with Mrs A. that his irritation had been
so intense as to be quite out of proportion to this minor incident.
She suggested that his wait at the Bureau that day, while she was
seeing another client, was very like the situation at home. He appeared
to have experienced the television set as a rival. This caused him to
associate his feelings with those he recalls having experienced whenever he imagined his parents' intercourse. 'Anger was quite useless
then; it only made matters worse between myself and my mother.'
Mrs A. commented on the way his childhood jealousy of his
parents still came between him and his wife. This he denied, replying
that he could now have intercourse when he felt like it and no longer
as a testing out of his wife's affection. When Mrs A. suggested that
this was another way of leaving his wife's feelings out, he said that
Mrs A. had made him very angry by making him realize that
whatever he did he could not have her sexually. Mrs A. said it felt
as if he could only prove his manhood to his mother and his caseworker by a sexual assault. His reply was: 'My mother has always
completely repudiated my sex by forcing me to withhold it, and it
feels as if I have to go to her in person and convince her physically
beyond reasonable doubt that I am a man and can have intercourse
with her.' When he was about eight, his mother had put him to bed
with his two sisters and a third little girl, wearing only a blouse. 'I
should have liked to have an erection but she made it impossible for
me by her assumption that I had no sex.' Mrs A. said that as he had
felt mother had denied his sexual feelings in the past, perhaps he now
needed to deny these in women.

On leaving, and quite out of the blue, Mr Cooper said he was going into hospital at the beginning of the next week, and was very sorry to have to miss his interviews. He left no opportunity to discuss with Mrs A. his evident anxieties and confused feelings about having to undergo an operation and having to expose himself to powerful male and female figures in the shape of the surgeon and nurses at the hospital.

This period of two months after the Christmas break has been an important one. Both partners attend regularly at the Bureau and the work with them goes on with parallel development and interaction in the four-person relationship which is now firmly established. Both Mr and Mrs Cooper are in their own ways re-experiencing their ambivalent feelings towards their primary love-objects, their mothers. Their phantasies about them still intrude into their marriage and disturb it; both are now striving to overcome this obstacle and to move towards a freer and more realistic relationship. Their feelings, and what they mean in terms of their sexuality, and in the relationship to the two workers who now represent mother-figures, can at this stage be fairly openly discussed with both clients.

Mrs Cooper, whose childhood experiences seem less compellingly vivid than her husband's, is beginning to move away from identification with him. She is now able to tolerate the sexual difference between them, and in spite of her ambivalences and anxieties, she has left the 'choirboy' behind and is trying to be a woman. She is less worried about her love for, and her anger with, her mother, and is finding more positive ways of identifying with her.

Mr Cooper still needs to test out his worker's acceptance of his aggressive dirty sexuality, divorced from feeling, and the sexual relationship with his wife must still be on his own omnipotent terms. The hate and anger which he experienced as a child when he imagined his parents' intercourse, seem to be rekindled by his own sexual feelings—and it is perhaps because of this that he must avoid them. Nevertheless, the decision to have his ear operation shows that he can now accept mothering from his wife. It also indicates his wish not to be as deaf and withdrawn as his father, and so to be a better and more effective husband. The prospect of the operation enables both to express their new attitudes. In mothering her sick husband Mrs Cooper can test her new femininity, and he can risk putting himself in her hands without completely surrendering his potency.

PHASE IV

A fortnight later Mrs Cooper came excitedly bursting into the room to tell Mrs B. what had happened. When her husband went into hospital she could hardly bear to let him go. She had wept on his shoulder, had loved him more than ever and felt forsaken and miserable after he left.

The next day he was sent home again because the surgeon had flu, and it was unbelievably wonderful to have him back so unexpectedly. They were both so happy—it was like a honeymoon. She felt quite exhilarated by the unexpected strength of her own feeling. Having reported this, her one idea was to get away to visit her husband, who was now back in hospital, having had his operation.

Mrs B., with very few comments, was sharing the relief that, at last, she could show feelings of sorrow, of sympathy, of love, which she had not been able to show in the past—and that something very important had happened between her and her husband. She cut the interview short and asked Mrs Cooper to give her best wishes to her husband.

*   *   *

Mrs Cooper missed the next interview; her husband had come home from hospital, and she wanted to look after him. When she came to the Bureau he was back at work, and she was pleased with herself for having coped so well. Talking about the operation, she said that 'he need not have worried so much about going into hospital for he was never quite helpless and could always look after himself'. This seemed important to her, but the feeling behind it, a mixture of concern, relief and ridicule, seemed so complex that Mrs B. did not take up the reference to the couple's shared feelings about what might happen to men in the hands of women nurses and only remarked on their achievements in having coped so well in a difficult time. The client then told Mrs B. with pride that she hardly worried now, was more relaxed, enjoyed life, and was loving and affectionate to her husband, about whom she spoke warmly.

It was their second wedding anniversary today; and she went on to talk about babies, and how they must be *really* wanted if they are to grow into happy children. She quoted a patient in the nursing home as having said: 'Two years is just the right time to start a baby.' Mrs B. commented with real pleasure on her client's evident wish for a baby, and the feeling that she was ready to have one.

After this there was a long silence, which the client broke to speak about the boy-friend who had attacked her. This time she talked about the incident with real concern for him, wondering why he did it. Was he jealous? Or was his pride hurt because her refusal to marry him made him feel let down in front of his friends? Mrs B., who could not see the connection between this and the rest of the interview, simply said that today Mrs Cooper did not seem to feel so much that she had provoked the attack, but was wondering what was going on inside the boy-friend to make him do it. No reply, a long silence, then the time was up. At the door the client said: 'I think I have missed my period for a day or two.'

After the break in interviews, during which she had been devotedly 'mothering' her husband at home, Mrs Cooper comes back pleased and proud about her achievements. She has found that she can love her sick husband and respond to his needs as she had wanted to with her sick father —and in her marriage can, without guilt feelings, realize her unconscious need to be 'better' to the loved sick man than she felt her mother was.

There is a new question, too: Is she going to have a baby? Although she only dares to mention this as she leaves, she hints at it in her choice of theme, and seems to use the session to test her caseworker's attitude and to explore her own feelings about it. It is her second wedding anniversary; her own mother was not at her wedding to give her sanction to become a wife and mother. Now she feels she has found another 'mother' who wants her to enter and to enjoy her marriage and the sexuality that had been fraught with guilt and jealousy. Both the idealized, kind, permissive mother projected on to the caseworker, and the rejecting, punishing rival of her unconscious childhood phantasies —are with her as she wonders whether she can be a mother too, and love her child.

Her thoughts turn to an earlier experience of conflict and jealous anger about her femininity—the incident with her boy-friend. Now that she begins to be more secure in the enjoyment of her wifely role, and may even have a child, she talks of the boy-friend, and of her husband, with a new mixture of concern and superiority. Perhaps it is, after all, her body—a woman's body—which is the important one and may arouse a man's envy while men's fears that women's envy might harm them now seem quite ridiculous.

Later we learn that it was during the unexpected week's grace before the husband's admission to hospital that Mrs Cooper conceived.

After his seven weeks' absence Mr Cooper came to his interview carrying some parcels which could be seen to contain young plants and seedlings, and with his pockets bulging with packets of seeds and little plants.

He seemed friendly and at ease and made only brief mention of his hospital experience. Then he said he had met Mrs B. outside on the landing. This had taken him by surprise, so that he was not sufficiently 'in control', and must have appeared to her like a 'small impotent boy'. When Mrs A. suggested that perhaps he needed to feel like this today, he mentioned a man at work, called Bill, whom he described as 'highly emotional and overbearing'. He said he resented Bill because he forced him into one or other extremes of behaviour—wholly controlling or wholly impotent. Oh, how much he would like to be 'just a happy-go-lucky chap—but this can never be'. For instance, if he sat quietly at home he blamed himself for withdrawing from his wife and shutting her out. Asked whether she resented this, he replied: 'Not at all, it is *my* fear that if I am just myself I will lose her. To be close to her mentally I have to be how she wants me to be or she will go away from me.' Mrs A. said he had been telling her that he could not be himself because he had to be how other people wanted him. He was silent for a few minutes and then said that he would like to alter so that his wife could go out towards him. But if she did, she might suck him dry—she held tremendous power over him.

Mrs A. showed his conflicting wish to get near to his wife which, at the same time, he made impossible by his fear of relaxing his control. When he smiled and nodded, she mentioned the little plants and seedlings, not because she had, at that time, any knowledge of his wife's pregnancy, but because she felt they were very significant. After describing the contents of his parcels and pockets, Mr Cooper said he did not really want Mrs A. to notice them; he intended to plant and to grow his seedlings in secret as he was terrified that his wife would criticize if anything should go wrong with them. She so adored him, as if the sun shone out of him and he dared not disappoint her, or show any enthusiasm about what he might achieve, in case she destroyed everything with 'one negative remark'. He had used the same phrase in earlier interviews when talking about his father. Now Mrs A. reminded him of this, asking why he had to be so secretive about his seeds? Why did he need to conceal his potency from his father, his wife and herself?

*   *   *

A fortnight later Mrs Cooper came straight from the hospital where she had had her pregnancy confirmed. On the way to the Bureau she had telephoned the news to her husband. She came in radiantly, wanting to be congratulated, and also congratulating Mrs B., to whom she brought her news as a present, saying: 'You will be more pleased about this than my mother.' She added triumphantly: 'Now I am an important person, and my husband will have to spoil me.'

After the first exhilaration, she showed some anxiety. First of all the vaginal irritation had returned and she was wondering why. Then there were anxious questions: how burdensome would the pregnancy be; how would she stand the confinement; what sort of a baby would she have?

Mrs B. was very pleased about the pregnancy, hoping that this experience would help Mrs Cooper to feel more positive about her femininity. She reassured her about her anxious doubts, implying that many women felt like that. For this was the last meeting for over two months—the Coopers were going home to the North and Mrs B. on her holiday immediately after their return. She tried, therefore, in this session to help Mrs Cooper to express more positive feelings for her own mother whom she would soon see and with whom she could now share the experience of her pregnancy and talk about babies. But the client would not talk about her mother, and would only look forward to her return to Mrs B. Her parting remark was: 'When I see you again, I'll be three months' gone.'

Mr Cooper is as usual little concerned with outer events. He makes light of the operation, says nothing about the extra week at home with his wife, and makes no mention of his wife's possible pregnancy. Instead he is preoccupied with his inner dilemma of having to be wholly controlling or wholly impotent. The connection with his wife's potential pregnancy which will change their lives, and the threatening knowledge that much of her mothering will soon go to their baby, is expressed in the seedlings, his 'babies', which he brings to his worker in this indirect way as a demonstration of his anxiety and confusion.

*Does he have to grow them in the dark and in secret to protect them
from attack and destruction? Is he doubtful whether his seeds will come
up and whether he is really able to give his wife a baby? Does he need
to rival his wife as a mother in growing babies himself? The safest way
to cope with these conflicting feelings seems to be to hide his potency
and to appear to be the 'impotent little boy', and this is what he is
doing with Mrs A. and Mrs B. and with his wife.*

*Mrs Cooper had arranged her hospital check-up before the meeting
with Mrs B., who is a most important person to her in the new situation.
She comes excited to her as to a 'good mother' who will accept her
pregnancy and share her womanly knowledge about it all. Her real
mother seems to be still representing the 'bad mother' to her, the forbidden rival for her father's love, who might be jealous of her daughter.*

*Mrs Cooper has learned to connect the return of her vaginal irritation
with hidden troubles. In addition to her doubts about her mother's
approval of her pregnancy, and her guilt for having dared to rival her,
the irritation may express the client's unconscious resentment against
the now undeniable fact of her husband's penetration. At the same time
it is an effective means of keeping him out: it is almost as if she is
saying to him: 'I don't want you as a husband any more. Spoil me, be a
good mother to me.' This may be one way to try postponing the now
inevitable demand on her to grow up and to become a mother herself.
Her difficulty in facing this may reflect her inability to integrate her
feelings about the bad, rejecting mother with her picture of the accepting, loving one—a failure which results in withdrawal from husband,
mother and caseworker, who all represent aspects of both.*

Mr Cooper spoke in the next meeting of how he was taking much
more of a 'back seat' as a husband and was releasing his hold on his
wife. He had felt practically no sexual desire for the last six weeks.
His wife was most probably pregnant. She seemed already preoccupied with fears of pain during childbirth and discomfort during
pregnancy. He added this in such a disparaging tone that Mrs A.
interpreted his feeling that he would cope with pregnancy so much
better if he were the woman.

He was unusually relaxed at this meeting and asked whether Mrs A.
had noticed it. She replied that evidently he was feeling easier both
at home and with her, perhaps because there was no need to prove
his manhood now that he knew his wife carried his baby. She did
not verbalize her awareness that the client was identifying with his

wife in the role of the pregnant woman, and could therefore sit back and relax.

Though he was offered an appointment for the following week, he said there was no need to come so soon, and that he would return in three weeks' time.

After the three weeks' interval he arrived early, and immediately said that he had been sitting in a café drinking tea and could have wept—he was feeling like weeping now. This sadness was interpreted as an expression of his need for a 'mother', who after all had not been so easy to give up for three weeks, especially as he knew that there was a long break ahead. His response was to complain of always having to be the strong dependable one, whereas he himself felt 'like a small child who has no shoulder to weep on'. He illustrated these feelings with an experience he had had a few days earlier when he and his wife had been baby-sitting for friends. One of the children started to cry and it was Mr Cooper who had to cope with the situation, helping the baby to be sick and then playing with him on the floor to help him to forget about it. He made it quite clear that he felt himself to be a much better mother than his wife, and Mrs A. accepted both this feeling and also the other side of the picture, namely, that he would prefer to be the baby himself. She wondered why the third possibility—that of becoming the father— did not seem to have occurred to him yet.

*   *   *

Mrs Cooper was looking very well when she came after the long holiday, and surprised and pleased at how well she felt. The vaginal irritation was never mentioned. She recounted with pride that she had not had a moment's sickness, no discomfort at all; was very energetic. She was very pleased with herself, basking in her elation at being 'the expectant mother', and wanting Mrs B. to share her pleasure in all this. She talked little about the holiday, and said, only in answer to Mrs B.'s question, that her mother was pleased about the pregnancy. Her husband was hardly mentioned in this and the next two meetings, which were entirely devoted to the topics of the baby, the preparations for it and the pregnancy, and were cosy little chats with Mrs B. as between two women who had achieved something together.

*   *   *

When Mr Cooper returned after two months, he was once again in a terrible rage with his wife, with Mrs A., with all women. The caseworker might be 'someone to talk to', but in other respects she was 'utterly useless' because she could neither change his wife nor help him to accept her as she was. His wife was more withdrawn than ever and they were drifting apart. She gave him no warmth or affection, or understanding or encouragement, and Mrs A., just like the psychiatrist who had treated him before, did not respect him, but only tried to undermine him. Anyway, she was only 'a bloody amateur'.

Mrs A., somewhat taken aback by the intensity of the client's anger, showed him how, when he was not loved exclusively, as just recently, while she had a holiday with her family and his wife was preoccupied with her pregnancy, he felt utterly rejected and bursting with rage.

He then told her that he had been on his firm's outing the previous week; his wife had not come because of her pregnancy. On the way home he had sat next to a pretty girl from work and they had kissed and cuddled—he responding spontaneously and warmly. He added wryly: 'she seemed to enjoy it'. The next day his wife noticed lipstick marks on his shirt; she commented on them, but showed no other reaction whatever, and this he experienced as a 'terrible insult' to his manhood.

Mrs A. smiled, saying that his wife's indifference to his flirtation made him doubt whether she cared for him, whereas his fury with Mrs A. had clearly shown how much he cared.

He made absolutely no mention of the baby this time.

In discussing these interviews, both caseworkers felt that although the pleasure and pride which Mrs Cooper had shared with Mrs B. had been a valuable experience to this young woman who had in the past so much denied her femininity, it was evident from the husband's material that it was time for her to recognize the impact which the pregnancy was making on their relationship, and to share these experiences with him.

Mrs B. had allowed her to keep him out of the discussions for many weeks, and had thus perhaps seemed to support Mrs Cooper's feeling that her pregnancy was of more concern to her mother (and her caseworker) than to the husband. By excluding her husband the client had, as it were, reaffirmed her loyalty to her mother in spite of this evidence of her marriage and of the sexual relationship with him.

At the next meeting Mrs Cooper again talked about nothing but the pregnancy, but Mrs B. detected a note of depression and flatness and asked what it was about. Was something worrying her? No response: a long silence. Then Mrs B. said perhaps the client did not quite know what to talk about today because in the last interviews she and Mrs B. had only looked at the things that concerned the baby; had never talked about the marriage and the husband, and had more or less pretended that pregnancies and babies had nothing to do with men. Perhaps it was thoughts about the husband which were on her mind today? What did he feel about the baby? Did he, perhaps, feel left out at home?

The client at once became defensive and angry and pretended not to understand. There was nothing for him to feel; 'The baby had not moved yet.' Mrs B. said that all her feeling now seemed to go to the baby, and she could not let the husband come close to her any more. At this Mrs Cooper was furious, saying: 'He has been complaining!' and then started to cry, and with mounting anger and a high-pitched voice, weeping all the time, she shouted: 'It's no fun having a baby! Men should have them, then there wouldn't be any!'

Mrs B. accepted her anger about the husband, and towards herself for spacing interviews and allowing the client to feel that now that the baby was on the way, the marriage no longer mattered; and to behave almost as though they had achieved this baby together and the husband had no part in it. The client became much calmer and then, shamefacedly, brought many instances of how her husband had recently been asking for affection and for her interest in him and his work, and how she had not been prepared to give it. How, in fact, she had been almost displeased at his achievements (he had just been promoted at work) and had resented them, for surely it was she who ought now to be made to feel 'special'. For example, he would telephone her and say he would be late because he had an important job to do, and she would reply, 'I can't possibly stay up and wait for you: I must have my proper rest now.'

In talking about this, Mrs Cooper was torn between feelings of compassion for her husband, guilt about rejecting him, and anger. Mrs B. looked with her at these conflicting feelings, and then suggested that during the last few months both she and the client had pretended that the fact of the pregnancy had solved all conflicts. Now it had become clear that there was a definite job which they needed to do together in sorting out these contradictory feelings and helping Mrs Cooper to bring herself and the baby into better relation with the husband. They jointly decided to meet again weekly. When Mrs Cooper left she was still tearful and confused.

*   *   *

By this time Mr Cooper was also coming weekly again. He told Mrs A. how his wife had come home weeping from seeing Mrs B. and how he had felt like saying to her: 'Don't fret, it doesn't really matter.' He restrained himself, however, and kept aloof, thinking: 'She has made her bed, let her lie on it.' Mrs A. discussed with him his need to punish his wife for withdrawing from him, and he was able to say that he had been quite touched by her anguish, and was now able to share things with her, for instance to tell her more about his work.

After that he could speak about the baby for the first time, saying he would be reliving his own problems through it. He was longing for it to be a boy, although he felt he would be intensely jealous, knowing that his wife would have intimate contact with the baby boy's genitals, and that she would accept the baby's messiness but not his own. Through the baby he would again feel himself a messy little boy whom nobody wanted to have anything to do with. Mrs A. added: 'least of all yourself'—and then talked with him about his conflicting feelings of identification and rivalry with the baby.

A week later he told Mrs A. how one evening he wanted to press his trousers and searched everywhere for a cloth. His wife made no move to get it for him, and he was unable to ask her, yet became more and more annoyed, frustrated and angry. Mrs A. linked this with the previous discussion in which he had so clearly shown his need to be accepted as the omnipotent baby, whose every wish was anticipated—or he would feel himself an unloved dirty little boy.

*   *   *

At the next meeting Mrs Cooper was happier and more relaxed, once again very much like a good girl who had managed to live up to her mother's expectations of her. She felt the good relations with Mrs B. had been restored.

The following week she began the interview by telling Mrs B. what a good housewife she was. She liked to keep her flat spotless, was a good needlewoman, and a conscientious wife who provided for all her husband's material needs. Mrs B. was still wondering why the client had to bring her this self-praise, which was quite out of keeping with her usual behaviour, when she started talking about the baby. She spoke anxiously of the disturbed nights one had to expect, the incessant demands, the dirty nappies. Mrs B. asked why she was so doubtful whether she could respond to the needs and demands of her baby, and of her husband. In reply, Mrs Cooper began to talk about her mother, who, when she came home from work, used to settle down straight away to her domestic chores and never had time to talk to or play with her little daughter. Depressed and unhappy, she asked: 'Will I be the same?' But before Mrs B. could answer, she went on to say that her husband had wanted to know whether the baby would be with her in the hospital. She had no information about this, but had answered without hesitation that the baby would be in another room and that he would not be able to see it at all! Mrs B. asked why she was so uncertain about her capacity to give the baby what it needed that she wanted to keep it away from herself and from her husband? Was she afraid that he would love the baby better than she? Mrs Cooper, almost as furious as on the previous meeting, shouted: 'Oh, he can have it; he can wash the nappies!'

Mrs B. remarked that today she could only see the demands and the messiness of the baby and denied everything which would give her joy and pleasure. It was almost as if she had to anticipate a hard and painful life just like her mother's. Mrs Cooper, now thoughtful and gentle, was wondering why she had to feel like that, and then went on to talk about her mother. It was true that mother had had a very hard life—but nevertheless she was very lucky. Both her children loved her and had turned out well, and had never given her any real trouble. Then she pondered: Why did her husband need such a special lot of love? His mother was not as busy as hers; she was a warm affectionate person, and yet he never seemed to have felt that he got sufficient love from her. So perhaps it wasn't always mother's fault if a child did not get enough—some children seemed to need more than *any* mother could give. Mrs B. said something about the phantasy of the 'ideal' mother, who gave always just what was wanted—but Mrs Cooper was not interested. She went on exploring her own thoughts: her husband's father worshipped him, and her own father worshipped her. Yet these loving fathers seemed quite powerless to give their children what they needed. Was this again the mother's fault? Did the mothers stand between the fathers and the children? Mrs B. here said that she was perhaps also talking about herself and her husband and their baby, wondering whether she had enough love to give to her husband, and whether she would be able to fill her baby's need and love it so much that she could tolerate her husband becoming important to it too, without fear that he might have more to give to the baby than herself, or that the baby might become more important than she was.

*   *   *

At the next meeting Mr Cooper discussed his sexual problems through the medium of the baby, and his wife's handling of its genitals. In this connection he recalled wanting to wet his mother with his urine in order, as he put it, 'to seal the union between us', but refraining because she would have disliked it and thought it dirty. Mrs A.'s understanding of his need to be accepted by her in spite of his dirtyness was implicit in the situation and did not have to be put into words.

With his wife, he had had a much better week, being more himself, and she less withdrawn and 'closer'.

In the following week he said it was something of a surprise to him to find that the disgust and embarrassment and rejection of dirtiness which he had always felt were his wife's and his mother's were really inside himself. About that time they visited friends who had a small baby, and the hostess brought this baby down and changed his nappy. Mr Cooper was overcome by a sense of disgust.

One evening, during the same week, he 'got an unpleasant surprise' when he discovered that not only was his wife still busy cooking instead of having his dinner ready, but, worse than that, she looked terribly untidy. When Mrs A. asked why he should be worried when his wife was not quite perfect for once, he replied 'it is because she is part of me!' Mrs A. wondered why he must experience both the baby when it was dirty and his wife when she was not quite perfect, as bits of himself?

*   *   *

During the next few weeks Mrs Cooper was clearly feeling much better and more secure. In the meetings with Mrs B. she talked with ease about her husband's and her own well-being and their growing contentment. At one period this security was somewhat threatened by the news that her brother's wife had had a baby boy who died after a few days. Mrs Cooper tried to convince herself and Mrs B. that, sorry as she was for her sister-in-law, the baby's death did not really concern her; it was in her sister-in-law's family that things went wrong, but she herself was so well that she was sure her baby would be all right.

When Mrs B. talked with her of her anxiety about whether she could have a healthy baby, the client said that the most difficult thing to bear in pregnancy was the loneliness. The baby was so utterly dependent on her, and nobody could share her responsibility. It really felt as if she and the baby inside her were all alone in the world.

Mrs B. accepted with her this alarming knowledge that she who, until recently, had been feeling so insecure herself must now bear such a burden of responsibility. But why did she have to isolate herself from her husband in her most important feelings—her present fears and her earlier elation? It was, of course, true that she had to carry her baby alone, but the anxieties about it might be eased and the joyful anticipation heightened by sharing them with the husband, just as they might be shared in the interview.

It was only eight weeks to the confinement when she came again. She had stopped work and was enjoying herself at home as 'a lady of leisure'. Although she started the interview in such a cheerful mood, a note of depression soon came into it. What would it feel like to be quite dependent on the husband—materially, physically, emotionally? She had never felt so dependent on anyone since early childhood. Mrs B. linked this fear of being dependent on her husband with the anxiety expressed at the last meeting of having the baby so dependent on her.

After this Mrs Cooper talked of her husband's kindness and understanding. He had urged her to go home for a holiday, had made all the arrangements for her to go next week. But, she added, he did not seem to want to know much about the baby and shuddered with horror when she wanted him to feel its movements. Mrs B. made no comment on these conflicting attitudes to her and the baby, but talked with her about the coming holiday with her mother.

This raised new anxieties—how would the sister-in-law, who had just lost her baby boy, feel about her coming? And mother, who had always had to work until her babies were born? Mother never had a husband she could depend on—no holidays for her! Mrs B. talked with the client about her feeling of guilt at having something that mother, sister-in-law and, perhaps, her husband had not. Mrs Cooper agreed that she felt very guilty, and would feel worse if she should have a boy baby. In fact she and her husband had been talking for many weeks about the baby as 'he' and she was preparing everything in blue, saying that 'Pink looks silly on a boy, but blue is all right for a girl.'

The client seemed reluctant to leave, and for the first time over-stayed her hour. Mrs B. commented on this, asking why she needed her caseworker so much just when she was going home to her real mother? When at last Mrs Cooper got up, she said, 'I am so glad you understand that I really am a bit worried about going home just now.'

* * *

For Mr Cooper the last months of his wife's pregnancy were a period of coming to terms with fatherhood. As if to clear the way for becoming his own kind of father he used the next five sessions to talk about his feelings for his own father and his relationship with him.

He introduced this phase by complaining that Mrs A. was always so patient and tolerant, never losing her temper or telling him to his face that he was 'just a nuisance' or 'just a dirty little boy'. When Mrs A. exclaimed: 'How like your father I am', his face lit up and he said with enthusiasm 'That's it! He would always gloss over any naughti-ness or dirtiness when I was small and pretend that it had not hap-pened. If only he had told me off and taken notice of my misdeeds!' And then, with a sigh, 'If only my wife were not so good!' Mrs A. spoke of his demand on her and on his wife to control him so that he would not carry out his 'dirty' sexual designs.

At the next meeting Mr Cooper began speaking about his manager at work who did not appreciate him. He was soon able to see that he despised the manager and that this applied to his father also, however much he had always tried to suppress these feelings. He brought other examples of father figures whom he despised and who had misused their authority, such as a teacher he knew who had been arrested for an offence against a boy, and a bus driver who nearly collapsed after having barely averted an accident.

He then said he was feeling very uneasy about criticizing his father: as he put it, 'I feel very threatened because my father's hold over me is loosening, and that means that my dirtiness and my bad temper and aggressiveness are coming up more.' However, during the week he had been much closer to his wife and shared his worries with her. Mrs A. suggested that in his marriage he was apparently able now to be more himself—there his father didn't interfere any longer!

When he came next time it was amazing to find him looking years younger, and this was confirmed by his saying how much more carefree he had been after last week's interview, although when he had left the building it was as if the ghost of his father was appearing to him, frowning and telling him how disloyal he was in throwing him off. Mr Cooper then spoke of his guilty feelings towards his father for going his own way, and his fear of 'plunging into the unknown and experiencing life as myself and not as my father'. He was now aware that he had needed to see his father as a strong, powerful, manly, compelling person, while in reality he was a rather weak man, who never lived fully, and whom he, his son, had to prop up by his love and devotion.

Then he told Mrs A. for the first time that he had been the only one of the four children who had left home and come to London. A few days before he was due to leave, he had his first anxiety attack at night, followed by an experience which seemed to him like an 'uncontrollable rage'. In this connection he expressed his resentment against his father for being 'so little of a man, so insipid', crying when he was saying good-bye to him on the station and making it so hard for him to leave him and make his own way in the world. Mrs A. then spoke of Mr Cooper's own impending fatherhood, and his need to become his own kind of father, and this appeared to mean a lot to him for he said: 'I have just had a feeling for the first time that we are two equals discussing something on the same level.' At the end of this session he told Mrs A. of his wife's prospective visit to her people at home, and his fear at being left both by her and by that father 'who had always been inside' like a friend to him.

A week later, Mr Cooper was in a tense and anxious state and straight away attacked Mrs A.: 'You have already stripped me of so much that had made me feel safe. What will you take away from me this time?' His wife was away and he was resenting the feelings of loneliness and longing for her for which he blamed the caseworker. He added: 'Now that I have got rid of my father inside me I have no one to help me to bear this loneliness.' He was really rather frightened by the intensity of his feelings for his wife since she had gone away, and said he felt 'a lost little boy, exposed and helpless'. Suddenly he said: 'If my father were still inside me I would not have to feel these things.'

Mrs A. suggested that, at the prospect of his wife's return, he had to internalize his father once more as a protection against his feelings for his wife. She did not tell him of her awareness that he may have sent his wife away because without the control of his internalized father, he did not dare to be alone with her.

In spite of the client's despair in the interview, it became obvious that he was coping extremely well with the many things which were demanded of him during his wife's absence, and that he could keep his anxieties at bay in his outward life.

The following week Mr Cooper reported a dream. In the dream he received a telegram which was folded, and on its outside were written the words 'with deep regret'. He said he felt these words were there to warn him, and to soften the shock, but when he read the message inside which said that his father had died, he 'had to help the grief' and only then was he able to cry. He added: 'I can feel nothing intensely, neither grief for my father's death, nor love for my wife.' Mrs A. showed him how guilty he felt towards his father. He seemed to feel that he could not love both his wife and his father—and that his love for his wife must kill his father.

He then enlarged on his feelings towards his father and towards his wife. She did not participate in the sexual act, and it was as though he masturbated in front of her and she looked on. This made him feel as if 'father was being dragged along as well, as if I just escape from him for a brief moment and then he gets me back and says, "You should not be doing that".' He repeated that his father had always made him feel that his love for him really should have gone to his mother; and he had felt like a girl or a woman who was mother's rival. His wife, he said, also made him feel as if he were performing a homosexual act with her.

All this was said under great pressure, and with a sense of confusion which was shared by Mrs A. She did not understand clearly why, now that his wife was becoming a mother, Mr Cooper had to use the image of his father as an obstacle in his relationship to his wife, just as earlier he had thus used the image of his mother. Indeed, the interplay of phantasies in which this client is seeing himself and his wife in always changing roles, as father, mother, boy, girl is most confusing and contradicting.

*   *   *

On the day after Mrs Cooper returned to London she fell ill with pneumonia. For two weeks her husband stayed at home to nurse her. When she came to see Mrs B. again it was only four weeks before the expected confinement. She was quite recovered, looking almost beautiful and surprisingly mature, but seemed detached in her attitude to Mrs B.

She spoke with great warmth about her husband, who had nursed her devotedly. He had insisted on doing everything for her himself although the District Nurse, who had called every day to give her injections, had offered to help with the nursing. Mrs Cooper kept on stressing how happy she was to be with her husband again, and how surprised she had been at her longing to get back to him, even while she was staying with her mother. Mrs B. said that the husband seemed to be just as good as a mother, in fact he was perhaps the best of all mothers just now. Mrs Cooper responded to this by speaking with uneasiness of her mother's apparent indifference towards the baby. Of course, it was not her first grandchild, so one could not really expect her to be overenthusiastic. Then, after a depressed silence, came an angry story of mother-in-law, with whom Mrs Cooper had stayed on her journey home. She had made her sleep in an un-aired bed—a thing that her own mother would never have done—and this had probably caused the pneumonia. Mrs B. linked Mrs Cooper's anger with her mother-in-law and the depressed feeling about her own mother; she spoke of the client's anxiety whether mother and mother-in-law really wanted her to be a mother too and would allow her to have a baby of her own. Perhaps it was this fear which had made her ill, and yet she really knew herself that the guilty frightened feelings which came up when she dared to rival her mother did not belong to the present situation, but to the past, when she was a little girl and worried about her feelings for father and mother.

Mrs Cooper seemed to accept all this; she was silent for a long while. Then she recalled how, last week, she had come with her husband to the West End to do some shopping during his interview with Mrs A., and had spent a lot of his money for the baby and for herself. She had felt very guilty, and when she met him again had asked whether he had wanted anything. He had replied, sulkily: 'Yes, a blue tie.' This had sounded funny because he had lots of ties—but she had realized how left out he must feel and that he was angry with her for thinking so much about the baby.

Mrs B. said that Mrs Cooper seemed to feel so guilty towards everybody for thinking so much about her baby, and that was perhaps why everybody felt so left out—adding, 'I, myself, felt left out today!' The client laughed and relaxed, and Mrs B. asked why the husband had so specifically wanted a *blue* tie. Mrs Cooper replied: 'I am sure it will be a boy. My mother wants a boy, my husband wants a boy,' and then, with a grin: 'The majority seems against me, so I'll have to make the best of it.' And in the door, with an affectionate smile towards Mrs B. 'Don't you think I'd better get him his blue tie straight away?'

*   *   *

During his wife's severe illness Mr Cooper acted as her devoted nurse and 'mother', and this was a set-back in his development towards fatherhood. When he came to Mrs A. he was worried because as soon as his wife showed signs of getting better he felt only one need, and this was to extricate himself from her and to get away from her. This seemed again to indicate that while his wife needed to be mothered by him he felt all right; it was more difficult to be the husband.

He then said that before her return it had felt to him as if his father was coming back instead of his wife. Again he associated this feeling with the sexual relationship with his wife which reminded him of the relationship with his father, except that the roles were reversed, he representing his father, his wife representing himself. Mrs A. asked why he made the association with homosexuality when, in fact, his wife was a woman and he was a man, and suggested that he might be afraid to acknowledge that they were different sexes for fear that if he were wholly to give himself to a woman, he would not be able to get away again. At this he said repeatedly: 'That is it; I cannot give myself to her.' He added that he had meant to tell Mrs A. that just as he was going out that night, he felt a 'great rush of tenderness' for his wife. The caseworker replied: 'It was safe to feel it at the point of leaving her.' This brought more material about the sexual act; 'I must make it mechanical and very quick, otherwise my father would take revenge.' He repeatedly stressed the connection between his father and his wife; she, too, wanted inter-course 'mechanical and quick'.

Mrs A. put it to him that the sexual act still remained for him forbidden, sinful, dangerous. Either he felt his wife as his father, then it became a homosexual act; or he made her, in phantasy, his mother, then he committed incest; or else he felt he was masturbating in front of his mother. Perhaps his worst fear was that he might not get out again, and might lose his penis. Is that what he felt would be his father's revenge?

Mr Cooper became sad, saying how desperately he and his wife had missed one another when they were separated, and yet now he had retreated from her once again. He described her illness and how she had surrendered herself to him 'body and soul'. He had found this very frightening and it disgusted him; it was like a 'dirty, sexual assault' on him. He added: 'I did not want that side of her.' Mrs A. repeated that they were both afraid of what they might do to one another if they were to live to the full extent of their feelings. He then said that his wife had invited him to use her bedpan—which he had emptied for her throughout her illness—and he had deliberately spilled some of his urine on the floor and 'forgotten' to wipe it up. Mrs A. said that perhaps he had had to act as the dirty little boy because he was too frightened to be an intimate husband.

The following week he seemed withdrawn and unhappy and said he felt 'heavy and as if in a wilderness' and 'as if thrown on to a scrap heap'. It seemed as if all women were after him and wanted something from him, adding: 'It's my penis they all want and I feel almost cornered.' His wife had come to town with him that evening to do some shopping and he got so frightened at all the women grabbing hats in one of the big stores that he had to leave in a hurry. Only with the greatest difficulty was he eventually able to say that his wife was buying things for her confinement and for the baby, and that he felt 'left out in the cold'. Actually she had offered to buy him something too, but that seemed just like 'giving a toy to a child to keep it quiet'.

After this he experienced the first anxiety attack since coming to the Bureau, and said it was the only time that he had ever been on the point of ringing Mrs A. during the week. It appeared that although his wife realized that he was feeling jealous of the baby, she had been unable to share his agony about it. Worse still, Bill, the chap at work, was ignoring him completely, and however much he

had tried to convince himself that this was of no importance, it had
contributed towards his night terror in which sweat was pouring
from him and he had the sensation of disintegrating completely, as
if his body was falling away from him. When again he repeated: 'I
do not really care about this chap's behaviour', Mrs A. replied with
much emphasis: 'but you do care.' He then described the incident
with Bill in more detail and it became clear that in fact it was he
himself who had been the rejecting one. Mrs A. remarked on his
apparent confusion about who was who, and linked this with the
previous interview in which he told her how in the relationship with
his wife he sometimes felt her to be himself, and himself to be his
father. She showed him again how frightening it had been to him to
reject his father and how he felt all the time that his father would
take his revenge and that he would be castrated as a punishment
either by the women or by father.

*During the last phase of pregnancy both Mr and Mrs Cooper
re-experienced, with great anxiety, their guilt about wanting to rival
the parent of the same sex, and being unfaithful to the parents by
loving their marriage partner and wanting to become parents themselves. Their painful doubts, his whether his father, hers whether her
mother, will really allow adult sexuality and let them become father
and mother in their own right, are expressed in their interviews.*

*It will be remembered that both Mr and Mrs Cooper were youngest
children; both of them seemed to feel that much of the love which was
given to them by the parent of the same sex should have been given
to the other parent. Neither of them were able to contemplate the
possibility that their parents might themselves have had a loving
relationship.*

*Both show their anger with their caseworkers, who have led them
into this dangerous situation in which they feel they have to oppose, and
possibly lose, the parents. At this point the workers themselves, who
have become involved for them with the images of the parents, have to
be kept at a distance.*

*Both clients transfer the most frightening aspects of their feeling
of the parents' hostility to other parent figures; for both experience
these feelings with such strength that they dare not admit them in
relation to their own parent. It is as if this were a battle of life and
death with their elders and either the parent or the child will have to
die. Mr Cooper feels that by loving his wife, and by becoming a father,*

he is killing his own father. Mrs Cooper, who probably went home to her mother with the hope of being able to identify with her, gets so ill that her own and her baby's life are in danger when this unconscious aim of her journey has not been achieved.

The period up to the baby's birth, though characterized by many ups and downs, nevertheless consisted mainly of looking at and working through much of Mr Cooper's ambivalence about his growing manhood and impending fatherhood. He showed a continuing development towards accepting himself in the new role which his promotion at work and his wife's pregnancy were forcing upon him.

In his relationship with Mrs A., too, there was a noticeable change. He no longer came as the worried, negative person that he had been in most interviews in the past, no longer needed to withhold his successes and achievements from Mrs B. There was, at this time, much testing out of his strength with her in the interviews, and then he would go away and try himself out at home and at work.

Interestingly enough, at that time he brought to Mrs A. his feelings and anxieties about fatherhood in terms of his work; he could not get himself to mention the baby. He was still much identified with the phantasy of the angry, vengeful father who needed to be placated with a never-ending show of love and appreciation; any criticism from workmates or from his wife was tantamount to complete rejection. At first he brought almost entirely negative feelings and was mainly aware of, and anxious about, the destructive potentialities in the 'father', the man in charge. There were frequent depressed comments such as: 'If anyone gets close to me, my nasty side comes up and destroys them.' Or: 'I cannot tell my workmates off, but in the end I blow up and go to excesses.' There were also questions such as 'Will I be able to give enough love and affection?'

Then, one day, Mr Cooper cautiously began to describe a table he was making at home. From his description, this table was evidently something of a masterpiece in which he had invested much love and creativeness; his wife had participated in its growth and was taking much delight in it. As he spoke of it he ventured: 'I don't know why I am telling you about this, but I feel it is important.' Mrs A.'s reply: 'Surely this is your child', delighted him, and he explained: 'Yes, that's exactly it. I can be creative too!'

Simultaneously he became aware of his anger with his wife for wanting to monopolize creativeness, for having been the one to grow the baby inside her. A few nights after this he awoke to discover himself hitting his wife on the stomach, 'trying to push them out'. However, she was not unduly upset and they were able to laugh about it. Mr Cooper, though able to cope with his envy of his wife, still felt apprehensive of his own potency and of the revengeful father figure. As he put it: 'Now that I have become aware that I can be constructive and creative too, I feel I have in a sense taken my father's potency away from him.' Mrs A. commented that he could nevertheless now bring his successes to her; perhaps she at least was no longer so dangerous to his potency. Mr Cooper burst out that he still could not bear the workmates' criticism of him, that he still could not take pleasure in his promotion to the most important department of his firm. Mrs A. asked him if he was afraid of being a better man than father. He smiled, saying: 'Even as a child I was always being told that I would go further than anyone in the family, but I never permitted myself success at school, except with my hands.'

A week later he came back in a fury, ready to 'send all women to hell'. He was angry because women now allowed him to be potent, thus exposing him to the full impact of his anxiety about the father's revenge. He had tried feverishly to escape from this by being protective and motherly towards his wife. But he was thwarted in this, because whenever she felt pain or discomfort she made it sound 'awful', yet would not let him help. Perhaps he even felt responsible? Anyway, he said: 'My wife at least gets something for her pain, while I shall go empty-handed.' What did he get out of it all? His wife had bought 'everything under the sun for the baby', whereas she had bought him only a shirt which he needed anyway, and which was the wrong colour!

While Mrs A. talked with him of these feelings of anger and frustration about the seemingly unrewarding roles of the husband and father, Mr Cooper surprised her by unexpectedly saying: 'You have made the baby real for me. I can now feel both the joy and the fear. The joy is because we shall be three, a real little family. The fear is about my being excluded. There will be the two of them, and me trailing along behind.' He then spoke about the baby as a real person, whose arrival would mean that his own needs and demands for love and care would have to be put out of his mind for ever.

'I'll only be the breadwinner!' was how he put it. Mrs A. did not accept this, saying that surely this was a phantasy, this picture of the husband and father who has nothing to give but the daily bread, who needs nothing whatsoever for himself, a kind of money-spinning robot.

The last meeting before the baby's birth was the final preparation for fatherhood and also for a break in the interviews due to the Christmas holiday. Mr Cooper used this session to gain reassurance about his relationship to Mrs A. Was he important to her even though she would not be seeing him for two weeks? Did she feel concern for him in spite of his growing potency? Was he significant even though it was not he who had the baby inside him? Would she respect him even if he were still the little boy sometimes? The clarity with which Mr Cooper could put these questions made Mrs A. feel that he had really answered them for himself and that he was prepared to bear the conflicts and contradictions which they involved.

*   *   *

During the last weeks of her pregnancy Mrs Cooper did not want to risk the journey to the Bureau. She asked Mrs B. whether instead of coming she could telephone her at certain times.

These telephone calls from a call-box, however, became superficial chats about the client's state of health (which remained excellent) and the progress of her preparations. In them she expressed throughout her gratitude to the worker, in an overpolite placating way quite unlike her usual manner. Mrs B. felt that these conversations were unsatisfactory and frustrating, but it was impossible to take up with the client on the telephone her sense of the client's withdrawal, and evident need to express only positive feelings, and to keep any anxieties or hostility to herself. It was this attitude of denial on the part of the client which made Mrs B. very uneasy about the fact that it was impossible to continue the meetings with Mrs Cooper during these important last weeks and thus have no opportunity to try to help her with her still evidently very ambivalent and guilty feelings.

Mrs Cooper was to have her baby in the middle of December. About the time the client was due to go into hospital for her confinement, Mrs B. was going abroad for three weeks. On her return she heard that the baby had been born only on the previous day. It had been sixteen days overdue, and had to be delivered by a Caesarian operation after an induction and three and a half days of unsuccessful labour.

It may be remembered how very doubtful Mrs Cooper was about herself as a woman and a mother—and how her unconscious fears that her own mother might not let her have a baby seemed to find expression in the serious illness after her last visit home. This visit and the illness had made the contact with her caseworker only intermittent during the last phase of her pregnancy. But, as Mrs B. came to realize, she too had become to Mrs Cooper a 'bad' mother from whom it was safer to stay away. That Mrs B. actually went abroad at this time may have confirmed the client's unconscious fear that her hostility and disloyalty were separating her from the 'mother' who meant so much to her.

When, later on, it became clear how much the client was aware of her difficulty in letting her baby come into the world, Mrs B. could not help wondering what might have happened if she had been available during the time of waiting, or if regular meetings with her client had been possible before she went away. Could she have helped Mrs Cooper with the fears and anxieties which perhaps made it so difficult for her to part with the baby?

PHASE V

The last phase of the work with Mr Cooper began with the birth of his son, and ended when both he and Mrs A. felt he had become sufficiently free of his infantile relationship patterns to be relatively secure in his roles as husband, father and wage-earner.

In this process the baby played a very significant part. Initially Mr Cooper used him as a means of bringing into the interviews with Mrs A. his own demands for love and also his fears of destroying the loved one with them. Whereas he experienced his baby's needs as legitimate, he constantly worried about how much he, as an adult man, was entitled to ask for. Things were, in fact, quite difficult for him when his wife returned home after her confinement, as she leaned on him a good deal, needing both moral support and help with the chores. These new and additional demands made him once more fall back on his old pattern. He was longing to escape this new burden of responsibilities by his customary withdrawal; instead he found himself taking over complete control from his wife at home. He was running everything and feeling the strain.

In his interviews at this stage, he readily accepted his resentment about 'being taken so much for granted', about having to give such a lot and, being unable to ask for anything, being given nothing. Soon, however, he was able to give up having to be so effective at home, and made it possible for his wife to take over more and more, with evident success. He began trying himself out by asking for things for himself, particularly at work and from Mrs A. 'I should like to ask you for something, nothing specific' was how he put it; his own demands were being experienced by him as less destructive. It was beginning to feel a little safer for him to be more of the baby himself, and, at the same time, his baby son's demands began to lose their terrifying aspect.

*   *   *

Soon after Mrs Cooper's return from hospital, Mrs B. decided to visit her. She was still very shaky after her difficult confinement, and extremely disappointed and ashamed that she had 'failed' to have her baby in the natural way. At first she could talk about nothing else. 'He didn't seem to want to come. Even when I was cut all open, the doctors had to heave him out, pull ever so hard. At least they didn't put me out, so that I could really feel he was coming out of me.' She went on to describe the waiting period, and the three days in hospital during which she got more and more scared, and expressed great anger with a number of women whom she blamed for having contributed to her 'failure'—neighbours who had frightened her with rumours, the 'brutal' midwife who broke her water, an unsympathetic nurse.

Mrs B. said how much the client must have missed her mother, or herself, during that time, and how she wished she could have been near. Then she admired the exceptionally beautiful baby, Peter. Mrs Cooper shared in this admiration and produced photographs of her mother with her brother as a baby to see the likeness. She spoke lovingly about the mother. It seemed that now that her baby was safely born she no longer felt any fear of her mother and was able to see her again as a good, much loved person. Then putting the baby into Mrs B.'s arms, she got herself ready to feed him, clearly pleased to demonstrate this achievement. She said that she had not thought she would be able to feed him, and was surprised that it was easy from the start and that she really enjoyed it. 'When I am feeding him I am at least sure that he gets what he wants.' Otherwise she was still very uncertain how to handle the baby, and anxious and worried about this and about her own weepiness when she 'ought to be so happy'. She also worried because the doctors said that she must not have another baby for at least two years—and her priest, whom she had asked how to avoid this, had offered no advice. At Mrs B.'s confident suggestion that the couple would work out their own way to cope with the situation, she relaxed and spoke with warmth about her husband, his great helpfulness and consideration. She told proudly of his recent promotion at work just a day before the baby was born, 'so we both were important'; she showed the table he had made and praised his ingenious contributions to the home. In fact, Mrs B. was struck by this couple's intelligence, co-operation and constructiveness, which was evident in the way in which they had made two odd rooms into a very comfortable home. Her surprise at this was an indication of how the Coopers had used the Bureau for help with the dependent and immature aspects of their personalities, and had kept their real achievements to themselves. During this visit, too, Mrs B. was very aware of Mrs Cooper's need to stress her failures before she could allow herself to bring anything good. Did she want to ward off attack and criticism, or avoid 'mother's' jealousy?

*   *   *

Mr Cooper was by now enjoying his baby, getting a sense of sharing him, taking him out in the pram because he wanted to and because his wife seemed pleased. Mrs A. recognized the significance of this new relationship with the baby boy for Mr Cooper. That he was able to accept him and to share his wife with him indicated his readiness to give up an omnipotent, all-exclusive relationship. At the Bureau, too, he felt for the first time that he was no longer so 'special' but had something in common with the other clients. 'I am one of the masses who have problems' was how he put it,. and he actually talked to other clients while waiting for Mrs A. He and his wife, he said, felt more 'like two children together', he no longer needing to be so all-knowing and controlling, and they were finding it 'quite fun to discover that often neither of us really knows the answer'. His wife, too, had less need to be so competent, and as they relaxed and shared their worries more the baby responded by being more contented.

One day Mr Cooper spontaneously remarked that he had come to realize how his 'efficiency' and his selflessness had been keeping his wife 'out'. He began to ask her to get some personal things for himself when she went out shopping. Mrs A. too did not have to be so perfect and was allowed to overlook or forget things sometimes.

As might be expected, there was another side to all this. Both Mr Cooper and Mrs A. were becoming increasingly aware that the time for termination was drawing nearer and that for both of them the process of giving up their relationship would not be an easy one. Termination is a kind of 'weaning', not only for the client but also for the caseworker, who must face her own ambivalent feelings about giving up a client at the same time as she has to help him to work through his ambivalence in the interviews. Mr Cooper now expressed his conflicting feelings about continuing to see Mrs A. in many ways. Being aware of, and uneasy about, his dependence on Mrs A., he one day spoke of an impulse 'to get free by walking out on you', only desisting because 'I thought it would please rather than hurt you'. Yet, in spite of obvious signs of growing revolt against his involvement with the caseworker he was very angry with her for making it possible for him to give her up. 'I really came to muck you up', Mr Cooper said once. And, another time, if Mrs A. was prepared to 'push him out', to let him go, she must care for him very little. This was so painful for him that he asked on three occasions for 'an extra long session of at least two hours'—apparently a last major attempt to resist the inevitable process of separation from Mrs A.—from the 'mother'.

From this point onwards, however, Mr Cooper began coming late to every interview, sometimes hiding his head in his hands and pretending not to notice Mrs A. as she came to collect him. Although he acted like an unwanted child, he also showed in innumerable ways his new and irresistible urge to grow up, to grow away from mother and to enjoy things on his own. This breaking away from the women, however, made him feel extremely guilty. In pursuing his own manly interests he still unconsciously felt himself to be rebelling against the mother, to be spurning her love, rejecting her, and this was frightening to him. It had felt so much safer to make the woman into the one who had rejected him. He felt guilty, for instance, when one morning he had gone off on his own instead of on the customary shopping expedition with his wife. Asked by Mrs B. why this felt so bad to him, he replied: 'It is because I want to enjoy things by myself!'

But Mr Cooper's attempts to enjoy things by himself, thus depriving a woman, were not altogether successful. This became even clearer when he began to talk about his sexual relationship. At this time he complained to Mrs A. about heat and throbbing in his feet and in his head, and it seemed that he displaced his sexual sensations to parts of his body where he could withhold them from his wife and yet this gave him no pleasure either. He made much of having only himself to fall back on, 'only my cigarettes to console myself with'. Eventually it became obvious to Mrs A. that he was asking her sanction for masturbation, permission to get satisfaction for himself as best he could, without women. As he put it: 'To get satisfaction from a woman is like forcing a camel through the eye of a needle!' When he again asked Mrs A. for a 'very long session', she pointed out to him that he seemed to be inviting her refusal in order to justify to himself his withdrawal from her and his attempts to enjoy his manly pursuits on his own.

Every subsequent interview began with Mr Cooper bringing something about his unwillingness or resistance to coming, and yet when this, as well as the feeling that he was not getting enough from Mrs A., was taken up with him, he would still get extremely anxious. Tense and often white as a sheet, Mr Cooper was suffering a good deal at this time, and he conveyed his feelings of helplessness to Mrs A. If her support were to be withdrawn, he would be exposed to all kinds of frightening demands. It was as if the knowledge that he must lose Mrs A. brought him up against his old conflict. He had to experience women as ungiving and rejecting—or allowing him what he wanted only in order to exploit him. Now that his wife was wholly dependent on him, he was overwhelmed by what he felt to be her 'extravagance', and by her assumption that he would be able to provide everything. On the other hand he talked of his 'unreasonable' anger even when his wife was not demanding but was letting him have his way. When she agreed to his buying an expensive camera, he felt as if she did not really want him to enjoy it but only to take snaps of the baby. When she was more responsive sexually he got so angry that he felt like hitting her. But if he were to abandon his sexuality and simply ask to be mothered by her, then he would feel 'like a dog nosing its way in while another dog (his baby) was being petted'.

*   *   *

When the baby was seven weeks old, Mrs B. again visited Mrs Cooper at home. Although she looked very much better, and this time took Mrs B. straight to admire the flourishing baby—once again she had a failure to confess first. She had weaned Peter because she had continued to lose blood since the operation and felt tired and weakened. The very day she gave up feeding, the loss of blood stopped, and now she felt she need not have done this. Peter seemed to miss it, and since he had been weaned, he sometimes wakened as if in a panic. He did this, just when she was telling Mrs B. about it—and Mrs Cooper picked him up within a split second, and hugging him to her, whispered: 'I am here, I am here!' Her reaction showed her anxiety but also the tremendous satisfaction that he needed her so much. When Mrs B. remarked on her pleasure at being so much wanted, she said that her husband sometimes teased her over her doubts before the baby was born about whether she could love him enough.

Peter had gone to sleep again, and Mrs Cooper wondered what it must have been like when she was a baby and her mother wasn't there to comfort her. Then she talked about her husband. He, too, could not really have felt secure with his mother—otherwise he would not still need Mrs A. so much. Or was there perhaps some need in him that no mother could fill? Would she herself be able to give him what he needed? Mrs B. felt that through Peter the client was trying to re-experience her own and her husband's babyhood, as well as her new motherhood.

Talking about her husband's needs, Mrs Cooper broached the problem of sexual intercourse; she said that although there were ways to get round the prohibitions which the Church imposed, her husband did not want to take any risks, saying her health came first. Was it possible to be close and happy together without a sexual relationship? She clearly asked for Mrs B.'s reassurance that even without sexual intercourse she and her husband could enjoy each other. When she felt that this had been given, she spoke most warmly about him and their happiness together. They now had quite a circle of friends, there were many things to enjoy. Soon it would be their third wedding anniversary—they had achieved much during the year! And now the spring was coming—they were looking forward to taking Peter out—'He will teach me to enjoy the sunshine.' With evident pleasure she said that her husband was seeing Mrs A. tonight, and when he came home the talks with Mrs B. would still be fresh in her own mind, and they would exchange it all. Mrs B. felt 'it all' meant chiefly her sense of relief at being 'allowed' to be happy with her husband without sexuality. When she left, Mrs Cooper said that she could now try to make the journey to the Bureau, if Mrs B. still wanted to see her. It might be a good thing for her to make sure that Peter could sometimes do without her. The client was evidently feeling her way towards doing without Mrs B.

*   *   *

Though Mr Cooper was continuing to bring into the interviews his terror of his greed, of his anger, and of destructive women, what he told of his life at home showed that there was more freedom and feeling in his relationships, particularly with the baby. At times he was 'consumed with love for him!' He was also now able to pursue his hobbies without experiencing this as quite so depriving and damaging to his wife. In his new and more responsible job at work he was encountering no difficulties and was very easily holding his own.

But whenever he talked about sexuality, Mrs A. found herself rather reluctantly faced with the realization that at their present stage of development adult genital sexuality was likely to remain a problem for this couple at least for some time. Mr Cooper himself made this clear when he said: 'Whenever I talk of sex, I feel as if I am in a long, dark tunnel, crouching and afraid.' Obviously sexual fulfilment still seemed frightening and unattainable.

We may ask ourselves how much caseworkers concerned with marital problems make their clients feel that the expected aim of successful therapy is the achievement of 'sexual normality' in the marriage? Here the two caseworkers had apparently conveyed something of this in the first phase of work; and not until both clients so clearly asked permission to avoid intercourse did they see how much of this request had been contained in the material of earlier interviews.

Having taken some kind of unverbalized permission from Mrs A. to pursue his own kind of sexuality, Mr Cooper became strikingly more relaxed and happy, and could say: 'I am no longer crouching in the dark tunnel, but have begun to explore it and to discover some light in it.'

Immediately after this interview, he purchased a very expensive camera and used it with skill, yet he felt guilt towards his wife, and towards his parents who were particularly hard up at the time. To Mrs A. he made much of having bought it to enjoy on his own and linked it himself with his newly sanctioned sexuality. 'It feels just like going with women, a new woman,' he said. He brought many associations and comments, saying that the camera also felt like his 'very own baby' or 'like a penis which, if I enjoy it, will separate me from my mother'. Mrs A. suggested that in fact he had gone a good way towards separating from mother and although this was still frightening to him, nevertheless he was discovering new compensations.

Mr Cooper then proposed fortnightly meetings instead of the weekly ones; and soon the intervals between interviews widened even more. He was looking brighter, younger, on top of the world, and brought less and less of his vulnerable dependent self to Mrs A. There were stories of pretty girls taking notice of him in the street. At the same time two anxiety attacks at night in which he felt as if everything, including his own body, was 'crumbling and disintegrating' showed his reluctance to give up a dependent relationship. He likened this experience to that of his baby 'whose whole world crumbles when his bottle is taken away from him for a moment'. When Mrs A. tried to show him that she understood his terror of separation, Mr Cooper responded by drawing her attention to how much 'on top' he felt in spite of the spaced interviews. There were long descriptions of jobs he was doing in the home and of decorating schemes which were being much appreciated by his wife.

A fortnight later he brought Mrs A. his photographs of his wife and baby, and gave her numerous examples of his increased communication with them. 'Things are moving inside me', was how he put it, and he rather timidly asked would Mrs A. still 'want' him when he was well? It was as if he asked, was it possible to be both tender and strong, to get love both as a child and also as a man?

Although both Mrs A. and Mr Cooper were aware that this conflict had not yet been resolved, they both felt that the time had come to stop meeting regularly. They jointly decided to end the interview without making further appointments for Mr Cooper and to leave it to him to ask for future meetings.

He did this at monthly or still longer intervals, bringing into the interviews evidence of his growing strength as well as of his eternal longing to be loved as a child.

*   *   *

During this same period Mrs Cooper had cancelled appointments which she had made with Mrs B.—with many apologies and very good reasons. When at last she came, Peter was almost three months old. She thought he was already getting his first tooth, and the Health Visitor had said that he was quite exceptionally advanced for his age.

Then she did what she had never done before: she asked what Mrs A. thought of her husband. When Mrs B. said this sounded as if she were asking for a report from his teacher, she laughed: 'Far from it, he is so very capable and grown up. I would never have believed he could do so much at home and for Peter.' It seemed as if she were asking Mrs B. whether either of them still needed the Bureau. She spoke about the way they shared Peter—her husband would do everything for him except change the nappies—and when asked whether he disliked this, she replied: 'No, but *I* am afraid he will stick the pin through.' In spite of her growing maturity and independence, she evidently had still to project on to her husband her own fears of injuring the baby boy's genitals.

Then with tremendous feeling and insistence she spoke of her decision not to toilet-train the baby too early: 'Let him have his peace and pleasure and not disturb him, even though that means that he messes me up sometimes.' When later she told of her husband's consideration in not wanting to give her another baby for the time being, and said how easy and affectionate they now were together, she spoke in the same tone of voice of the baby's and the husband's 'peace and pleasure', and Mrs B. felt her relief and satisfaction in this new relationship with husband and baby boy in which she could tolerate and enjoy the 'messiness' of both and find some means of dealing with her envy of masculine sexuality.

The couple were planning to go home to their parents early in the summer and Mrs Cooper was much looking forward to showing Peter off. Nevertheless, she expressed uneasiness about her mother's reception of them, saying disparagingly: 'She will probably cry over him.' And, a bit later, angrily: 'If mother had had more children, I would have known about babies and that would have saved me a lot of trouble.'

When Mrs B. suggested discontinuing interviews after the holiday, Mrs Cooper's reaction showed the same ambivalence as in relation to her mother. She left this interview saying that she would start another pregnancy as soon as possible: 'I have to do that to come back again to the Bureau.' Yet she kept none of the dates which Mrs B. offered her later. Each time she telephoned with affectionate messages and apparently valid reasons for cancelling, always asking for another appointment.

When in the end she came, Peter was six months old. He was doing wonderfully, but his mother's proud accounts were mingled with guilt about her preoccupation with him, and his playing her up, leaving her no time or energy for her husband. She mentioned in particular Peter's screaming whenever her husband wanted to be affectionate. Uneasily talking around this, Mrs Cooper began to wonder whether by disturbing her husband's advances Peter was perhaps expressing some of her own feelings. She then went on to speak anxiously about 'giving the husband his due', 'risking another baby'. Mrs B. discussed with her how she may be feeling Peter's screaming almost as an expression of her own protest against her husband, and then spoke more generally about the way parents and children interact with each other. At this Mrs Cooper began to talk angrily about her mother, and her parents-in-law, all of whom had 'let her down' on her holiday. Mrs B. said that the client seemed to feel that no parent, including herself, had shown her how to be the 'right' sort of mother, the 'right' sort of wife. Inevitably she was left to solve her own problems, and to work things out for herself.

In this and subsequent meetings which took place infrequently and at long intervals, Mrs Cooper continued to talk about her contradictory needs and her ambivalent feelings towards Mrs B. Although she now wanted so much to be independent and to be not only a loving mother to Peter but an affectionate wife to her husband, she found this difficult: 'I really know it all myself,' she said, 'but I still need your help to bring it into the open.' Or: 'I still have to try out with you how things sound which I want to say to my husband.'

The date for final termination has not yet been fixed. It seems that it will not be long now before she can come for the last time.

After two years of casework with the Coopers (the husband had approximately 60 and the wife approximately 45 interviews) both clients have to face with their caseworkers the fact that many of their difficulties remain unsolved.

In this last phase of work, interviews have been spaced at longer and longer intervals. Now that the contact is about to be terminated, the clients bring to their caseworkers their feelings of relief that they are 'grown up' enough to be independent of substitute parent-figures, but also their resentment and grief at being left on their own, and inevitable anxieties about those problems which they will have to face alone.

Both Mr and Mrs Cooper have responded well to the work at the Bureau, and that is reflected in their fuller and more gratifying life. They look almost like different people, infinitely more mature, stronger and happier. Mr Cooper in particular is almost unrecognizable. He has lost the hurt, victimized look and his colourless appearance. He must have put on considerable weight, looks more alive, with a twinkle in his eye, and gives the appearance of being surer of himself, a man of some standing.

Mrs Cooper is no longer the 'good little girl' who was always worried and anxious. She looks very much a mother now, someone to be respected and reckoned with. To the intuitive insight which was so striking in the inhibited girl has now been added a conscious striving towards increased understanding.

To see them and to hear how well they cope at work and at home, and about the well-established circle of friends and their hobbies and domestic achievements, gives the impression that they are now quite 'all right'.

Both have moved towards more adult roles in life and have achieved this in their own individual way and at a different pace. Yet the similarity in their development and in the conflicts that remain for each of them in their marital relationship is most striking. It confirms the caseworkers' first impressions that these two people married each other because they are so much alike; this may be both a help and a hindrance to their future development.

Their caseworkers, who know how much has been left undone in spite of the couple's achievement, have to face their own ambivalent feelings about letting their clients go. They are helped by the knowledge that growth is a continuing process, and that the Coopers may now be sufficiently free within themselves, so that the natural impulses for further growth and development are less impeded.

Problems of Maturation in Marriage. The Four-Person Relationship and the Caseworkers' Group

PART III

Problems of Maturation in Marriage:
The First-Person Relationship and
the Caseworkers Group

Problems of Maturation in Marriage

In the marriages we have described, the partners were people of varied personality and background, and on the surface their lives presented widely differing pictures. Nevertheless, although to the caseworker each client's story as it unfolds seems vivid in its uniqueness, certain recognizable themes recur again and again, as out of the wealth of detail the contours begin to emerge, and behind the words of the interviews familiar themes make themselves heard. Some of these themes have been illustrated in the five cases presented, and we must now attempt to take them up in a more general way and ask what were the common problems which brought these couples to seek help, and what dynamic processes seem to have been taking place both in the development of their marital difficulties and in the moves they made towards more satisfactory adjustment. Marriage is a relationship which presents special opportunities, and specific difficulties, to each individual, as in certain ways it is patterned by the previous relationships which he and his partner have experienced in earlier life. Within the developmental framework outlined in the opening chapter we can now briefly consider some of the inherent sources of marital conflict, and some factors in marital choice, together with the growth of the relationship and the maturation of husband and wife.

Love relations are the natural media for the growth of personality, providing in their intimacy and particularity the to-and-fro of unity and separation, likeness and difference, through which each human being feels his identity established and supported.

We have described in Part I how, first through the psycho-physical relationship with his mother, and then in his dependence on the close day-to-day contacts in the family circle, the growing child's awareness of himself and others develops, and his immature perceptions and phantasies are modified under the test of repeated experience. In these early years the foundations are laid of belief in the creative possibilities of relationships with others, as he learns that the people he loves and needs are reliable, and that he too has something to give. They will be securely laid in so far as these first relationships not only provide for his physical well-being, and give him repeated satisfactions, but can also withstand the intense and often destructive nature of the feelings which the demands and frustrations inherent in them evoke, in both parent and child.

The child's dependence always involves him in conflict with his parents, and inwardly, in ambivalent and conflicting feelings towards them—just as they too feel both delighted and exasperated by him. The relationship between parent and child can never remain static, and can never be fully satisfying to either for long. The natural reciprocity of instinctual seeking and giving is in all human relations a limited one: civilized parenthood, like civilized marriage, is the fruit of personal maturation. So, although in the infant's first relationship with his mother the instinctual needs of both are to some extent complementary, and in the mother's feeding and tending of her baby both can feel deep gratification, even this primary unity is by no means complete. The long process of becoming a separate person has begun, and the child has to renounce, little by little, his claim on his mother's body, and the measure of control of the parents which babyhood gives him. Frustration of the omnipotent demands of infancy goes hand in hand with the development of new capacities, however, and is a stimulus to growth and emotional response, as the child seeks to relate himself to others, and to gain increasing control of his environment.

The early years bring particularly intense conflicts and anxieties, as the child's smallness and dependence still give him a claim to intimate affection and bodily contact with his parents, but make him subject also to their control, which he feels and resists as he grows active, curious, and aware of 'me' and 'mine'. As his powers of movement, observation, speech and physical control develop, new sources of pleasure, excitement or tensions are discovered day by day in the ordinary activities of play and mealtimes and bedtime and going out, and are associated with 'being good', 'being naughty', with 'having' and 'not having' his loved people. The yearning for complete unity with the loved, needed person, and its frustration, the longing for dependence, and the drive towards the satisfaction of independence and achievement, remain throughout life. Indeed, much in the marriage relationship itself is wrought of the play of these opposite impulses—the regressive search for a 'self-less' primary intimacy, and the drive towards individuation and responsible adulthood.

According to the ways in which feelings are expressed or dealt with in the family, and his parents' handling of him, from the first the child builds up his characteristic patterns of response and behaviour, as his inherited capacities and temperament allow, in his striving to win and keep his parents' love, and to orientate and express himself within the family group. The extent to which he is able to involve himself with people and things around him, and the ways in which he will do so, will depend considerably, as has been said, on the nature of the intense inner relations which have been established from infancy with the phantasy images of the parents as the internalized 'good' or 'bad', gratifying or punishing objects of his primitive perceptions. His feeling about himself as 'good' and loved, or 'bad' and rejected or destructive, vis-à-vis his parents and others, will vary with the balance of the positive and negative elements in these inner relationships.

We have described how the 'oedipal' phase, of awareness of his parents' relationship and of sexual difference, involves the child in the dilemma of rivalry with both father and mother, in a three-person relationship which can be very disturbing for him. The case studies have demonstrated how the unconscious residues of experience of this phase of childhood, with its intense gratifications, frustrations and anxieties, may have a powerful influence on the individual's later attitudes towards adult sexuality, and on his behaviour in his marriage, and feelings towards his own children.

* * *

When adolescence and genital development bring a resurgence of sexual drives which are more consciously experienced, marriage may, however, seem to offer an escape from the frustrations and rivalries of the relations with parents and siblings, with fresh possibilities, both of a new independence, and also of return to the real or phantasied security of the earlier intimate dependency. The adolescent seeks someone to love whom this time he can really have to himself; and a relationship in which he can explore, express and discover himself, and can achieve adult status, and, as an essential part of his growing-up, the sexual satisfactions which so far have been denied him. This search represents a further phase of the long and complex process of weaning and separation from the parents. This time the unconscious incestuous love-aims have to be relinquished, and the deep attachments to parents and siblings are gradually transferred, first fragmentarily in the intense but often transitory relations he forms with friends or older people of either sex, then more wholeheartedly to the one he seeks to make his life partner.

For these reasons the impulses to growth and maturation again involve the individual in conflict, both in outward relations, and in himself. Since the young person, however independent he may be in terms of money or his way of life, is still emotionally bound to his parental family, the apparent or actual withdrawal of his attachments to his parents may be painful, both for them and for him. The expression of his maturing sexuality may be disturbing to them; while in so far as his own experience of his sexuality in childhood, and his perception of his parents' relationship, aroused anxiety or conflict, his own uncertainties about it will be increased. At this time, with the developing strength of instinctual drives, much of the unconscious content of the love relations with the parents becomes dynamically active again. Besides intensifying the tensions at home, it will also be brought into play in the new relationships of adolescence. In the storms and enthusiasms of these years some working out of the conflicts from the earlier phases of attachment to his parents enables the young person to achieve a further measure of emotional independence. His work and social activities help him to find his own place in society and new roles outside the family. Marriage may be his chosen way of attempting to change his role within the family and of expressing his drive towards emotional and sexual maturity.

*   *   *

Most people feel that in getting engaged and married they are taking fateful and irrevocable steps which will bring about profound changes in their life and personality. Outward changes must indeed be made: engagement brings planning and preparations for a home together, and getting to know the other family. New prospects open: the possibilities of life together are different, and richer. Marriage promises an immediate extension of experience; new status and privileges, as well as new responsibilities.

The changes involved affect many areas of activity, and take place at all levels of consciousness, but the outward happenings and the inner adjustments to them do not keep step with one another. The wedding and its rituals, the honeymoon, and the house-warming may help to symbolize for the young couple their separation from the parental homes, the union of their lives, and the assumption of their new roles of husband and wife. But the inner acceptance of these changes comes about through deep and complex readjustments which go on at a much slower rate, and piecemeal, as the relationship between the married pair develops.

In getting married, husband and wife are faced with the task of psychological growth and reorganization on three fronts: vis-à-vis their parents, in themselves, and in relation to the new partner. These adjustments are closely interdependent, and take place within the whole nexus of relationships which has evolved between each and his parental family, and are forming between the couple and their in-laws. The dynamic organization of the personality of each before marriage has been based on the relations, conscious and unconscious, with their parents, and with siblings, relatives and others; and thus in both two- and three-person patterns, with both their own and the opposite sex, and mainly in patterns of dependence or rivalry. In these, a variety of roles has been learnt and played, and a working equilibrium and partial self-sufficiency have generally been achieved.

Courtship and marriage lead not only to the establishment of a new outward way of life, of sharing house-room and possessions and experience, but also to the organization of a new inner psychological economy, this time in a reciprocal relationship with one person only, of the opposite sex and of about equal maturity or immaturity. This will have to replace, for the husband and wife, many of the supportive aspects of their former relationships, and at the same time to allow of the development of new, adult, responsible social and sexual roles. Where adolescent difficulties have been particularly severe, courtship or marriage may be a desperate attempt to deal with the conflicts about dependence or rivalry. The partner may be important as an instrument, rather than in his own right as a person to love; as offering an opponent to the parents, or a way of escape, rather than as a life partner. Many of the very young couples who reach helping agencies seem to have married out of conflicts with their parents rather than from any real feeling for each other. In such cases, although during the courtship the couple often embark somewhat compulsively on a sexual relationship in which they feel themselves suited, once they are married the deep anxieties concerning the parental figures still have to be reckoned with, and they often find themselves unable to enjoy their relationship any longer. Either may be resentful of the other's dependence, or anxious about his indifference, and both equally furious at being 'landed for good' with a wife or husband or baby.

The anxieties and ambivalences which commonly arise during engagement may, however, signify the beginning of a more real commitment of the pair to each other. Some conflicts between the demands of the various systems of relationship in which each is already involved and the demands and prospects of the new one will inevitably arise. This period is valuable in so far as it allows for some close testing-out of whether these can be reconciled. There is time for some resolution of the parents' uncertainties: the boy who is 'not quite our daughter's type' may prove to be capable and amusing; the 'rather ordinary little girl' may be a less disturbing daughter-in-law than her more obviously attractive rival. Although there is generally a good deal of illusion in the view the engaged pair have of each other, there is time, too, for some testing of how far their hopes of each other, and of themselves in the relationship, are well founded, and how far the dreams and potentialities that each brings from the past are likely to be realized if they marry. The tensions of this period may stimulate change and growth, each partner using the other to help him free himself a little more from his dependence on his parents, and from some of the rigidities and limitations which have been set by his experience, and by the subjective picture he has of himself and of his home. The discovery of another family culture, and the continuing encounter with another personality with its own network of relationships and its particular needs and expectations, can help each in the development of their new roles as husband and wife, as their own characteristic relationship begins to take shape.

The natural drive towards maturation and the fulfilment of these roles is, however, always offset by the need of each personality to maintain its own equilibrium, and to resist any change which seems to threaten this; and by the persistence and often compelling strength of unconscious systems structured in the past. Thus, while marriage may bring about a move from home and signify independence of the parents, each partner will generally also try to maintain the balance he has established, not only in his present and conscious relations with father and mother but also the inner balance established in the unconscious relations of earlier phantasy, which are still the corner-stones of his personality. So in general the young person will seek a partner who can help him to gratify some of his present needs and his hopes for the future—for companionship, support, sexual satisfaction, social status—but who will also fit in with the relationships of the past. Thus the old patterns can be sufficiently integrated with the new for him to retain as it were his full identity in the marriage. Included in this are needs, expectations and responses based on both his actual and his phantasy-relations, with both the real parents and the phantasy-images; and not only the person he now feels or wishes himself to be but also the forgotten but internalized *dramatis personae* of childhood, and all that he felt he was in relation to them. The nature of the phantasy-images, and the strength of these inner relations, will be, as the case studies have shown, of particular significance in determining the partners' choice of each other, and the varying ways in which the marriage develops.

*   *   *

In general, people feel that they know well enough why they marry: they can approve of, or identify with each other, and feel that together they can work out the kind of life they want. The basis of their choice always includes important unconscious motivations in terms of their past experience, and their drive for integration. It is just these unconscious elements which make for the sense of magic in their love for each other, or their powerlessness to resist the desire for each other, albeit against rational judgment or the doubts of relatives or friends. For the universal biological drives which unite husband and wife have their counterpart in the psychological need of each for the other, for a 'symbiotic' relationship which will be, on the emotional as well as the physical plane, both stabilizing and stimulating, providing a field for experience and a means of growth and integration. In their life together, each will offer the other opportunities for satisfaction and self-development in some directions and, since no two people are made exactly to measure, will also deny or restrict the other in some directions. They will develop their roles as husband and wife, and as parents, according to the mutual psychological system which establishes itself between them. Just how much will be realized and integrated of the potential 'wholeness' and the manifold capacities and tendencies of each personality, and what will remain dormant or be frustrated, can never be altogether predicted. But the choice of a marital partner is never haphazard. In choosing this man rather than that, the girl next door rather than the girl at the office, there seems always, for both partners, an unconscious basis for the hope that this particular person will help them to solve their own unique psychological problems, and some hope of possessing or achieving, in or through the personality of the other, what they have not been able to realize in themselves or in their previous relationships.

At both conscious and unconscious levels they will find correspondences and differences which make possible the transference to the new partner of feelings for the important people of the past. There may be in the partner half-recognized likenesses to a parent or sibling or friend, or similarities of background which make for continuity and easy adjustment; or there may be differences which seem to provide elements that were desired but lacking in previous relationships, or to put right what had gone wrong in them. The decisive factor may even be the absence of any apparent link with past experience, and the promise of 'a fresh start' on a new basis. The natural hope and expectation is that, in marriage, the frustrations of the past can be left behind, while the satisfactions of earlier relationships can be found again, and the familiar situations on which security has depended can be reproduced.

The vital need to incorporate in the new relationship the positive elements of experience and feeling, and to control or exclude the destructive negative elements, may be felt in every area of it. As the couple set up home and work out the management of their shared resources and spend time together, it may be expressed at all levels of the relationship: for instance, in the wife's buying household things 'like mother's' or 'better than we had at home', or getting the husband to make morning tea 'as father always did' (or 'never did'); or in the husband's wanting his wife to be well-informed enough to be interested in the career in which his parents could give him no support. And, more importantly, it will be felt in terms of the relations with the phantasy-images from the past. The partner may unconsciously be chosen to represent some of the 'good' aspects of the parents of either sex, not only as they were in reality but also as they were idealized in phantasy. Each partner will hope also to be able to play his own role as husband or wife, father or mother, after the pattern of these 'good' images, and will be distressed if the partner's response does not support him in this. Thus, in a quite specific way, the genital love-aims which could not be realized in childhood in relation to father and mother can to some extent be fulfilled in marriage, and love for the partner will be enriched by echoes of the deep loves of earlier years.

The interlocking in the marriage of the dynamic elements of past relationships, the transference of expectations and responses, the exchange of projections, and the continual interplay of phantasy between the partners, make for much of its stability or tempestuousness or frustration. In so far as the relationship patterns and phantasy images of the married pair 'fit' in positive ways, so that each can accept from the other, and embody for him, the 'good' or desired roles, positive and mutually gratifying bonds will be established between them. Provided that these roles can express real qualities of the partners, and are not based on idealization or demands which cannot be maintained, each can find in them reassurance of the partner's goodness and his own love. This will act as a powerful counter-balance to outweigh the anxieties and disappointments they must also experience in the relationship.

The very attempt to preserve the needed good in past relationships, to protect the object of love from greed or hate or jealousy, or the personality from pain or disruption, may, however, in marriage perhaps even more than in other relations, create the conflicts which sabotage it. Where much frustration and anxiety was experienced in the original love relations, and could only be dealt with by 'splitting', and repression or projection of the destructive hate, or the denial of the painful feelings, later relationships may be possible for the individual only on the same terms. We have seen in the case of the Webbs and the Prices how, although a precarious balance in a two-person relationship may be established where the mutual projection is complementary, it remains inherently conflictful, and a more mature integration may be very difficult for the partners to achieve. Even a relatively well integrated person may remain under a compulsion to re-create and live out, in later relationships, situations which mirror the unconscious, negative aspects of his childhood experience or phantasy, as if in a continuing effort to achieve or maintain control of the destructive elements in them.

We have seen evidence in all the cases studied of how, under stress of childhood conflicts, threatening feelings—such as hate for a loved but frustrating parent, or guilt-laden sexual impulses—were thrust out of consciousness or remained embodied in the child's unconscious phantasy, as the defensive resources of personality were organized to achieve some adaptation to the situation at home. It seemed that later for each pair, when they met, these defences were mutually supportive, and their phantasy worlds were sufficiently complementary for each partner to be able to offer the other a relationship in which this particular adaptation was viable. This at first made the marriage seem safe and even promising, as the balance between conscious and unconscious, positive and negative, elements in the personality, on which its stability and cohesion depend, could be maintained.

Initially, both Mr and Mrs Clarke felt their choice to be a hopeful one. They sought in their partners some positive resemblances to the people loved at home, and had good grounds for expecting that in the relations with the partner they could avoid the painful ambivalence of the feelings they had had for their parents. Mr Clarke saw his wife as a woman who was able and intelligent like his mother, but was less dominating and more capable of tenderness. Mrs Clarke, in turn, could see in him the brilliance of her father, but felt him to be potentially more effectual and reliable than either father or brothers. Nevertheless, their unconscious negatively charged phantasies about their own destructiveness in the relationships at home were also expressed in their choice, and in their attitudes to, and expectations from, each other. Each had chosen a partner who could also take, or be placed in, a role which evoked familiar anxieties, and they were thus both thrown back on a defensive pattern of behaviour, and could neither allow themselves, nor help the other, to develop a more positive reciprocity. Mr Clarke tried to escape from his mother's dominance and her threatening love, but could only deal with his ambivalence and his anxieties about his aggressive masculinity by putting his wife in the mother's place as the dominant one and maintaining his defence of resentful ineffectiveness. Mrs Clarke accepted the accustomed role of the capable, responsible supporter which was offered her, and could thus continue her denial of her own dependence and her reparative mothering of the ineffective male, at the price of continued anxiety and considerable frustration.

Mr and Mrs Cooper's marriage showed a similar interplay of needs, defences and phantasies. Each offered the other the positive and reparative role of the 'good' father and mother of their idealized phantasy—he was 'always kind', gentle and reliable; she dutiful and housewifely—in an 'unconscious agreement' to keep out of awareness, and out of the relationship, those feelings of passionate rivalry and of dependence which they felt to be so dangerous, and to control the sexuality which held for them a burden of anxiety and guilt. At the same time each had also perpetuated in their marriage the negative aspects of the earlier relationships—Mr Cooper's hate of the needed woman who rejected and controlled his sexuality, and Mrs Cooper's fear of femininity and her destructive jealousy of the male—and was held in the 'straitjacket' of an inhibited response structured by the anxieties of these unconscious dilemmas.

This rigidity of behaviour is, indeed, a measure of the anxiety which is contained in the unconscious phantasies; and such marital 'collusions', where the inflexibilities of the one partner are needed by the other for the maintenance of an equally restricting defensive organization of his own, can result in the most intractable and painful situations. Often there exists also a foundation of real affinity and goodwill which only makes the playing-out of the negative phantasy all the more distressing and baffling.

Such re-enactment may, nevertheless, sometimes be a useful one which can help the individual to come closer to the marital partner, and also, at unconscious levels, to get into better relationship with the frustrating or dangerous aspects of the love-object of his inner world. As has been said, there is room in the marriage for a good deal of testing out of phantasies, especially those concerning the aggressive and sexual components in intimate relationships. So if a woman, for instance, has grown up to feel that she can be loved only on condition that she is 'clean' or 'good', she may be anxious about any expression of her 'dirty' impulses or 'bad temper'; but if her husband is more at ease with his body and with his ambivalence he will perhaps be able to help her towards a freer and better balanced relationship. This requires a degree of flexibility on both sides, however, and the toleration of some anxiety and frustration, such as were not possible in the marriages described, where neither partner dared put their phantasies to the test.

Inevitably, marriages based on such 'collusions', which frustrate the drive to mature, and in which conscious and unconscious needs may be at variance, leave the partners anxious and disastisfied. The primitive phantasy elements remain unmodified and dynamically active, an ever-present threat to the stability of the personality and the relationship, and often manifest themselves in physical symptoms, disturbances in the children of the marriage, or in family crises at times when change and readjustment are necessary.

It is beyond the scope of these pages to consider the many variants of neurotic marital and family interaction with which caseworkers are familiar, or to follow the marital relationship further in its cycle and trace the development and change in its dynamic organization as children are born and grow up, parents die, and the partners readjust in middle and later life. We can concern ourselves here only with some of the central difficulties which beset our clients in becoming husbands and wives.

* * *

It seems that many of those who come to the Bureau, having taken the step of getting married, experience a recoil, and, like the Clarkes and the Coopers, cannot go further with the differentiation and development of their adult masculinity and femininity, although they consciously wish it. It will be remembered that it was in their sexual relationship that these two couples were brought up against deep antagonisms and anxieties which they could only deal with by withdrawing all feeling and inhibiting their response.

The Robinsons came later in their marriage, but they were similarly held in a restricted response to each other by anxiety and conflict about sexuality. Although each needed the limitation the other put upon the relationship—Mrs Robinson perhaps could not have trusted herself to a more assertive man, nor Mr Robinson have married a more dependent and feminine girl—each at the same time resented it, and all their activities and pleasures were spoiled by fears lest 'giving' might mean 'giving in' or 'giving up'.

The difference between men and women, their reactions, their roles and what they do to each other, are the burden of half the complaints and jokes and intimate conversations of the human race—but it is only from the standpoint of a secure sexual identification that we can say, 'Vive la différence!' The complaints and jokes also express the eternal anxieties, jealousies and uncertainties about adult genital functioning, and sexual adequacy or inadequacy. Underlying all marital problems are the unconscious anxieties of husband and wife about the implications of adult sexuality, and what it may cost them, or do to the partner, if they differentiate and develop their reciprocal roles. These anxieties, and the resulting sense of uncertainty and confusion about how masculinity and femininity can be safely and satisfactorily expressed in the marriage, reveal themselves in many guises, and by no means always specifically in a 'sexual problem'. They constitute the central themes of counselling work with all clients, from the simplest to the most sophisticated, and may emerge at any age, or at any stage in a marriage. The cases have shown how in spite of their conscious feelings of bafflement and frustration a couple may be unable to help each other, and may cling for a long time to the kind of defensive 'unconscious agreement' we have described, for fear of putting to the test their phantasies about what a more mature role-taking may involve. We have seen from the cases, too, how uneven and how slow a process this testing-out invariably is, and how long it may take for a couple to work through the individual problems which are restricting their relationship with each other.

*   *   *

We have spoken of the all-or-nothing, absolute character of the child's experience and responses; of the untempered nature of his loves and hates, and his inability, as yet, to bear the tensions of inward conflict. When he is beset by the stress of contrary impulses, or opposed perceptions which he cannot reconcile, he can often only deal with them by trying to get rid of the one or the other by pushing it out of awareness or projecting it on something external to himself, and thus minimizing the conflict within himself. In adult life, when a couple cannot reconcile the conflicting or unwelcome masculine or feminine elements in their personalities in marriage, some solution of the problem of sexual differentiation may be sought in the same 'either . . . or . . .', 'yes or no' manner.

So in the course of their interviews at the Bureau husbands or wives will often reveal, directly or indirectly, a quite vivid conception of a man who is 'a hundred per cent masculine' and a woman who is 'utterly feminine'. They feel that this is what a husband or wife should be, and that their own inability to achieve this degree of differentiation is what is making their marriage 'wrong'. These conceptions of masculinity and femininity are invariably somewhat unrealistic, and themselves contain contradictory qualities. They represent perhaps the cultural images of man and woman, the inherited experience of the polarities of masculinity and femininity in all their varied aspects—man as hero, father, the fighter and the sage; woman as both nymph and matriarch—and perhaps owe something too to current ideal social stereotypes. The client will often strive to bring them together in a picture of marriage 'as it ought to be', in which the husband has authority, makes decisions in every sphere and is the initiator, provider, protector—and invulnerable; while the wife is dependent, sexually attractive and yielding, but at the same time a competent housewife and devoted mother.

When a couple find that in their marriage the wife is, for instance, the better organizer and manager of money or that the husband has more patience with the baby, they often feel with deep anxiety that this is not how it should be, and not what they want. Yet these capacities in the other may at first have seemed most desirable— often because they were qualities which each felt uncertain of possessing in adequate measure himself. But when they are married, the wife's good head for figures or the husband's skilful mothering may worry them, and often give rise to intense resentment, as if the expression of the desired attributes by the one makes it impossible for the other to share or express them, or is further proof of his or her own inadequacy as a man or a woman. Either may feel he 'can't compete' in certain spheres, although he ought to be able to; or that he is pushed into playing the wrong role: 'I know I ought not to leave him to cope with them (toddlers) such a lot, but he makes me feel I'm doing everything wrong'; or: 'The mortgage arrangements are his job really and I hate having to see to it all.' There is often the underlying feeling that marriage ought to have made them into a 'real' man and a 'real' woman, and disappointment at finding themselves just as uncertain about their masculine and feminine capacities in their marital roles as they were when they were single, or even more so. Often this is seen as the partner's fault; the wife will say, 'If only I could really depend on him I shouldn't have to see to it all', or the husband, 'If only she'd let up a bit I could do more', or 'If only she were (sexually) more responsive I should be all right.' And the hope or phantasy may be secretly cherished of being 'different with the right man (or woman)'. But both the wish for a more 'manly' or 'womanly' partner, and the conviction that this would make everything 'all right', and enable them to become more masculine or more feminine themselves, are illusory. Neither has, in fact, chosen a partner who more closely represents his ideal of masculinity or femininity, although he must certainly have met such people; for each may need thus unconsciously to avoid a situation in which he might be confronted, and have to respond, with the 'proper' masculinity or feminity of his phantasy, which also has its unwelcome or even terrifying aspect, and which he therefore fears, both in himself, and in the partner.

In any case, the task of sexual differentiation and adjustment in marriage is not simply one of becoming 'wholly' masculine or feminine in relation to the opposite sex, as thus envisaged. It also involves the working out of an equilibrium between the masculine and the feminine traits in each of the partners, and the accommodation of these in the relationship in such a way as to afford an adequate degree of satisfactory self-expression for them both. On the one hand husband and wife must accept their different and complementary sexuality, and develop their basically appropriate role in relation to each other; but at the same time each must come to terms with their own and the other's essential bisexuality, so that their 'opposite' tendencies too can be tolerated, and used creatively in the marriage, or in some other sphere of activity which can complement it.

The central and universal aim of marriage is the realization by the spouses of their manhood and womanhood in a psycho-sexual relationship through which a new family can be created and nurtured. But this living out of their biological destiny will not in itself be satisfactory, in our society at least, unless it can be through a relationship which allows also for self-fulfilment in a more individual sense—the expression of the whole personality of each, with its unique quality and range of response, which may include both masculine and feminine traits.

There is a clear, though by no means absolute, physical difference between the sexes, which is biologically determined from the moment of conception. Male and female have their distinctive characteristics, and forms of expression of the sexual drive, and the individual will develop physiologically in a more or less highly differentiated way according to his genetic inheritance. But there seems no such clear psychological differentiation: qualities of mind and feeling, behaviour and responses, are capable of development by either sex, and can develop through relations with, and identifications with, both. Such characteristics, for instance, as reticence or sympathy, or passivity or aggressiveness, though some are more characteristic of one sex than of the other, or may in some cultures be considered to be more appropriate in the one sex than in the other, are in fact common to both in varying degrees. They may be developed or not, and felt as appropriate or acceptable, or not, according to the temperament of the individual, and the family situation and the society in which he grows up.

From his first year the child will strive to find his identity as boy or girl, and to align himself with father or mother, brother or sister. His idea of what man and woman are, and of their roles and ways of behaviour, builds up slowly, first on the basis of his own family pattern—in which perhaps a father does something important but unknown at 'the works', and talks little and never loses his temper, while a mother stays at home, shows her feelings about everything, has babies, and always prepares the meals and arranges the family outings. (Or it may be an 'inverse' pattern in which the father takes the important roles at home.) This will be extended and enriched by his experience of other families, and people he meets and hears about, at all stages of his development. Nevertheless, the individual's conscious and unconscious expectations of himself and his partner as husband or wife will remain patterned to some extent on the roles taken in the family of origin. This will also include the 'opposite' of them which may be felt as more desirable. Thus his parents' relationship is, for the individual, normally the prototype of adult sexual relationships.

The ways in which his perceptions of sexual difference, and of the parents' relationship, become associated for him with his feelings and phantasy; the particular modes of expression of, or defence against, the intensity of his own need or anxiety or jealousy, in the early years when he is trying to orientate himself within the three-person relationship with the parents, will form the basis of his attitude towards his own sexuality and, later on, to his partner's. We have seen in the case studies that the achievement of a positive and appropriate sexual identification, and a flexible adjustment in marriage, may be difficult where the conflict and distortion inherent in these perceptions have remained unmodified by later experience, and where the unconscious childhood phantasies in which they are incorporated have persisted in their compelling power.

The child's understanding of his parents' relationship will at first inevitably be distorted and phantasy-laden, often carrying the projections of the intense needs and responses of his infantile love and hate, and constructed according to the primitive logic of his guesses about intercourse and impregnation and birth and death. For whatever he may or may not ask about, and be told about, he will answer for himself, in terms of his own feelings, his urgent questions about sexual matters, and the parents' roles. The parents' attitudes and behaviour towards each other and towards the children in the family, and changes in the family situation, may as we have seen be interpreted by a child, particularly in critical phases of his development, in terms of his unconscious preoccupation with his own relationship with father and mother, and his own sexuality.

It may, for instance, be evident to the small boy that the mother has breasts and can have babies, and can be loved for her power to cherish and create and 'make things better' at home in a thousand small ways. But the spheres of his father's potency may be less evident. And as we have seen, where the father's role is not very effectively taken, so that the mother is experienced as the dominant partner, it may be difficult indeed for the boy to feel assured of his father's masculinity, and to assume his own. Or it may be equally difficult if the father is felt to be too harsh in his dominance. Similarly the small girl, who has neither breasts nor babies, nor even a penis like her brother, may unconsciously feel that the mother she loves is cruel in denying her these wonderful possessions, and may have difficulty later in identifying herself with her as a woman and a mother. Thus the child's primitive phantasies about the adult genital organs with their mysterious powers will become invested with the intense ambivalence of the oedipal phase of childhood; and may become associated also with the experience and phantasies of the earlier phases of infancy, and the problems of dependence and aggression and control which were then experienced in relation to the parents.

The child's speculation about what goes on in his parents' relationship, and between them in the scenes, companionable or tender or angry, from which he is excluded, will similarly be coloured by his love and need of them and his envy of their relationship. He may project the jealousy and hate this gives rise to, so that the sexual act he instinctively knows about, or may actually see or hear, may seem to him dangerous or destructive. Or he may, if he has, or longs for, a particularly close bond with one or the other, unconsciously feel responsible when they disagree, or if circumstances separate them in any unusual way. Thus there may be much unconscious anxiety or guilt connected with his sexual phantasy and his feelings of love and dependence. In a variety of ways he will try to deal with these conflicting elements. Anxiety about the parent's relationship often brings about a denial of their sexuality, so that the child who has shared his parents' room can assert in later life that 'nothing really went on between them'. This may again carry the unconscious fear that it was he who deprived them of their pleasure, or prevented the arrival of another baby. If there is in reality a severe degree of conflict or hostility between the parents, the anxieties are less likely to be resolved, and his phantasies of their intercourse as cruel to the mother or damaging to the father are less likely to be modified by the reassurance of repeated evidence of the parents' love and loyalty, or by a more realistic understanding of the nature of sexual relationship. Sexuality may thus remain associated for him with anxiety and hostility, and the element of guilt or the primitive sadistic nature of his phantasies may make it extremely difficult for him in later life to fuse his sexual impulse with feelings of love or pleasure. He may need, as the cases have shown, to deny his own sexuality to some degree, or to control it or his partner's very rigorously in his own marriage.

At the same time, the child's sex, and manifestations of sexual interest or feeling, may be very important to his parents, especially if they have experienced considerable conflict about their own, or feel frustrated or deprived in the relationship with the spouse. They may need to deny or to control or even to stimulate the child's sexuality, and their attitude may add to his uncertainties about his sexual identity, and about how 'safe' or how destructive his impulses really are. An intense wish for a child of a particular sex may sometimes indicate conflict or narcissism in the parent which will express itself in strongly ambivalent feeling towards the child, or hostility if the wish is disappointed: for instance, if a woman who longs for a boy to express the masculinity she envies or cannot allow her husband has to welcome a baby girl who confronts her all over again with her own 'castration'; or if she wants a docile little girl-doll to mirror her image of herself and has to deal with a vigorous, demanding male child who may seem an uncontrollable and damaging invader. These attitudes to their own and to the child's sex will communicate themselves to the child, who may find it difficult to identify himself appropriately, for thus he must risk 'becoming' the unwanted child, and perhaps also being like the 'bad' rejecting parent. The girl whose parents wanted a son, or the youngest boy of three whose father had hoped for a daughter, may comply to some extent with the rejection of their own sex; and the girl may react by tomboy behaviour or the boy by a polite passivity, as if in an endeavour to be what they feel is desired.

The child's attitudes to sexual difference and relationships, and to his own sexual identity, will thus be structured largely by his perceptions of their meaning in the family. As he grows, he will inwardly identify himself to some extent with both parents, as he feels they are 'good' or 'bad', and it is important to him to be like them, or different from them. And in relation to both he will try out varying modes of response, according to his need to win their love or to assert himself against them, and to the pressure of their varying and perhaps conflicting demands on him.

In the middle years of childhood and even in adolescence the boy and girl may relate to the parents and each other in a fairly undifferentiated way—the girl, for instance, cycling with her brothers or cleaning the car with father, and the boy helping mother with the washing-up or household shopping. They will also learn to take the role of either parent to some extent in relation to the other: normally, for instance, a boy will be protective and 'look after mother' if the father has to be away from home, or a girl will learn to cook the meal for father if mother is out. In ways like these they will identify themselves with the parent both of their own sex and of the opposite, and feel that they have much of both father and mother in them.

Where family life is impoverished by the disability or actual loss of one or other parent, a child may, however, have little or no opportunity of relating freely to an 'ordinary' mother and father and of experiencing the reality of their own living relationship and differentiation within and outside the home. Or it may be that the particular nature of the parents' relationship makes a positive sexual identification with the parent of their own sex difficult: for the sensitive boy, for instance, who can only act the passive, masochistic 'wife' to his bullying father; or the girl who has to take the place of the father for a widowed or deserted mother.

For many reasons the roles of ordinary, stable, good-and-bad father and mother may be unfamiliar, and the memories and images of the parents may be distorted by phantasy or by the need to deny the disturbing elements in them. Thus the roles of husband and wife, and the expression of masculinity and femininity, will have very different significance for each individual. His ability to take these roles in ways which will be satisfying, and will allow of growth and change, will depend very much on how love, hate and sexuality are connected for him, and on how safe or how destructive he unconsciously feels the sexual elements in his relationships to be. The case studies have illustrated how the achievement of a positive and appropriate sexual identification will depend for each spouse not only on the actual nature of his parents' relationships—as they provided a more or less acceptable pattern for him to follow—but on his own unconscious interpretations of the parents' relationship, and of his own with them; thus on the nature of the parent images he internalized, and the balance of positive or negative feeling associated with them. The Clarkes, Coopers and Robinsons all came from stable families with affection and loyalty between the members, and good standards of care and behaviour, but the imbalance which they felt existed between their parents' masculinity and femininity, their anxiety about whether either was harming the other or causing him/her suffering or frustration, and the denial or 'collusion of silence' about some of the important aspects of the family situation—aggression with the Clarkes, sex with the Coopers, for instance—had given rise to much unconscious anxiety in them concerning the 'goodness' and 'badness' of their own sexuality, and the destructive power of their sexual wishes towards the parents, or jealous envy of them. Similarly, the particular situation vis-à-vis their siblings of the opposite sex had given rise to considerable jealousy, and circumstances had served to substantiate rather than to dispel the unconscious guilt about hostile wishes towards them. (It will be remembered that three of the five wives had brothers who were in some way incapacitated; and that three of the husbands expressed envy towards their sisters, who they felt had gained their parents' love—and the mother's especially—without having to make any effort to 'earn' it.) With the Robinsons, in particular, their confused and distorted impressions of their parents' relationships to each other, and their hopeless endeavours to compete with the sibling of the opposite sex in winning the parents' approval, are clearly reflected in their uncertain conceptions of their own roles as husband and wife and parents, and in their anxieties about their own sexuality. Mrs Robinson even wondered whether she might not 'turn into a man', and Mr Robinson was equally anxious for reassurance about the 'feminine' side of himself. We have seen how the achievement of a more mature adjustment involved some working over and testing-out of these part-real, part-phantasy perceptions of the childhood relationships. In so far as the individual can come to terms with his parents' sexuality, and 'allow' them their unity and relationship, and feel that the loving elements in it outweigh or counterbalance the frustrating or destructive ones, he will be able to express his identifications with them positively in his own marriage. How important it was, for instance, to Mrs Robinson to have evidence that her parents were often happy in the marriage which she had at first to interpret as a martyrdom for the dead mother towards whom she had felt so guilty herself. Mr Clarke, too, acknowledged with relief his mother's deep dependence on the father whom in phantasy he had felt he might all too easily hurt or supplant. Husband and wife need to be able to feel that the parents can allow them their sexual inheritance also, and that they are neither stealing it from the parents nor harming them by assuming the adult roles. These generally unconscious anxieties, residues perhaps of the infantile inability to conceive of 'sharing' or inheriting these roles, were strikingly manifested in the Cooper's marriage. Mrs Cooper was seriously ill during her pregnancy, and felt this was her mother-in-law's doing—perhaps thus displacing both her fear of, and her guilt towards, her own mother. And Mr Cooper dreamed vividly of his father's 'death', and felt that this released him from his bonds of dependence—but it was also the phantasied price of his own adult masculinity and fatherhood.

*   *   *

These universal psychological problems, the natural jealousies between the generations, and tensions between the sexes, are dealt with in many cultures by the maintenance of a social structure in which the accepted characteristics and roles of the sexes are clearly differentiated, and the transitions from one stage of growth to the next are given communal recognition. In the rites, for instance, through which boys and girls are initiated into adulthood in some primitive communities, the guilt or resentment can be collectively dealt with, and status, attitudes and behaviour are prescribed for the young adult by tradition. In our own time 'initiation' is a haphazard and private process which parents, school, Church and place of work deal with as they may. The marriage ceremony remains to give sanction and support to the couple taking their new and acknowledged roles of husband and wife, to link them with the traditional values of the community, and to establish the relationship legally as a permanent one which will thus provide a secure setting for their development and mutual adjustment and for the upbringing of children. But the ceremonies of the wedding cannot give the experience of sufficient sanction if a couple are too heavily burdened with conflict about taking these roles, nor enough security if their anxieties about being able to love, or worthy to be loved, are too deep. The inner problems of sexual identification and rivalry, and of the balance of love and hate in relationships, have to be striven with individually, and together, in each marriage.

Although the cultural fluidity of our own day allows for perhaps a freer and richer development of individuality within the marital relationship than was formerly possible, the greater intimacy and exclusiveness of the small family and the very opportunities it offers for the fusion and sharing of roles may actually tend to intensify these problems, and to make the establishment of a gratifying give-and-take between the partners in some ways more difficult.

In many urban communities there is often little distinction either at work or at home between the roles of husband and wife. Both partners may be earning, perhaps in similar jobs, both sharing the running of the home and the care of the children. In the actual organization of society there may be little to give each any external help in maintaining and developing his or her sexual identification. Once they are married, neither may have much opportunity to continue to engage in activities with his own sex, which can both support the 'appropriate' identification and also provide some satisfaction of the 'opposite'—as for instance sport may both reassure a young man of his masculinity and also satisfy his unconscious need for homosexual involvement; and time at the hairdressers and the baby clinic, or intimate gossip with her neighbours or work-mates, may do the same for a woman.

Many of those who come to the Bureau have withdrawn, perhaps on account of their insecurity in their marriage, and their uncertainty in relation to both their own and the opposite sex, into a degree of social isolation which means that these supports are not available to them outside the home. The marriage has thus to serve as their main defence against the homosexual trends or 'opposite' identifications. This, however, makes them all the more vulnerable to any threat from the partner, and they cannot risk expressing these within it. For instance, the husband may feel a danger in identifying too closely with his wife, and losing his 'proper' role as a man. He may accordingly refuse to participate in anything he considers 'her job'. If this means, for instance, leaving her to cope single-handed with the children and the washing-up while he reads a technical magazine, it will generally be resented, and may provoke retaliation in the form of attack on him, or withdrawal from him—which he in turn may interpret as an attack on, or a rejection of, his masculinity.

So a vicious circle of mutual hostility may be set in motion. Or a wife who wanted a child in the hope of 'proving' herself as good a woman as her sister or neighbours, may then feel too anxious about herself and her own mothering to be able to allow the husband any share in caring for it, interpreting his moves towards a relationship with the baby as 'spoiling' or 'interfering'.

At the same time, each may fear the power of the other sex, and not only avoid any situation which might lead to rivalry in the desired 'appropriate' role, as in the instance above, but also strenuously resist recognizing any dependence on the partner. The anxieties involved in differentiating and developing their masculinity and femininity will be dealt with in a variety of ways which restrict interaction in the relationship. Sometimes it may be by the kind of rigid defensive separation of the 'proper' spheres of interest of husband and wife just described; sometimes by an equally rigid refusal to countenance the expression of their sexual and emotional difference. The wife, for instance, may cling determinedly to her pre-marital insistence on 'equal partnership' and 'fair shares', resisting the husband's efforts to be protective or to dominate in any way. Or the husband may react with resentment and withdrawal to his wife's emotional dependence on him, and with irritation to her impulses to mother him, and succeed in frustrating her equally effectively.

To involve themselves more wholly with the partner, both by a freer sharing and closer identification which can include their 'likeness' and accommodate their bisexuality, and by a fuller acceptance of their 'difference', and different roles, and needs from each other, may seem too much to risk. If they have in phantasy interpreted the parents' relationship as destructive, they may need unconsciously to keep rigid control of the 'bad' sexual organs, both their own and the partner's, or as it were to deny their existence. Or the original repressed envy of parent or sibling may be re-awakened by the proximity of the partner: the husband's penis, or the wife's pregnancy, as was the case with the Coopers, may stimulate anxiety and anger rather than love. Or to separate the roles may sometimes seem to mean only loss, as to Mrs Robinson being 'only a woman' meant 'losing all I value in myself'; or in Mr Cooper's fear of being 'only the father—the breadwinner'—as if to be whole and happy they must keep all of the desired attributes (or both the 'good' parents) inside themselves, without possibility of sharing and expressing them in a differentiated way.

It seems, too, that sometimes each fears the discovery of his strength or his weakness, in exposing not only his own demands but also the partner's; and not only his own incapacity to give what is expected, but the partner's incapacity to satisfy him. The choice of a partner who is not very responsive, and therefore need not be really loved or surrendered to, and can in fact be kept as it were outside the personality, the visible and partially controllable embodiment of the frustrating elements, is often, as we have seen, both an attempt to avoid, as well as a repetition of, the frustrations, the humiliations or the disasters of earlier love relations. 'I've always had to stand on my own feet', 'I'm afraid of what it might lead to', 'Women will just make a fool of you if you let them', 'To love is to lose' express the underlying anxieties about re-entering a closer dependence. Thus, where love and sexuality evoke powerful elements of phantasy, or are associated unconsciously with painful experience, the partners may feel that the only available roles besides these of strictly limited committal are the dangerous extremes of their immature perceptions. To give way further to deeper impulses may seem to entail either a return to the helpless love, or rage, or dirtiness of the frustrated child, or else taking on—or confronting in the person of the partner—the primitive phantasy-aspects of the parent images—perhaps a violent or vengeful 'father', or an irreparably damaged 'mother'.

Where these negative aspects of feeling are not too threatening, most couples after marriage enter a phase of exclusive dependence on each other, as the 'two-person identity' establishes itself between them; and the security and intimacy of the relationship can provide a foundation of gratifying experience. If at this stage each partner can feel on the one hand sufficiently supported in the responsible 'work' of building the home or a career and preparing for a family, and on the other hand can find sufficient reassurance of mutual need and pleasure in the regressive 'play' of love-making, the dependence can be tolerated, and the relationship can develop creatively. Even though some of the satisfactions of this phase may be based on a degree of idealization or denial, its real achievements may offset some disillusion and encourage the partners in their efforts to struggle through the difficulties of readjustment in succeeding phases, and test and discover what they really have to give each other.

As we have seen, however, where there has been quite severe

frustration or insecurity in childhood, a return to a loving relationship can reawaken the buried dependency needs in all their intensity. The very partner who at first seemed self-sufficient and undemanding may be the one to reveal alarming 'weakness', or sexual greed, jealousy, or 'hysterical tempers', as he struggles again with the infantile desire to possess and control the loved person absolutely and *make* him or her give what is sought. We have seen in the cases described how the phantasy of 'oneness' with the loved and all-loving person may be brought to life in marriage; and how with it may come a correspondingly intense experience of disappointment and anger at the realization of the partner's separateness and essential difference, such as was expressed in Mrs Clarke's: 'If I don't love him, I hate him!' and in Mr Webb's outbursts of violence, and Mr Cooper's inward sense of anger with 'all women'.

Such experience, however, of the partner's inability to tolerate the regressive, self-abandoning dependence, or omnipotent control, which are desired, may represent a fresh effort to deal with the unsolved problems of separation, and a 'weaning' from the phantasy ideal which is projected on the partner. The discovery that even this hate does not sever the relationship, and that hurts to the partner may be healed, and damage made good, can be immensely reassuring and diminish anxiety about the destructive strength of the demands of love or impulses of hate. We have seen how some testing-out and enactment between the partners of their hate, as well as their love, can lead to a better integration of the negative elements in their relationships, a clearer perception of the partner, and increased tolerance of the inevitable frustrations and ambivalences of the marriage.

Indeed, just as sexual union depends on the acceptance of sexual difference, so the frustration of the primitive absolute love-aims, except perhaps in the momentary self-abandonment of intercourse, and relinquishment of the ideal phantasy as the object of love are the conditions for the developing unity of an adult interdependence.

The Four-Person Therapeutic Relationship and the Functioning of the Caseworkers' Group

Our aim in writing this book has been twofold: to share what we have come to understand about marriage in the light of our experience with the many couples who have come to us over a period of years and also to show the particular way in which we have tried to use this understanding on their behalf. We are, of course, not the first writers on marriage to base our understanding of the relationship on the psycho-analytic theory of personality development, and this theory also forms the conceptual basis of the clinical work done in a number of social and medical agencies besides our own. What may be unique is the setting within which we work, and this is in itself an indication of the way in which we have both gained our experience and sought to adapt it to the needs of our clients.

In foregoing chapters we have briefly considered those aspects of psycho-analytic theory which are particularly applicable to the study of marriage, that is to say, the ways in which everyone since earliest childhood develops to a greater or lesser degree the capacity to tolerate the tensions necessary to sustained relationship. In the case presentations we have tried to show something of marriage itself as a developing relationship and as an important aspect of the process of maturation in each individual and how, as such, it both demands further growth and provides the setting for it. It remains for us to attempt a more generalized account of our setting and our casework methods, certain aspects of which need more detailed consideration: in particular the four-person therapeutic relationship, the functioning of the caseworkers' group and the role of the psycho-analytic consultant.

From the cases which have been discussed it will already be apparent that the couples who come to us differ widely, particularly in their degree of maturity. Some of them have a relatively low capacity to tolerate frustration and anxiety and easily become panic stricken, living more or less from crisis to crisis. Others, with greater maturity, manage well enough until some inner or outer change occurs creating a disturbance in the relationship which is beyond their capacity to get through alone. We have suggested that while some couples seem never to be aware of being in conflict and others, although aware of difficulties, do not turn to outside agencies, those who do seek help may also be those who are, at some level, aware of the potentialities for growth inherent in conflict.

In some instances the disturbances which seem to threaten the stability of the relationship can, in fact, be related to a point of manifest change and growth within the marriage such as the birth, growing up, or marriage of a child or the death of a parent. But in other cases the words 'disturbance' or 'crisis' seem quite inappropriate. Many marriages have simply settled into a frustrating and repetitive pattern of relationship which leaves the partners feeling depressed and unable to communicate satisfactorily with one another or to find any joy in their life together. But whether the difficulties for which help is sought can be described as critical or chronic, within them may always be discerned, however dimly at first, the groping by each partner towards a more integrated self. Therefore, if casework is to be effective, any situation which the clients bring must in this sense be regarded as purposive. Although a true evaluation of the unconscious striving within the marriage will take time, the caseworker's initial acceptance of this standpoint will in itself be therapeutic. Her conviction can seem to the client, in the midst of his muddled unhappiness, like a steadying hand offering him an opportunity to take stock of his situation afresh.

We have already outlined some of the normal phases of individual development and given an indication of some of the difficulties which may occur if these are obstructed. The symptoms which have developed in a marriage may give some clue as to where obstructions lie and what in the individuals and in the marriage has to be clarified or reconciled before healthy psychological growth can be resumed. The relationships made at the Bureau between the client and the caseworker, and in the four-person relationship between two caseworkers and the marriage partners, provide a framework within which such an assessment can gradually be made and a medium within which growth can continue. These two functions of diagnosis and therapy are never clearly separate. Just as in early growth the child's individual needs and ways of developing may only be understood through the attuned attentive relationship of parents or teachers, which relationships also create the environment within which the child will grow, so the relationships created at the Bureau have the same dual purpose.

It will have become apparent from the cases already studied that we rarely make any attempt to elicit from clients an orderly 'social history', but learn 'what we can from the client's own impression of his present situation and of his life history and from the manner in which these are presented. What we are told is frequently highly coloured and a subjective account of emotional experiences rather than a factual description of events. The extent of distortion gradually emerges through the nature of the client's relationship with us, which may sometimes be used for reliving important relationships from the past which the client may also have reconstellated in the marriage. The value of our intervention therefore largely depends, on the one hand, on our ability to remain aware of how the clients are relating to us as well as with the marriage partners and, on the other, on our ability to communicate with them in a way which is meaningful and dynamic.

In the first interview with Mr Robinson, for instance, we have seen how the caseworker sensed underneath his co-operative attitude her client's unconscious need to destroy; she experienced with him the weight, not only of his despair, but also of his hostility. From this experience she was able to understand something of his difficulties and the problems in the marriage. We have seen how she used this understanding in determining her response to her client. In other words, the caseworker's observations of her own reaction to Mr Robinson gave her some indication of what he was trying to turn her into, which subsequently not only helped her to understand about his inner world and the projections that he would need his wife to carry, but also determined her own approach to the task of helping him to withdraw these projections and to find their meaning in himself.

To achieve this understanding, rational and irrational forces in both client and caseworker were brought creatively into play. It was not a mere ego relationship, not just an explaining on the part of the caseworker or client. It involved much more of the personality of both. It is true that all relationships exist on a more than conscious rational level, but the fact remains that the unconscious components are given more or less attention according to the circumstances and the purpose of the relationship. At the Bureau, where the purpose is to establish a relationship conducive to growth and to enable a redistribution of psychological forces to take place, and where this is the sole aim of the relationship, it is obvious that the irrational component in both client and caseworker needs constant attention; the more so, perhaps, because the work is focussed on adult sexuality and the emotionally charged marriage relationship. Much of what the caseworker must be aware of and deal with in her client is unconscious and highly dynamic and liable to evoke in herself, in response, attitudes and demands of an uncompromising nature of which she must seek to become equally aware. To help this awareness of her own involvement and possible distortion, there is first and foremost the constant exchange of impressions between the two caseworkers in the four-person relationship. These exchanges are quite as important as the interviews themselves.

Mr Robinson's caseworker was able to balance her assessment of her client's basic pattern of relationship with the picture which his wife's caseworker gained from her client. Both clients had experienced the parents of the opposite sex as singularly destructive but exciting figures, and the intensity of fear and longing centred on these images, which each partner brought into the marriage, were seen, felt and discussed by the two caseworkers. The significance of the deaths of the parents of the same sex became high-lighted in these discussions, and the caseworkers were enabled to see more clearly what their task with this couple might be. This does not mean to say that, in the course of such informal discussions, the caseworkers evolved a plan of campaign to pursue with their clients. Any imposed plan would vitiate the caseworkers' efforts to find out how their clients tend to use relationships. The pattern of work must be initiated by the clients, although the caseworker will, in a sense, through her awareness of what is happening, remain in control. This awareness is necessary also to enable her to respond in a way which will expose rather than corroborate the basic misconceptions upon which so much of her clients' behaviour will be based. It has also to be borne in mind, and it cannot be repeated too often, that these processes take time and that the distortions or unconscious assumptions arose as a defence against intolerable anxiety and so cannot be given up 'on demand'.

We have seen that the Robinsons in contrast to others described, began almost immediately to share their interviews quite consciously. Very often this is not so, but the sharing is indirectly expressed in behaviour at home. In all cases it represents a new means of communication, the clients are using the caseworkers, or rather their images, to convey ideas to each other which have been too difficult to approach before. Reports about these communications, whether brought directly or indirectly to the caseworkers, also help their understanding of the total situation and of their own involvement in it. In the case of the Robinsons, not only was a more meaningful relationship soon established between them, but all the exchanges between caseworker and clients, between the two caseworkers, and between the marriage partners, combined relatively quickly to produce a more conscious understanding of the relationships involved. One might say that by the exchange of impressions, in which the phantasies were allowed full play, the total perception of reality was strengthened.

It is clear that in order to keep their vital self-awareness and to understand, as far as possible, the extent to which their own involvement may be distorting their understanding of their client's difficulties, the caseworkers need a medium in which they, too, may develop and feel free to involve themselves in relationships. Without such freedom it would become very difficult for them to avoid working in mental blinkers which would prevent them from seeing anything except the rational content of their client's complaints and fears, and of their own anxieties. The group provides a setting in which these anxieties can be aired and tolerated. Caseworkers have an opportunity to discuss their cases in conference, but the constant gain in casework experience which this provides is seen as incidental to the vital atmosphere created by the group which can be internalized so that workers carry it with them to their clients. It is essential that this atmosphere should be predominantly accepting and supportive so that the workers can be spontaneous in their discussions, knowing as they do that these will reveal hidden aspects of their own personalities. But, in so far as the group avoids a destructively critical attitude it must, nevertheless, make demands on its members, the chief being for a disciplined and discriminating attitude to their work.

Caseworkers demand from their clients a considerable amount of moral courage when they ask them to assimilate a fresh understanding of their predicament. They demand, in effect, that their clients shall sacrifice the unreal picture of themselves behind which they may have taken refuge for a long time, although, for our clients, this refuge has ceased to be a peaceful shelter. They need some assurance that life more in the open can be risked, but usually begin by demanding another unreal picture behind which both client and caseworker can take refuge. There are certain kinds of cases in which it is especially difficult for the caseworker not to do this, as we have discussed more fully at the end of the Price case. If in this instance, instead of stressing the need for Mrs Price to withdraw her projection from her husband, the worker had suggested she might try to be 'understanding' or 'be kinder' to him, most likely Mr Price would have reacted unfavourably, and Mrs Price would have returned to her caseworker angry and disappointed, saying that her husband accused her of being 'bossy' or 'condescending'.

When this happens it may be that the client senses the unconscious 'bossiness' in the caseworker. If, however, the caseworker can manage without the image of herself as a helpful person, and tolerate her own anxiety about being useless, ungiving and therefore apparently destructive, the client has a chance to recognize the possibility of facing his own anxieties more openly. He might then identify with his caseworker as the person who can see herself more realistically.

It is often with those clients who have the least differentiated ego that caseworkers are most tempted to be 'helpfully' directive. Yet Mr Webb, who was so much at the mercy of his phantasies, was immeasurably helped by his caseworker's unshakeability in this respect. By showing him that she could remain intact in the face of his destructive phantasies, the caseworker implied her knowledge, her experience and her emotional security. She offered her client the safety of a well-differentiated ego, and a sense of proportion which was not overthrown by his phantasy. This safety was lacking in the marriage relationship. His wife used to get swept into his phantasies and so increased his terror, but by the caseworker's ability to remain invulnerable it became gradually diminished.

Clients often put great pressure on their caseworkers to respond to them in a pseudo-parental way, as if they were in a position of authority. If the caseworkers' responses are to be of any lasting value to their clients, they know that they must withstand this pressure. It is not at all easy to do. As will have been evident from the case studies, the caseworkers frequently find themselves colluding with their clients in just such an unreal relationship: unreal because it implies the ability and readiness to take responsibility for the direction and management of the client's life, to take care of him.

In some settings this might be an appropriate attitude, but at the Bureau usually it is not. It would be wrong to infer from this an inflexibility that demands that casework should always follow a certain pattern. There are, of course, times when sharing in a phantasy for the sake of making contact with a client is really creative. Each combination of client and caseworker will, in fact, constellate a different relationship, and one that varies as the case proceeds, but the validity and appropriateness of the various 'methods' thus put into practice can be verified only by conscious scrutiny.

The four-person and caseworker-group relationships help to keep this scrutiny continuously alive. From a casework point of view, such unconscious collusions as inevitably occur can often be fruitful, since it is not their occurrence but the continuous lack of awareness of it which can be damaging to the work. The caseworkers' ability to protect themselves from too much pressure, to use these collusions creatively and to find their way back to a different attitude within the casework relationships depends largely on the atmosphere of the group. This atmosphere is the product of the relationships in the group, including that with the consultant psycho-analyst who attends the case conference and whose attitude to the group is vitally important. Unless the consultant is willing and able to lay aside his traditional role of 'knowing best', which his authority and knowledge might allow, such a laying aside would be impossible for the caseworkers themselves. The consultant also has to withstand pressure. A group inevitably looks to him to take the authoritative role, to issue directions and be responsible for casework in a way which, again, might be entirely appropriate in other settings. Even in this relatively sophisticated group this demand unconsciously persists, as does its corollary: that is the group frustration at the consultant's refusal to adopt an authoritative role.

The caseworkers often experience within themselves what they must at other times meet from their clients. Sometimes their frustration will lead to a rejection of the consultant. His time, his experience and his individual way of participating in the group discussions is rendered 'useless'. Caseworkers know very well what this feels like. A conference may be held in which the consultant is firmly kept out. The caseworkers talk in a lively and knowledgeable way which offers him no real opening and no encouragement to join in. Then, in the middle of a bit of theorizing, a caseworker may be struck by the similarity between her own behaviour and that of a particular client whose elaboration of material may have seemed, at times, to be aimed at something other than an elucidation of his problems. Other members of the group will be struck by this too, but as it is not a therapeutic group in any technical sense, no interpretations are offered. In other words, the widening of consciousness which in fact does take place within the group is not its direct aim. The direct aim is the understanding of the cases presented.

When a member of the group becomes aware of a situation such as the one described, she becomes aware, also, of the attitude of other members of the group, including that of the consultant. She becomes aware that his response to the 'rejection' as to the 'demands' is primarily one of respect for the real needs of the group. This does not mean that he has to understand these needs all the time, or to pretend to or even to make very concentrated efforts to do so. As in the casework situation, this is not a mere 'ego' relationship. During the time which the consultant gives to them he belongs to the group and allows himself to become involved with them, relating at various levels of consciousness in the same way as the caseworkers have to allow themselves to become involved with their clients. The fact that there is more than one consultant, and that they all have different ways of relating to the group, is also very important because it stresses the need for each caseworker to find her own individual way, so that the 'internal therapist' is something which really grows from within and is not an imposed imitation. In other words, although in the group and in the casework situations there are many similarities, there are also many differences, but the task which must take place within the transference is the same, namely that of recognizing the conflicting demands so that both caseworkers and clients may become freer to discover, within themselves, those impulsive and creative capacities which they incline to disown and which, when reintegrated, can help them to find a way through their existing difficulties. In both sets of relationships there is the need to internalize, not an authoritative figure, but rather that of an attentive friend who will discuss things from a disciplined standpoint. That is to say, someone who does not need to reject problems by actively suggesting solutions or give way to the infantile pressures which they produce; but whose experience and knowledge enables him to bear the tensions, the depressions and the chaos.

An important part of the analyst's contribution to the group is his capacity, based on this experience and knowledge, to believe in the creative possibilities inherent in a conflict situation and to wait until these emerge. Again and again the material presented at a conference, and the freely associative way in which the group considers it, will appear just as muddled and as tentative as the casework interviews themselves. Sometimes the consultant has nothing to say to the group; this may be because of shared depressions when everyone sits in silence, or he may feel out of touch with the group which goes on working without him. At other times, everyone will be lively and full of ideas which are genuinely creative. But, as a rule, there are neither such distinct ups nor downs—just a solid plodding through the case material.

This setting, which is used to foster growth in both clients and caseworkers, must now be considered in comparison with the family unit in which similar processes take place, and with which the work is ultimately concerned. In making such comparisons we are constantly aware of the significance of a living relationship. It would seem to be where and when relationships are not sufficiently realistic, and therefore cannot act as a corrective to the child's exaggerated and often frightening phantasies, that difficulties in development become so disproportionate. We have already seen in the Clarke family how the son's phantasies of an overwhelming mother, in themselves a normal part of his development, reached a paralysing intensity. If the phantasies could have been tested against the reality of the parental relationship, they would have assumed more manageable proportions. In this case, because of the somewhat limited relationship between the parents in which only the father's admiration and approval of the mother's achievements were acknowledged and in which his and their own resentments and feelings of deprivation had to be denied, the children lacked a vital opportunity to experience that negative feelings are necessary components in any relationship and are not finally destructive to it. We have seen how these phantasies were reduced in the course of Mr Clarke's contact with his caseworker and how this client gradually came to accept this negative feeling as a normal part of his relationships, especially with his caseworker and his wife. He no longer needed to keep them completely separate and was eventually able to tell his caseworker how badly he felt about her 'abandonment' of him before the joint meeting. We have also seen how useful it was, in this particular case, that the negative and positive feelings could, at the beginning of the contact, continue to be kept separate by being split between the wife's and Mr Clarke's own caseworker until the client had acquired sufficient security to bring them together himself.

Throughout the contact, Mr Clarke tested out the relationship between the two caseworkers; that Mrs A. did not defend her colleague or join with him in attacking her, was a vital part of his therapeutic experience. It was important that a live relationship, in fact, existed between the caseworkers throughout, and that they were able, within the security of their own group, to discuss the case with feeling, to share their uncertainties about its outcome, and to endure at times quite divergent views about the process. Just as a flexible attitude on the part of and in the relationship between parents is of such importance to children, so we feel that too great an emphasis cannot be placed on the necessity for a flexible attitude on the part of and in the relationship between caseworkers at the Bureau. They have to avoid, so far as they can, any fixed ideas of how a marriage should be or of how the casework should develop. As we have seen, again with the Clarkes, the wife, after an initial period of contact, stayed away for some time, until there came a point at which she was able to resume contact and work intensively. Later, the workers were able to see how very important this temporary breach in the relationship had been to the marriage. If the wife had been forced by her caseworker to face her own needs, to carry her own depression and illness before the husband had acquired sufficient confidence and strength to bear this, the effect on the marriage might well have been disastrous. Although a redistribution of forces and a resumption of growth might have taken place within each individual as a result of their individual experience, it might not have taken place as it did within the marriage. Because the wife's caseworker sensed the need of the marriage without, at the time, fully understanding it, she had to take the risk of losing contact with her client before she had fulfilled one of the primary tasks in casework—that of helping her client to accept her own need. So many clients can only come saying they need help for the sake of the children or of the other partner, and no real development can begin to take place until they are able to feel that their own needs are valid and not destructive, but, on the contrary, of value to the marriage.

We can translate this back to the group setting and say that the caseworkers have also to learn to value their own individual need of the group. The regular and valuable time which the psycho-analyst consultants give to the group, which the group in turn give to each other in case conference and in individual case discussions, is a measure of the value and meaning this association has for them. We have seen how, in the Clarke case, the caseworkers had to bear their own and each other's uncertainties about the way in which the work was progressing, and the way in which their different ways of working might be affecting their clients. The flexibility required of them would, indeed, have been hard to maintain without the support of a group itself sufficiently tolerant of, and welcoming to, individual differences and development. Inevitably the group will fail sometimes in this, just as the caseworker will sometimes fail her client.

We have seen, in all the cases studied, how the relationships established at the Bureau vary from caseworker to caseworker according to their different personalities and skill. Each caseworker's individual technique is also varied according to the client's needs. In the case of the Robinson's for example, both caseworkers decided, almost at the outset, that a specific kind of response would be appropriate. In this case, each caseworker, in her own way, took up the opposite role to that which she felt had been cast for her by her client. One could make a comparison between this and the way in which parents often find that the best means of helping their adolescent children is to take an opposite role; when the adolescent feels rebellious they may offer more responsibility, and when he is trying to be over grown-up they recognize his dependent needs. This adaptability requires a sense of security and a lively imagination on the part of the caseworkers, as it does on the part of the parents, who, by necessity, have to communicate with their children at different levels and in different ways according to their ages and understanding.

The second and third cases, for instance, were in some ways different from the others although worked by the same caseworkers who can be seen relating to the clients in a somewhat different way. At first more time was spent talking to them in terms of the realities and phantasies which they brought of the 'here and now' situation, both within the marriage and with their caseworker, than in making attempts to link these for them to past relationships and childhood assumptions. Mr Webb, for instance, seemed unable to see Mrs A. as anything but a good although terrifying woman whom he had to placate and obey, apparently the opposite of his descriptions of his wife. Yet the caseworker sensed that these two pictures were complementary and were a clue to his muddled and unsatisfactory relationships with women. This knowledge helped her in the difficult task of accepting without too much fear the stories of violence and the signs of injury which Mr Webb continued for some time to bring to her. In fact, it was almost impossible at first for this panic-stricken client to listen to anything his caseworker might say. Nevertheless, the fact that she did not reject his problems with 'advice', but was manifestly trying to find the meaning in his compulsive behaviour and that she in fact believed it was meaningful and valued her client sufficiently to make such efforts on his behalf, were in themselves communications of therapeutic value. They enabled Mr Webb gradually to relax and to begin to relate to his caseworker as a real person instead of as the terrifyingly 'good' object which she had originally appeared to him.

We have seen the same means of communication at work with the Prices. A great deal of the wife's present-day conflict with her husband and daughter were understood by the caseworker in the light of her client's earlier experience, but for the most part the discussions were simply in present-day terms. The character of these discussions became very dramatically changed, however, after the client had been enabled to accept and express the value which she had come to place upon them and upon her caseworker.

We have already considered in the previous chapter how the conflict of demands made by our society concerning sexuality, for instance, where the Church says one thing and the newspapers another, make the process of maturation more difficult although more rewarding than in less complex cultures. Many of our clients have, in fact, suffered particularly from the fragmentation of society and they find themselves often very disorientated and cut off from any channels through which they can keep in touch with traditional values or be free to develop and share their own. For such people, the fact that, at the Bureau, the marriage relationship is recognized as the centre of the therapeutic intent may itself be a help. They know that the object is to help them to reorientate themselves in this relationship which is seen as offering possibilities for increased satisfaction, support and growth to both individuals. In this way, the idea of the Bureau, as well as the individual relationships which are made there, may provide for some people the sanctioning and initiating body which has been lost to them in the community.

Interviews at the Bureau lack the exclusiveness of some other therapeutic techniques, particularly analysis. Even if the second partner does not come, there still remains an emphasis on the marriage. This may make things more difficult for those very deprived clients who need to experience an exclusive and very individual relationship, such as analysis, to stimulate and foster their growth. Clients who feel that they have experienced very little or perhaps too extended a period of close mother-child relationship are the ones who find most difficulty in giving up their longing for this very dependent state. For example, Mr Cooper, in spite of a long period of individual therapy before starting at the Bureau, still needed to continue this pattern with his caseworker for some time.

There are also those clients whose own degree of flexibility demand further growth but whose partner's rigidity has become quite unassailable. It is often possible for such a couple to remain together, affording each other valuable support, particularly where the more flexible partner can be helped to find some further means of expression and growth, perhaps outside the marriage, which is not too threatening to that relationship. But in the occasional case, where the beginning of a change in the one partner has come to represent such a threat to the other that the growing partner takes on for the other one, and for himself, the character of an altogether destructive figure, nothing seems able to get through this mutual delusion.

In such cases, where the marriage is in fact irretrievably broken, the task which emerges may be that of helping the healthier partner to overcome the intense feelings of guilt and anxiety which such a situation necessarily activates. To help such people to regain confidence in their capacity for relationships is a very important function for any social service, particularly if, as is often the case, there are young children involved. Clients are faced at this point with the familiar problems of differentiation. They have the usual need to give up their dependence on a phantasy figure and to re-establish their own identity, but in this instance there is no marriage to contain the readjustment and a mourning period needs to be gone through.

There is an added difficulty in these cases in that those clients who have more than average neurotic difficulties are liable to compensate for their pain and failure by a belief in some form that they are both different from and better than other people. Though often verbalizing only their misery and sense of inadequacy they will, in fact, hold tenaciously to this inner conviction of superiority, and it becomes one of the brakes on progress counteracting more realistic drives towards growth and maturity. Many clients at a late stage in case-work say angrily, 'You are trying to make me into an ordinary woman just like every other housewife in the road', or 'You are trying to take my identity away from me', or, in one client's words, 'You are taking my magic away from me'. Indeed, magic is probably the right word for these beliefs, which have been retained because the client's actual life has not seemed to provide sufficient satisfaction or sufficient security to enable him to discard them. This problem is not such a difficult one where there is still a marriage in existence. In such a case, clients are helped by their increasing satisfaction in the marriage itself, and the growing confidence on the part of each, that in his marriage he has something which is both special to him and unique in itself, with a reality and a value of its own. Where the caseworker is working with only one client, whom the bitter experi-ence of an irrevocably broken marriage has probably driven further into his phantasy world, this may present a very serious barrier and it may be a long time before his new adjustment to life can give him sufficient confidence to face his emotional problems. Meanwhile, the caseworker is faced with the client's intensified demands and lacks the support and safeguard of the four-person relationship.

It is in these few cases, because of our particular setting, that we as caseworkers find ourselves most burdened by doubt. We are often in danger either of sharing with our client the feeling that to demand consideration for oneself is essentially destructive, or we may keep up a pretence that this is not an individual problem, that the work is still centred on the marriage, and that we are just seeing the client through legal proceedings or something of that sort. But, in fact, it is very important for the clients that we should be able to face with them the reality of the breach, and the need for individual help.

Whatever the circumstances in which clients come to us, however, our aim remains essentially the same, that is to help them to achieve a more realistic relationship to their environment in general and a more realistic conception of themselves and of their marriage partners. We cannot enable them to solve their emotional conflicts, as these are a condition of living and can never be fully resolved, but we can help them to face these feelings which they have had to deny and which have consequently created for them a burden of guilt and anxiety. If, within the personal relationship of client to caseworker, clients can permit their anger and distrust to come into relationship with their love (and it may not always be the latter of which they are first aware), then this unconscious burden will be reduced and this will in turn result in a more satisfying relationship between the marriage partners.

The lessening of guilt brings an increased capacity to communicate with and to accept communications from each other, and when a real contact begins to replace a rigid repetitive pattern of relationships, the growth process is re-established. In other words, the clients come originally torn by the conflict between their creative and destructive forces and beset by the underlying fear that the destructive forces will prove the stronger. The more anxious they feel about this the more desperate is the struggle to keep any destructive feelings away from the new and important relationship at the Bureau. If within this setting clients can experience the stability of a relationship within which they can work through the nub of their ambivalence and really learn that love can survive hate, then they no longer need to hold on so rigidly to their defences. The balance of forces becomes changed, energy is released and growth can continue. If the case-worker has succeeded in freeing some of the growing points within the clients, there is every prospect that a developing process will be set in motion and that it will be one that the couple will continue for themselves. Such a process will, however, never continue at an even rate nor be separable from conflict and regression. The impelling force which makes for progress and growth is always opposed by the human need to cling to or go back to familiar situations. As each individual prepares for the important steps forward in his life, such as getting married, becoming a parent, or losing one, he is liable to be disturbed by feelings which would seem more appropriate within his primary relationships and which may alarm him by their infantile intensity. Although through the exploration of his feelings at the Bureau anxieties may be lessened, as new situations create new problems a number of clients feel the need to return to talk things over again. This may be for one or two sessions only.

It is very usual for clients gradually to transfer their feelings from the caseworkers to some other object, a baby, a new job, a better home, and it may be that if such clients return later it will be to make a further attempt at integration. Such renewed contacts are considered by the caseworkers as valuable and rewarding. They also provide a means of following up cases and are a comment on the basic experience which the client has had at the Bureau.

Many clients come with an illusory hope of returning to a state of complacent bliss. It may be a hope which they originally carried with them into marriage. They say, 'I thought when we married everything would be all right.' We can help them to bear the realization that all human solutions are partial ones, that they will never be completely freed from pain and conflict and that, however much their personalities may grow and integrate, there will always be a sense of loss and friction encouraging further growth.

One of the important factors in helping worker and client to terminate will be the ability of both to relinquish the hope of finding an ideal solution and to leave many questions open. Clients 'let go' in a variety of different ways, mistrustfully, angrily, gladly, sadly or triumphantly according to their type of personality and mode of growth. As termination approaches they will often return to their original pattern of behaviour with the caseworkers. Both client and caseworker may then feel despondent and imagine that this is exactly 'where we came in'. In fact, this is not so. When the client first came to the Bureau his unconsciousness created a barrier in his relationships, including that with his caseworker, which will at termination have broken down to the extent to which the caseworker has succeeded in helping him to become more conscious. Client and caseworker will be aware of the greater freedom in their relationship and in the relationship between the married couple. They know that this freedom represents a shared gain and a shared loss, similar to that between parents and children, as the children grow and both face the ending of one sort of relationship and the beginning of a new one. These changes are accompanied by feelings of regression and progression, loss and gain, mourning and rejoicing even to the point at and after which the children finally leave the parental care. It may be at this point that parents become more poignantly aware of their children's capacities or incapacities and that the children feel most strongly their need to have, or to do without, parental support. In the same way, hitherto hidden strengths or weaknesses often emerge in individual clients and in their marriage relationship at the point when termination is first discussed, as though the impact of the threatened separation had brought them to light, so that the process of termination, with the promise and challenge which it holds for the future, becomes a fruitful and dynamic part of whatever coming to the Bureau has meant to the clients and their marriage, as a total experience.

REFERENCES

No attempt has been made to draw up a bibliography of works on the subject of marital problems nor a complete list of source material. This is merely a selection of works in which will be found some of the basic theory and understanding of interpersonal relationships on which the work of the Bureau has been based.

Abraham, Karl (1919), 'Ejaculatio Praecox'. *Selected Papers on Psycho-Analysis*. London: Hogarth Press.
—— (1920), 'Manifestations of the Female Castration Complex'. *Selected Papers on Psycho-Analysis*. London: Hogarth Press.
Balint, Michael (1957), 'The Doctor, His Patient and the Illness'. London: Pitman Medical Publishing Co., Ltd.
Deutsch, Helene (1947), *The Psychology of Women*. London: Research Books Ltd.
Dicks, H. V. (1953), 'Experience with Marital Tensions seen in the Psychological Clinic'. *Brit. J. med. Psychol.*, Vol. 26, pp. 181-196.
—— (1957), 'Mental Hygiene in Marriage'. *Royal Soc. of Health J.*, Vol. 77, No. 9.
—— (1959), 'Sexual Problems in Marriage—the Psycho-Dynamic Aspects'. *Proceedings of the Royal Society of Medicine*, Vol. 52, No. 867.
Fairbairn, W., and Ronald, D. (1952), *Psychoanalytic Studies of the Personality*. London: Tavistock Publications.
Fordham, Michael (1957), *New Developments in Analytical Psychology*. London: Routledge & Kegan Paul.
Freud, Sigmund (1922), *Introductory Lectures on Psycho-Analysis*. London: George Allen & Unwin.
—— (1905), 'Three Essays on the Theory of Sexuality'. *Complete Psychological Works of Sigmund Freud*, Vol. 7. London: Hogarth Press.
—— (1905), 'Fragment of an Analysis of a Case of Hysteria'. *Complete Psychological Works of Sigmund Freud*, Vol. 7.
—— (1909), 'Analysis of a Phobia in a Five-year-old Boy'. *Complete Psychological Works of Sigmund Freud*, Vol. 10.
—— (1909), 'Notes upon a Case of Obsessional Neurosis'. *Complete Psychological Works of Sigmund Freud*, Vol. 10.

Freud, Sigmund (1914), 'Remembering, Repeating and Working Through'. *Complete Psychological Works of Sigmund Freud*, Vol. 12.

—— (1925), 'Some Psychological Consequences of the Anatomical Distinction between the Sexes'. *Collected Papers*, Vol. 5. London: Hogarth Press.

Isaacs, Susan (1948), *Childhood and After*. London: Routledge & Kegan Paul.

Jones, Ernest (1953), *Sigmund Freud, Life and Work*. London: Hogarth Press.

Jung, C. G. (1953), 'Two Essays on Analytical Psychology'. *Collected Works*, Vol. 7. London: Routledge & Kegan Paul.

—— (1953), 'The Practice of Psychotherapy'. *Collected Works*, Vol. 16.

—— (1953), 'The Development of Personality'. *Collected Works*, Vol. 17.

Klein, Melanie (1957), *Envy and Gratitude: A Study of Unconscious Sources*. London: Tavistock Publications.

Klein, Melanie, and Riviere J. (1939), *Love, Hate and Reparation*. London: Hogarth Press.

Sutherland, John D. (Ed.) (1958), *Analysis and Contemporary Thought*. International Psychoanalytical Library, No. 53. London: Hogarth Press and Institute of Psychoanalysis.

Thompson, G. (1949), 'Abnormal Psychology in Relation to the Emotional Development'. *Modern Practice in Psychological Medicine* (J. R. Rees, Ed.). London: Butterworth.

Wilson, A. T. M. (1949), 'Some Reflections & Suggestions on the Prevention of Marital Problems'. *Hum. Rel.*, Vol. 2, pp. 233-251.

Winnicott, D. W. (1958), *Collected Papers*. London: Tavistock Publications.

INDEX